PSYCHOLOGY LIBRARY EDITIONS: MEMORY

Volume 21

NEUROPSYCHOLOGY OF THE AMNESIC SYNDROME

NEUROPSYCHOLOGY OF THE AMNESIC SYNDROME

ALAN J. PARKIN AND NICHOLAS R. C. LENG

Routledge
Taylor & Francis Group
LONDON AND NEW YORK

First published 1993 by Psychology Press

2 Park Square, Milton Park, Abingdon, Oxon OX14 4RN
711 Third Avenue, New York, NY 10017, USA

Routledge is an imprint of the Taylor & Francis Group, an informa business

First issued in paperback 2016

British Library Cataloguing in Publication Data
A catalogue record for this book is available from the British Library

ISBN 978-1-138-97700-6 (pbk)
ISBN 978-1-84872-403-7 (hbk)
ISBN 978-1-315-77828-0 (ebk)

Publisher's Note
The publisher has gone to great lengths to ensure the quality of this book but points out that some imperfections from the original may be apparent.

Disclaimer
The publisher has made every effort to trace copyright holders and would welcome correspondence from those they have been unable to trace.

Neuropsychology of the Amnesic Syndrome

Alan J. Parkin and Nicholas R. C. Leng
Laboratory of Experimental Psychology,
University of Sussex, UK

LAWRENCE ERLBAUM ASSOCIATES, PUBLISHERS
Hove (UK) Hillsdale (USA)

Reprinted 1994

Lawrence Erlbaum Associates Ltd., Publishers
27 Palmeira Mansions
Church Road
Hove
East Sussex, BN3 2FA
UK

British Library Cataloguing in Publication Data
Parkin, Alan J.
Neuropsychology of the Amnesic Syndrome.
—(Brain Damage, Behaviour & Cognition Series, ISSN 0967-9944)
I. Title II. Leng, Nicholas R. C.
III. Series
616.85

ISBN 0-86377-200-5 (Hbk)
ISBN 0-86377-201-3 (Pbk)

Typeset by J&L Composition Ltd., Filey, North Yorkshire, UK
Printed and bound by BPC Wheatons Ltd., Exeter, UK

Contents

Brain Damage, Behaviour and Cognition

Developments in Clinical Neuropsychology

Series Editors

Chris Code, University of Sydney, Australia
Dave Müller, Suffolk College of Higher and Further Education, U.K.

Published titles

Cognitive Rehabilitation Using Microcomputers
Veronica A. Bradley, John L. Welch and Clive E. Skilbeck

The Characteristics of Aphasia
Chris Code (Ed.)

Neuropsychology and the Dementias
Siobhan Hart and James M. Semple

Acquired Neurological Speech/Language Disorders in Childhood
Bruce E. Murdoch (Ed.)

Neuropsychology of the Amnesic Syndrome
Alan J. Parkin and Nicholas R.C. Leng

Clinical and Neuropsychological Aspects of Closed Head Injury
John T.E. Richardson

Acquired Apraxia of Speech in Aphasic Adults
Paula A. Square (Ed.)

Cognitive Rehabilitation in Perspective
Rodger Wood and Ian Fussey (Eds)

Forthcoming titles

The Neuropsychology of Schizophrenia
Anthony S. David and John C. Cutting (Eds)

Unilateral Neglect: Clinical and Experimental Studies
Ian H. Robertson and J.C. Marshall (Eds)

Series Editors' Preface

From being an area primarily on the periphery of mainstream behavioural and cognitive science, neuropsychology has developed in recent years into an area of central concern for a range of disciplines. We are witnessing not only a revolution in the way in which brain–behaviour–cognition relationships are viewed, but a widening of interest concerning developments in neuropsychology on the part of a range of workers in a variety of fields. Major advances in brain imaging techniques and the cognitive modelling of the impairments following brain damage promise a wider understanding of the nature of the representation of cognition and behaviour in the damaged and undamaged brain.

Neuropsychology is now centrally important for those working with brain damaged people, but the very rate of expansion in the area makes it difficult to keep up with findings from current research. The aim of the *Brain Damage, Behaviour and Cognition* series is to publish a wide range of books which present comprehensive and up-to-date overviews of current developments in specific areas of interest.

These books will be of particular interest to those working with the brain-damaged. It is the Editors' intention that undergraduates, postgraduates, clinicians and researchers in pyschology, speech pathology and medicine will find this series a useful source of information on important current developments. The authors and editors of the books in this series are experts in their respective fields working at the forefront of contemporary research. They have produced texts which are accessible and scholarly. We thank them for their contribution and their hard work in fulfilling the aims of the series.

Chris Code and Dave Müller
Sydney, Australia and Ipswich, U.K.

Preface

Interest in the amnesic syndrome has grown substantially in the last two decades. Clinical psychologists have become increasingly involved with the assessment of memory disordered patients and the planning of rehabilitation strategies. Within psychological science, studies of amnesic patients have been at the forefront of attempts to understand the neural substrate of memory and behavioural studies of amnesia have become highly influential in a number of theoretical areas.

These developments suggested that it would be timely to produce a handbook embracing all aspects of investigation into the amnesic syndrome. In particular, we saw the need to provide for both the clinician, whose primary concerns would be assessment and the clinical features of the various patient groups presenting amnesia as the primary deficit, and the scientist, whose interest would warrant an account of the empirical findings plus some guidelines on theoretical matters.

The book has three distinct parts. In the first we provide a theoretical background from within which the amnesic syndrome emerges as a distinct entity, followed by an account of the various assessment techniques used to define various features of the syndrome. Following from this is an account of the findings relating to the varying aetiologies of the amnesic syndrome. We then present a discussion of some of the theoretical issues surrounding the amnesic syndrome. The final chapter discusses current approaches to non-interventive treatments.

The preparation of this book had a somewhat unusual course. It was started at the University of Sussex and then worked on by one of us (A.P.) at the University of Canterbury, University of Western Australia, and the

University of Otago. In the process of production, this book has been through three different word processing systems and our thanks go to Lida Graupner, Yumi Hanstock, Sylvia Turner (Sussex), Mary Platts, Mike Teale and Denis Brown (Perth) for all their help in producing the book.

Many people have helped in the production of this book. Narinder Kapur and John Richardson both read the entire manuscript and offered many valuable comments. Frances Aldrich, Chris Code and Veronica Bradley also read and commented on various parts. Thanks must also go to our many clinical colleagues who have referred patients and helped us with our investigations—in particular, Caroline Barry, Jane Blunden, Veronica Bradley, Richard Greenwood, Narinder Kapur, Christopher Lee, Barry Longmore, Brenda Mumford, John Rees, Susan Scott, John Spencer and Mike Tossell. We must make a special mention of Nikki Hunkin, whose recent work on aetiological variation in amnesia provided us with much clinical and theoretical material. Finally, we must thank all our patients and their relatives for helping us in our investigations.

1 Defining the Amnesic Syndrome

A syndrome can be defined as a set of symptoms that persistently co-occur and must be considered as a consequence of some systematic breakdown in an underlying system or systems. The syndrome concept is used widely in medicine to delineate sets of clinical features that, collectively, indicate a specific diagnosis. Endocrinologists, for example, recognise Cushing's Syndrome—a cluster of symptoms including myopathy, growth arrest and osteoporosis—as indicative of adrenal disease. The syndrome concept is also applied to behavioural disorders whether or not there is a known organic basis. A good example is Gille de la Tourette's Syndrome in which the patient is afflicted with various forms of tics and uncontrollable tendencies to produce obscenities. This disorder used to be considered in purely psychiatric terms, but recent neurological findings now indicate that it may be related to specific neurological impairment (Singer & Walkup, 1991). Consequently, the appearance of the syndrome now indicates a brain abnormality that may, at some future point, be treatable.

Within neuropsychology, which in this book is defined in the more narrow sense as the investigation of psychological deficits following brain damage in humans, the syndrome concept has also been used to describe patients who all experience the same pattern of psychological deficits. However, a number of neuropsychologists have expressed doubt about the validity of neuropsychological syndromes on the grounds that psychological deficits rarely if ever show the consistency of medical syndromes (e.g. Caramazza & Badecker, 1991) and that, as a result, it is misleading to group patients together in purely neuropsychological terms. There is considerable strength in this argument. Earlier this century, Gerstmann identified a syndrome comprising left–right confusion, finger agnosia and dyscalculia. The co-occurrence of these deficits caused much excitement, not in the least because of the unexpected perspective they gave on the nature of human arithmetic ability! However, subsequent investigations have undermined the reality of this syndrome and with it those interesting speculations on one aspect of human cognition (Gardner, 1977).

The title of this book indicates that we, at least, still adhere to the concept of a neuropsychological syndrome—a view that we share with many neuropsychologists (e.g. Zurif, Gardner & Brownell, 1989). Our view is that the term *amnesic syndrome* still has a high level of descriptive adequacy, in that it identifies a group of patients whose various memory impairments exhibit a degree of consistency that is sufficient for them to be thought of as suffering from the same basic form of deficit. This is not to say that important differences do not exist both between and even within specific groups of patients—a fact that is repeatedly emphasised in our descriptions of different patient groups presenting the syndrome. All we contend is that the term amnesic syndrome specifies, at a certain level, a regular pattern of memory impairment associated with damage to particular brain structures.

A TAXONOMY OF MEMORY DISORDERS

The amnesic syndrome is one of a variety of memory disorders encountered in clinical practice. To understand the position of the amnesic syndrome within the overall range of memory impairments, it is necessary to consider a taxonomy of memory disorders. In attempting to produce a taxonomy, a number of approaches can be considered. Kapur (1988a) adopts an *aetiological approach*, categorising memory loss in terms of the illness or trauma that caused the deficit. This scheme has its merits, in that it allows the nature of memory loss associated with any illness to be accessed directly. A disadvantage, however, is that functional similarities between patients of different aetiologies may not be emphasised. At the other extreme, amnesic disorders can be classified in purely behavioural terms. This was the approach adopted in the experimental studies of the amnesic syndrome conducted by Warrington and her colleagues in the late 1960s and early 1970s (e.g. Baddeley & Warrington, 1970). An important corollary of this was to move amnesia research out of a neurological framework, in which the primary concern was the relationship between lesion site and deficit, towards a consideration of amnesia in terms of functional deficits and psychological theories of memory and learning. A behavioural definition of amnesia radically simplifies the problem of studying amnesia, but sufficient evidence has accumulated to show

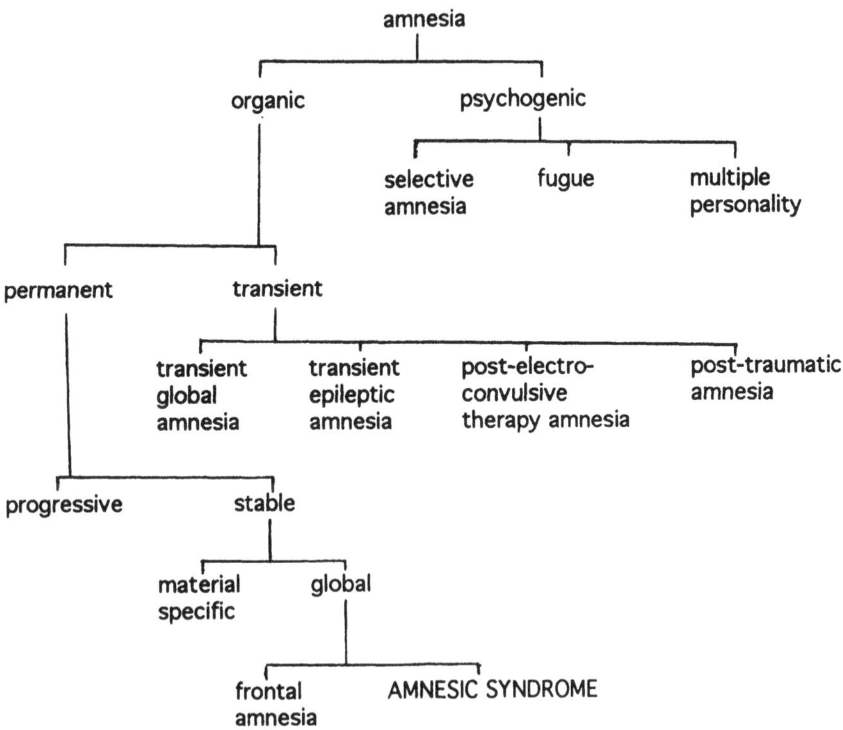

FIG. 1.1 A taxonomy of memory disorders.

significant variation in different aetiologies of amnesia. This led us to adopt an approach to the classification of memory disorders based on aetiological criteria, but this emphasis does not mean that our primary concern is the relation between lesion site and behavioural deficit. Rather, the association of different aetiologies with differing patterns of neurological damage allows, on *a priori* grounds, the possibility that patients from differing aetiologies have different functional deficits because the various neuro-anatomical sites associated with memory function may subsume different aspects of the memory process. Adherence to aetiological criteria thus serves as an heuristic in the task of understanding possible functional differences in the nature of human memory disorders.

Figure 1.1 shows a taxonomy of memory disorders. The scheme makes a fundamental division between an *organic* disorder, in which the patient's memory disorder can be attributed unambiguously to a brain lesion or metabolic deficiency, and *psychogenic* disorders, where the memory deficit is assumed to have a psychiatric origin.

Psychogenic disorders come in a number of distinct dissociative or hysterical deficits. Hysterical states can vary in their severity, ranging from *selective amnesia* (e.g. an inability to recall a specific set of life events, such as combat experience), through to a complete dissociation between self and memory. In this latter, *fugue* state, patients may deny all knowledge of their past, fail to identify even close relatives and, in some instances, adopt a new personality. Many case reports of fugue exist (e.g. Wong, 1990), but empirical studies of this puzzling disorder are very rare (however, see Schacter, Wang, Tulving & Freedman, 1982).

Multiple personality is another rare psychogenic disorder and one whose diagnosis is fraught with difficulties. Kenneth Bianci, "The Hillside Strangler", was responsible for a number of murders but maintained that they had been committed by his other self "Steve". Bianci fooled a lot of people for a long time, but systematic observation of Bianci by psychologists, particularly Martin Orne, eventually exposed Bianci's elaborate and well-researched malingering. In genuine multiple personality disorder, the patient compartmentalises different sets of personal experiences by attributing them to two or more separate individuals that exist within the patient. Coons, Milstein and Marley (1982) describe the case of "Lucy", a young girl who developed four personalities, each of which was used to describe a particular dimension of her disturbing past. Like fugue, multiple personality has received little scientific investigation, although two recent studies have attempted to elucidate the nature of this impairment via experimental means (Nissen et al., 1988; Schacter, Kihlstrom & Kihlstrom, 1989). A recent review of psychogenic amnesic states is provided by Kopelman (1987a) and the issue of multiple personality is specifically dealt with by Putnam (1989).

Within organic memory disorders, a division can be drawn between those that are transient and those that are permanent. *Transient* disorders take a number of distinct forms (Markowitsch, 1990), the most common being *transient global amnesia* (TGA), in which the patient exhibits the symptoms for between 1 and 24 hours (e.g. Hodges & Ward, 1989). The cause of TGA is still an open question. Fisher and Adams (1958) proposed that epilepsy was the underlying factor, but subsequent studies report that epileptic seizures are rare in TGA sufferers. A psychiatric cause is also unlikely because TGA sufferers lack the typical predisposing features of a psychogenic amnesic state (e.g. adverse life events). Most authors subscribe to the view that TGA has an ischaemic origin (a sudden reduction in cerebral blood flow), a theory consistent with the higher than average incidence of migraine in TGA patients (Markowitsch, 1983; Hodges & Warlow, 1990a).

Temporal lobe epilepsy can also cause transient loss of memory, known as *transient epileptic amnesia* (TEA). The occurrence of a grand mal seizure will cause a temporary amnesic state as well as loss of memory for events preceding the fit. Complex partial seizures, in which the patient is cognitively impaired but not rendered unconscious, can give rise to amnesic episodes including bouts of aimless wandering known as *poriomania*. It is tempting to consider TEA as being similar to TGA but, as Kapur (1990) has pointed out, there are good reasons for arguing that the two forms of memory disorder have important differences (see also Hodges & Warlow, 1990b).

It is well known that electroconvulsive therapy (ECT) produces a transient amnesic state, *post-ECT amnesia*, which usually ameliorates within about 12 days of treatment. Like TGA, ECT-induced amnesia has many similarities with the amnesic syndrome and controversy surrounds the issue of whether ECT causes permanent deficits in memory. There are abundant anecdotal accounts of people claiming permanent disorders of memory as a result of ECT, but controlled studies of ECT and memory indicate no long-term harmful effects (for a review, see Weiner, 1984). Possible reasons for this discrepancy are that large group studies may often conceal a few peculiarly susceptible individuals; people complaining of long-term ECT-induced amnesia may also be having memory problems for other reasons, such as continuing depression or the effects of their medication; patients who had poor memories prior to ECT may also tend to monitor their memory more carefully and incorrectly attribute these normal memory lapses to the effects of treatment (Squire and Zouzounis, 1988).

Symonds (1962) has stated "that it is . . . questionable whether the effects of concussion, however slight, are ever completely reversible". Supporting this view, Stuss et al. (1985) have shown evidence of impairments in a substantial number of closed-head injury victims who were judged to have made a full recovery. Similar findings have been reported by McMillan and Glucksman (1987) and Leininger et al. (1990), but it is important to distinguish these residual deficits from the period of profound memory loss and disorientation following closed-head injury which is termed *post-traumatic amnesia* (PTA). During this period, there is a marked inability to learn new material (anterograde amnesia) and loss of memories formed before the injury (retrograde amnesia) will also be observed. An interesting phenomenon associated with PTA is that, as the overall condition ameliorates, the retrograde deficit "shrinks", in that with the passage of time, the impaired memories become restored in a temporally organised sequence with more remote experiences returning prior to more recent ones. At the point of full recovery, the patient only experiences amnesia for the events immediately preceding the head injury (Benson & Geschwind, 1968).

In *permanent* disorders of memory, the patient's memory function does not recover and these disorders can be classed as *stable*, because the deficit remains clearly unchanged across time, or *progressive*, in that the deficit worsens as the illness (e.g. Alzheimer's disease) develops. Figure 1.1 indicates one more division within stable disorders, that between *material-specific* and *global*. In a material-specific disorder, the patient's lesion is usually unilateral and selectively affects the ability to remember certain classes of information. Most commonly, material-specific deficits are associated with unilateral cerebrovascular accidents (CVAs) and unilateral lobectomies. Right posterior lesions, for example, can give rise to selective problems in remembering pictorial and facial information, whereas left hemisphere lesions can give rise to verbal learning deficits. Although less common, unilateral subcortical lesions can also give rise to material-specific memory impairments. One might also include in material-specific deficits disorders in the immediate processing of phonology. These disorders have attracted particular interest in recent years because of the evidence they provide about the fractionation of the putative memory system that underlies conscious mental activities (for accounts of these deficits, see Mayes, 1988; Vallar & Shallice, 1990).

Global disorders are divided into the *amnesic syndrome* and *frontal amnesia*. As the name suggests, the latter group comprise patients who have suffered memory loss following damage to the frontal cortex. This form of memory deficit is disabling but not of sufficient severity to be called an amnesic syndrome. In Chapter 8, we will encounter this form of memory disorder in our discussion of memory loss following ruptured aneurysm of the anterior communicating artery, but the reader should also note recent studies suggesting that frontal amnesia may be a feature of the memory deficit underlying schizophrenia (e.g. Goldberg, Weinberger & Pliskin, 1989; Parkin & Stampfer, in press).

THE AMNESIC SYNDROME

In our taxonomy, the amnesic syndrome is defined as a permanent, stable and global disorder of memory due to organic brain dysfunction which occurs in the absence of any other extensive perceptual or cognitive disturbance. One of the most striking features of the amnesic syndrome is the wide range of different aetiologies that can give rise to it and its association with damage to several different brain regions. Aetiologies include closed-head injury, penetrating head injury, cerebral infarction, sub-arachnoid haemorrhage, hypoglycaemia, hypoxia, tumour, Wernicke's disease, other metabolic disorders and herpes simplex encephalitis. Describing the amnesic syndrome as a global disorder of memory is somewhat misleading because, when studied in more detail, it becomes clear that several forms of memory are left intact in amnesic patients. However, before this point can be fully appreciated, it is necessary to digress and briefly consider current theorising about the organisation of human memory.

A Model of Memory Organisation

Figure 1.2 shows what has become known as the "modal" model of memory, so called because it is still thought that most experimental psychologists would agree with its basic assertions. Somewhat confusingly, the principal feature of the model is *modularity*, a concept currently very much in vogue within cognitive psychology. Derived from the ideas of theorists such as Marr (1982) and Fodor (1983), modularity refers to the view that any system within the brain exists in the form of separable modules which interact with each other to achieve some overall complex function such as memory. Modularity is thought to convey advantages on an organism because it allows, in evolutionary terms, modifications or additions to one part of the system without the need for concomitant change in other modules.

Many neuropsychologists assume that the various modules occupy different anatomical locations (e.g. Ellis & Young, 1989). Armed with this assumption of *neurological specificity*, patients with brain damage constitute a powerful database from which to deduce the modularity of brain processes. Central to this approach is the principle of *double dissociation*. This can be

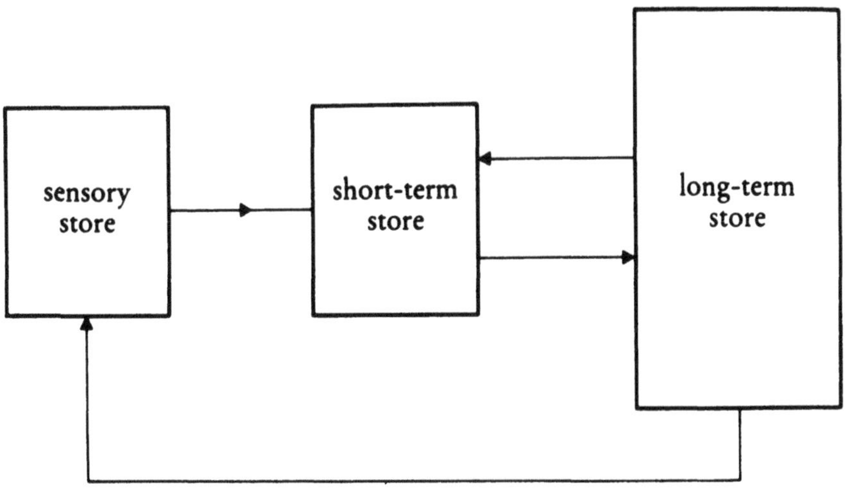

FIG. 1.2 The modal model of memory. Reproduced from Parkin (1987) with the permission of Basil Blackwell Scientific Publishers.

understood simply by imagining a particular brain process that is thought to be the joint product of two modules, A and B, each of which is assumed to carry out a subset of the required processing operations underlying a function. The value of this assertion can be verified if patients can be observed who show a behavioural deficit consistent with the preservation of A but loss of B and vice versa. However, it should also be noted that modular theorists are also impressed by *one-way dissociations*, in which one ability is consistently impaired despite normal function in another.

In Chapter 8, we will consider the importance of amnesia research in debates about the modal model but, for now, we will restrict ourselves to an introductory description of its various components. New experiences first impinge on *sensory memory*, a set of modality-specific storage systems in which raw perceptual information generated by the senses is held for a short period of time (approximately half a second for visual information and a few seconds for auditory information). Clinical assessment of sensory memory is not normally carried out. Furthermore, patients exhibiting deficits in this form of memory tend to be classified as suffering perceptual rather than memory deficits.

Information passes from sensory storage into what Atkinson and Shiffrin (1968) defined as the *short-term store* (STS). Other accounts of memory have also identified a similar structure but called it *primary memory* (Waugh & Norman, 1965) or the *central processor* (Craik & Lockhart, 1972). Although each of these accounts differs, they are united in identifying a limited capacity memory system that provides the substrate of our conscious mental experience and it is this which we will call STS. The capacity of STS is what we typically refer to as our span of awareness or *immediate memory*, and it is important to distinguish this concept from *short-term memory*, which is an atheoretical term specifying retention of information over a relatively short time period. At a clinical level, immediate memory is most commonly measured using *digit span*, a task in which the subject has to repeat back in the same order a series of digits that have been spoken by the tester. Normal individuals can manage about seven digits with a range of plus or minus two. However, more recently, tests on non-verbal memory span have also been introduced (see Chapter 2). Short-term memory can be tested in a variety of ways (e.g. free recall of word lists, recognition of pictures) and a purely consensus approach suggests that intervals of up to 5 min can be considered "short-term", although there is no theoretical reason for this.

Unfortunately, recent neuropsychological investigations of patients with immediate memory problems have shown that digit span is not a definitive measure of STS capacity. Shallice and Warrington (1970) report the case of K.F., an aphasic patient who had a markedly reduced auditory verbal digit span despite near-normal performance on other measures of immediate apprehension. This selective deficit has now been observed in a number of patients who otherwise appear to have no immediate memory problems (see Mayes, 1988; Vallar & Shallice, 1990), and led to the view that STS is not a unitary structure, but a collection of specialised sub-components held together by a common attentional mechanism. At the forefront of this theorising is the working memory model of Baddeley and Hitch (1974) and its revision by Baddeley (1986). Within this model, the deficit exhibited by patients like K.F. is attributed to the impairment of a specific articulatory sub-component which is crucial for certain mental operations.

Although STS is now considered to be non-unitary, it is still accepted that information contained within it is maintained in some form of active storage, i.e. its presence depends on a pattern of maintained neural activity. Information passes from STS, and hence out of awareness, and eventually reaches the long-term store (LTS) where it becomes *consolidated*, i.e. transformed into some permanent neural substrate that does not require continuing activity for the memory to be retained and, subsequently, serves as the basis by which that information is retrieved. The passage of information out of conscious awareness should not be thought of as co-extensive with the occurrence of full consolidation. Consolidation, as a biological process, is not well understood, but it is likely to take longer than a few seconds. Thus information that has just passed from consciousness into LTS is not, *ipso facto*, consolidated. Unconsolidated information is vulnerable to any event which disrupts the neurophysiological processes of the brain and the temporal extent of this vulnerability is still an open question. However, the finding that mild head injury victims can remember all but the last few minutes before their injury suggests that a degree of consolidation may be achieved quite rapidly.

LTS contains all the permanent memory acquired by an individual. Partly as a result of studying amnesic patients, it has been proposed that LTS has a number of separable sub-systems concerned with different kinds of stored information, but agreement on the exact nature of these different systems has not yet been reached. Tulving (1985; 1989) has proposed that LTS should be subdivided into three memory sub-systems: episodic, semantic and procedural. *Procedural* memory is the least controversial of these systems and is defined as knowledge that is inaccessible to consciousness. As a result, procedural memory can only be expressed indirectly through some form of action and is most readily exemplified by the representation of motor skills which, when well established, are difficult or impossible to describe consciously. Experienced typists, for example,

FIG. 1.3 Examples of closure pictures.

cannot define the sequence of finger movements required to type a word without carrying out those movements first. The grammatical knowledge used in the production and comprehension of language can also be considered procedural, as is the perceptual knowledge underlying our ability to identify closure pictures such as those in Fig. 1.3 when we encounter them for a second time.

Within Tulving's scheme, *episodic* memory is the record of personal experience which allows us to recount specific events in our lives and maintain a continuity with the past. *Semantic* memory, in contrast, consists of our linguistic knowledge, rules, concepts and other knowledge that allows us to function in the world. The contents of semantic memory are all assumed to have derived from specific episodes but, with the passage of time, these memories have become independent of any record of the original events that gave rise to them. Thus recalling knowledge acquired through past experience no longer depends crucially on recalling those experiences. Tasks involving the learning of verbal information are episodic rather than semantic. Consider a short experiment in which a subject is given the words DARK, CRUSH, HANDLE and SKY to remember. Ten minutes later, the subject recalls only DARK and SKY. Failure to remember CRUSH and HANDLE is not a failure of semantic memory because, if presented with these words, the subject could identify and comprehend them easily. What has failed is the subject's ability to recall those words that were presented at a particular time, i.e. they were part of the list-learning episode.

Not everyone agrees with Tulving's tripartite division of LTS. Cohen and Squire (1981) argue that one cannot reliably classify all knowledge as either semantic or episodic. For example, a statement that we worked hard at university could be derived from episodic recollections or from general semantic knowledge about oneself. Difficulties such as these have led some workers to suggest that episodic and semantic memory are really a single entity known as *declarative memory*, which, in contrast to procedural memory, is defined as knowledge that can be consciously accessed and expressed verbally or in some other symbolic means.

These kinds of theoretical difficulties have inspired an alternative approach to the division of memory. Rather than specify putative structural divisions, it proposed that LTS should be characterised in terms of the demands various tasks make on the memory system (Schacter, 1987). Within this system, *implicit memory* refers to any memory task that does not require conscious recollection of a prior learning episode. Procedural memory, as defined earlier, fits neatly into the definition of implicit memory, as introspection shows us that performance of a well-practised skill does not involve any recollective experience before it can be carried out. Explicit memory, in contrast, is defined as memory requiring the recollection of specific past events. Explicit memory equates nicely with our previous definition of episodic memory. This leaves just semantic memory tasks to be accommodated within the implicit/explicit dichotomy. At first sight, semantic memory tasks (e.g. categorising a word as either "animal", "vegetable" or "mineral") would seem to meet the criterion of implicit memory because no specific reference to a past episode is required. However, in making the response, the subject is aware, in some general sense, that their ability to answer derives from prior conscious experience—an introspection that does not accompany the use of procedural memory. As a result, semantic and procedural memory tasks are not easily thought of as functionally equivalent.

At this point, we will not attempt any conclusion as to which of the above descriptive frameworks provides the best account of LTS phenomena. We will simply note that there are various ways to describe the divisions of LTS and we will make use of these differing terms as appropriate. The term "semantic memory", for example, is extremely useful because it delineates, at least for cognitive psychologists, a particular set of phenomena related to language and general intellectual function. Its use is therefore justified even if it cannot be distinguished unambiguously from episodic memory. Similarly, the terms "implicit" and "explicit" memory have value because they provide a reliable and theoretically interesting contrast between two sets of memory tasks, even though not all memory tasks fit neatly into the distinction.

Defining Features of the Amnesic Syndrome

The above framework enables us to list the features which we and other investigators of memory deficits consider to be the defining features of the amnesic syndrome:

1. No evidence of impaired immediate memory as measured by tasks such as digit span.
2. Semantic memory and other intellectual functions, as measured by standardised tests, largely intact.
3. A severe and permanent *anterograde amnesia* (impaired memory for new information) exhibited on both tests of recall and recognition.
4. A degree of *retrograde amnesia* (loss of memory acquired in the period before brain damage), which may be extremely variable across patients.
5. Intact procedural memory, notably motor skills, and usually some evidence of an ability to form new procedural memory.

Aetiological Variation and the Neuroanatomy of Memory

Over the years, neuropathological studies of amnesic patients have provided a great deal of evidence about the neuroanatomical basis of human memory. Initially through autopsy studies, such as Victor et al.'s (1971; 1989) classic study of the Wernicke-Korsakoff Syndrome (Chapter 3), and more recently as a result of *in vivo* neuroradiology (e.g. Press, Amaral & Squire, 1989), it has been possible to identify, with a certain degree of accuracy, the particular brain structures vital for normal memory function.

The first critical structures are the medial temporal lobes of both the right and left hemispheres, and within these areas the *hippocampus* has been particularly implicated in memory function. The second brain region lies within the *diencephalon*, a structure beneath the cerebral cortex comprising two principal structures, the *thalamus* and the *hypothalamus*. Studies of amnesic patients, particularly those with Wernicke-Korsakoff Syndrome (see Chapter 3), have regularly implicated the *dorso-medial thalamic nucleus* (DMTN) and the *mamillary bodies* in memory function. Despite occupying different regions of the brain, the structures we have so far identified form part of the *limbic system*, which is show in Fig. 1.4. The significance of this interrelationship is returned to in Chapter 8.

The Rest of this Book

The remaining chapters of this book are concerned in different ways with the neuropsychology of the amnesic syndrome. Chapter 2 provides an overview of assessment methods, which includes both a discussion of clinical assessment and arms the reader with terminology that is essential for understanding much of the evidence discussed in subsequent chapters. Thus, even if you have no clinical interest, Chapter 2 should still be read. Following on from this are a series of chapters describing different patient groups presenting the amnesic syndrome. Because of their predominance in the literature, some patient groups have a whole chapter devoted to them (e.g. Wernicke-Korsakoff Syndrome, Chapter 3; herpes simplex encephalitis, Chapter 6). Other patient groups are linked together in aetiologically appropriate groupings. Each of these chapters provides an explanation of aetiology and an account of neuropsychological deficits. Memory impairment is obviously the focus of our account, but attention is also paid to related cognitive impairments such as those associated with frontal lobe dysfunction. Chapter 7 describes the pattern of memory loss associated with aneurysms of the anterior communicating artery, a patient group that has only recently been directly implicated in studies of the amnesic syndrome and one which provides scope for considering memory

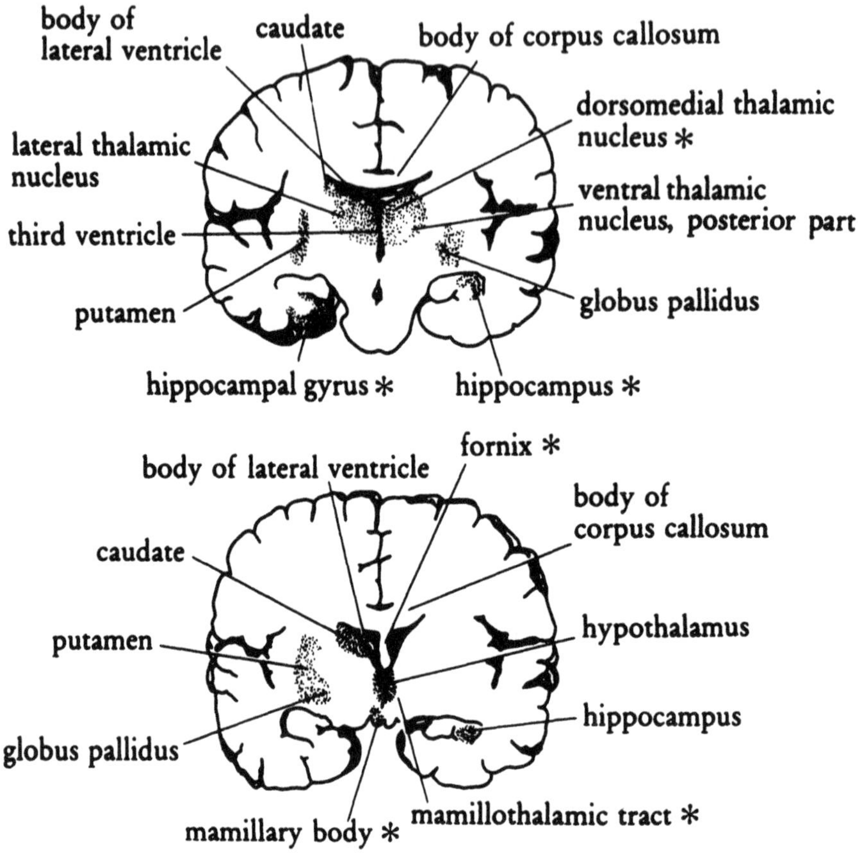

FIG. 1.4 Diagram showing the various structures of the limbic system associated with the amnesic syndrome (indicated by asterisks). Reproduced from Butters and Cermak (1980) with the permission of Academic Press.

loss arising from lesions that are primarily frontal in nature. Each of these chapters is also illustrated by example case histories from our own research experience. Chapter 8 provides a discussion of major theoretical issues surrounding the investigation of amnesic syndromes and a final chapter considers the prospects for remediation.

In writing this book we decided, for two reasons, to exclude any detailed discussion of patients with an amnesic syndrome arising from closed-head injury (CHI). Despite their tragic frequency, CHI patients have not been very prominent in studies of the amnesic syndrome (however, for an exception, see Tulving, Hayman & MacDonald, 1991). The reason for this is that CHI patients with amnesia often present other cognitive impairments which make interpretation of their memory deficit very difficult. Secondly, CHI is a major topic in its own right and is perhaps better dealt with by texts directly addressing it (e.g. Richardson, 1990). For similar reasons, we have also omitted dementing illnesses. Dementing illnesses present our society with a major therapeutic and social problem. The memory deficits associated with these devastating illnesses are perhaps the foremost cause of management problems in the psycho-geriatric population. There is now substantial interest in the nature of memory impairments in dementia and the possibilities of remediation. Although there are similarities between memory disorders in dementia and those found in patients with the amnesic syndrome, a full account of these disorders is again outside our present scope. However, the interested reader is referred to a number of recent accounts of memory loss in dementia (e.g. Morris, 1991).

2 Assessment of Memory Disorder

The accurate and systematic assessment of memory disorder is vital, both to the researcher and to the clinician. In conducting experiments on amnesic patients, it is important for the experimenter to characterise both the qualitative and quantitative features of the patient sample. This is essential if meaningful comparisons are to be made between groups of patients within the same study and with results obtained by other researchers. In particular, interpretations of results obtained from studies comparing different aetiological groups are difficult without adequate quantitative measures of the memory deficit that are independent from the experimental measures. Clinically, memory assessment should profile the patient's abilities and disabilities, measure change in memory function over time, and predict memory functioning in everyday life.

The study of memory is one of the core areas of experimental psychology, and therefore one might expect that the development of memory tests would be closely allied to developments in the associated theoretical field. However, as Loring and Papanicolaou (1987, p. 341) note, given

> the importance of memory evaluation in contemporary neuropsychology, one would expect a considerable degree of sophistication on the part of the professionals performing these assessments, both in their approach to the phenomena of memory and in the assessment procedures they select. Regrettably, however, many neuropsychologists appear to believe tacitly in a variant of a familiar theme; that is, memory is that quantity that the Wechsler Memory Scale measures. Similarly, when employing newer measures attempting to parcel memory into different components such as

> storage vs. retrieval (eg. Selective Reminding Procedure), they fail to remember that an unambiguous operational definition of a psychological construct is completely independent of construct validity.

With this view in mind, we will now consider various procedures for the assessment memory function.

Wechsler Memory Scale

The Wechsler Memory Scale (WMS: Wechsler, 1945) was one of the earliest attempts at measuring memory using psychometric methods and it is still widely used both clinically and experimentally despite repeated criticism of its inadequacies (e.g. Erickson & Scott, 1977; Prigatano, 1978). The WMS comprises seven sub-tests—orientation, information, mental control, digit span, logical memory, visual reproduction and paired-associate learning—although the latter three are often administered on their own. There are two forms of the test, enabling more accurate reassessment, but form 1 is used far more than form 2. Major shortcomings of the WMS include an absence of recognition and remote memory tests (both functions that may show selective sparing in memory-disordered patients), an absence of delayed retention and limited non-verbal memory content. However, the Boston revision of the WMS (Milberg, Hebben & Kaplan, 1986) now includes a recognition test and has generally improved the WMS for use with neurological patients.

The individual sub-tests also have various shortcomings. The mental control sub-test seems to have little to do with memory function. The visual reproduction test is easy to verbalise but, more importantly, factor analysis studies have indicated that it loads most heavily on visual-perceptual motor ability unless delayed testing is used (Larrabee, Kane & Schuck, 1983). Logical memory presents with a number of scoring difficulties (e.g. verbatim *vs* gist measures: Loring & Papanicolaou, 1987) and the patient's performance will suffer if he or she is momentarily distracted, anxious or has difficulty concentrating. Also, because the two stories are read consecutively, there is the risk of proactive interference impairing performance on the second one, although, in this case, one must note that the second story of form 1 is more difficult to recall *per se* (Henry et al., 1990). The paired-associate learning test has easy pairs, which can easily be guessed at (e.g. up–down) and are therefore not very informative, and hard pairs (e.g. obey–inch), which amnesic patients rarely learn. Interpretation of this sub-test may therefore be biased by floor effects and there must be doubts about combining easy and hard scores to form a single measure.

In its original form, the WMS sub-test scores are combined to produce a memory quotient (MQ) which was assumed to be directly comparable to the Full Scale IQ (FSIQ) measure of the Wechsler Adult Intelligence Scale (WAIS: Wechsler, 1955). However, modern conceptions of memory reject the idea of a unitary system and, for this reason, the MQ measure is reported less and less frequently by clinicians. None the less, given the characterisation of amnesia in terms of impaired episodic memory in the presence of relatively preserved language and intellect (see Chapter 1), it is commonplace for studies to cite FSIQ–MQ discrepancy scores as a means of indicating the "purity" of a patient's amnesic syndrome. Aside from knowing what MQ is functionally, there are two additional difficulties. First, FSIQ and MQ (assessed by immediate retention performance) are highly correlated and, secondly, the normative populations used in developing WAIS and WMS cannot be considered comparable (Larrabee, 1987; Richardson, 1990). The FSIQ–MQ discrepancy is also problematic because nothing is known about its distribution. It is sometimes suggested (e.g. Weiskrantz, 1985) that a 15 points discrepancy should be the minimum value indicating a deficit. However, the reasoning underlying this is not clear, because appropriate descriptive statistics do not appear to be available for MQ (Knight & Longmore, 1990). These problems have not been generally addressed, although the high correlation between FSIQ and MQ can be largely overcome by using Russell's (1975) modification (the "Russell Revision of WMS"), which includes delayed testing of logical memory, paired-associate learning and visual reproduction.

Given limitations such as these, the WMS seems far from ideal but we would argue that its administration is worthwhile. It is relatively quick to administer, provides a screening measure sensitive to severe memory impairment, with failure on immediate logical memory, and hard paired-associates, generally good indicators of an amnesic syndrome. There are also substantial normative data available for the WMS. D'Elia, Satz and Schretlen (1989) recently appraised these data in terms of seven methodological criteria including quality of sample, scoring and age distribution. Their study cites the most appropriate data for American populations and several alternatives are recommended including norms for non-American English-speaking subjects. Finally, FSIQ–MQ discrepancy scores may have some value as a first approximation of memory impairment and, as we shall see at various points, it provides a reasonably consistent index of the amnesic syndrome.

Revised Wechsler Memory Scale (WMS-R)

The revised Wechsler Memory Scale (WMS-R: Wechsler, 1987) begins with an extended orientation/information section. It retains some of the

WMS sub-tests—digit span, logical memory, paired-associate learning and visual reproduction—but the items have in many cases been changed, or increased, and the scoring criteria improved. Sensitivity and reduced correlation with IQ are addressed by including delayed recall versions of these sub-tests. A non-verbal memory span task, visual paired-associate learning and a visual recognition test involving geometric visual patterns are also included. The results from these tests are used to calculate various indices, each with a mean of 100 and standard deviation of 15: a general memory index, a verbal memory index, a visual memory index, a delayed recall index and an attention/concentration index. Roth, Conboy, Reeder and Boll (1990) have carried out a factor analysis of WMS-R and identified three distinct but highly correlated factors—attention/concentration, immediate memory and delayed recall. Thus, these results suggest that the ability of WMS-R to differentiate visual and verbal memory is questionable.

The manual (Wechsler, 1987) provides a table of intercorrelations between WAIS-R Full Scale IQ and WMS-R sub-tests and between each of the WMS-R sub-tests by age. Logical memory, both immediate and delayed, appears to correlate most highly with WAIS-R FSIQ, but the correlations between FSIQ and visual reproduction and digit span also tend to be quite high. A table of intercorrelations between indices is also provided. General memory correlates very highly with delayed recall. The correlations between verbal memory and visual memory are very low in the younger age groups, but they are higher in the older ones. The remaining intercorrelations range from 0.41 to 0.66 and are fairly stable across the age range. In addition to age-related norms, the examiner is able to compare a patient's performance with memory-disordered groups of various aetiologies such as Korsakoff's Syndrome and closed-head injury. The WMS-R is clearly an improvement over the WMS, although it is wise to use it with additional tests of recognition memory.

From a practical viewpoint, the WMS-R takes much longer to administer (45–60 min) than its predecessor. A short-form is specified but this unavoidably omits delayed retention testing, an important advantage of WMS-R over WMS. For these and other reasons, clinicians may well continue to use WMS, particularly the Russell revision which has recently undergone re-standardisation and modification (Russell, 1988).

Recognition Memory Test

Warrington's (1984) Recognition Memory Test (RMT) consists of two sub-tests, one involving memory for words and the other for faces. For each sub-test, there are 50 items shown individually for 3 sec, each followed by forced choice recognition. As a measure of recognition, the test provides a useful adjunct to the WMS. The test is easy to administer, age- and sex-related norms are given, and there is a good range of scores available. Also, by use of verbal and non-verbal material it is possible to detect material-specific deficits.

There are, however, some drawbacks to the RMT. Controls, particularly younger people, perform close to ceiling on the task. As a result, a young, mildly impaired patient may not be detected. Parkin et al. (in press a) offer one solution to this problem by administering the test upside down, so as to lower overall performance and provide greater scope for detecting differences at the higher end of the performance range. Problems also arise when testing severely impaired patients beause they all tend to perform at chance (Warrington & Weiskrantz, 1982), thus minimising the informative value of the test and its use as a patient-matching criterion. In addition, no inter-rater or test–retest reliability data are reported, practice effects have not been investigated, and there are no parallel forms of the test (for an extensive critique of RMT, see Kapur, 1987).

An alternative form of recognition test is the "Continuous Recognition Memory" (CRM) procedure which exists in several versions (e.g. Hannay & Levin, 1988; Kimura, 1963). In this test, the subjects view a sequence of items and their task is to differentiate between repeated and non-repeated items. These tests are useful because they make minimal demands on verbal and motor responding and, by the use of appropriate materials, they can also detect material-specific deficits. The CRM is also useful in that it can yield measures of both sensitivity and bias in recognition memory, whereas RMT is only a measure of sensitivity.

Complex Figures

An additional and often used test of visual memory is the Rey Complex Figure (Rey, 1964) and the alternative prepared by Taylor (1979) for re-testing. The subjects are initially required to copy the figure and the manner in which they do this can be a measure of visuo-spatial ability (Ogden, Growden & Corkin, 1990). Figure 2.1 shows data from two memory-impaired patients on the Complex Figure Task. Learning is incidental and free recall of the figure, usually undertaken between 10 and 30 min after learning, provides a measure of retention. The complex figure is somewhat difficult to describe and this, combined with the use of incidental learning, make the figure a reasonable test of visuo-spatial memory. A problem, however, is that the performance of memory-disordered patients can often be severely impaired and interpretation is sometimes difficult because frontal lobe disturbance can result in disorganised copying which might exacerbate basic memory difficulties. Test–retest performance is also complicated because delayed recall of the

(a)

(b)

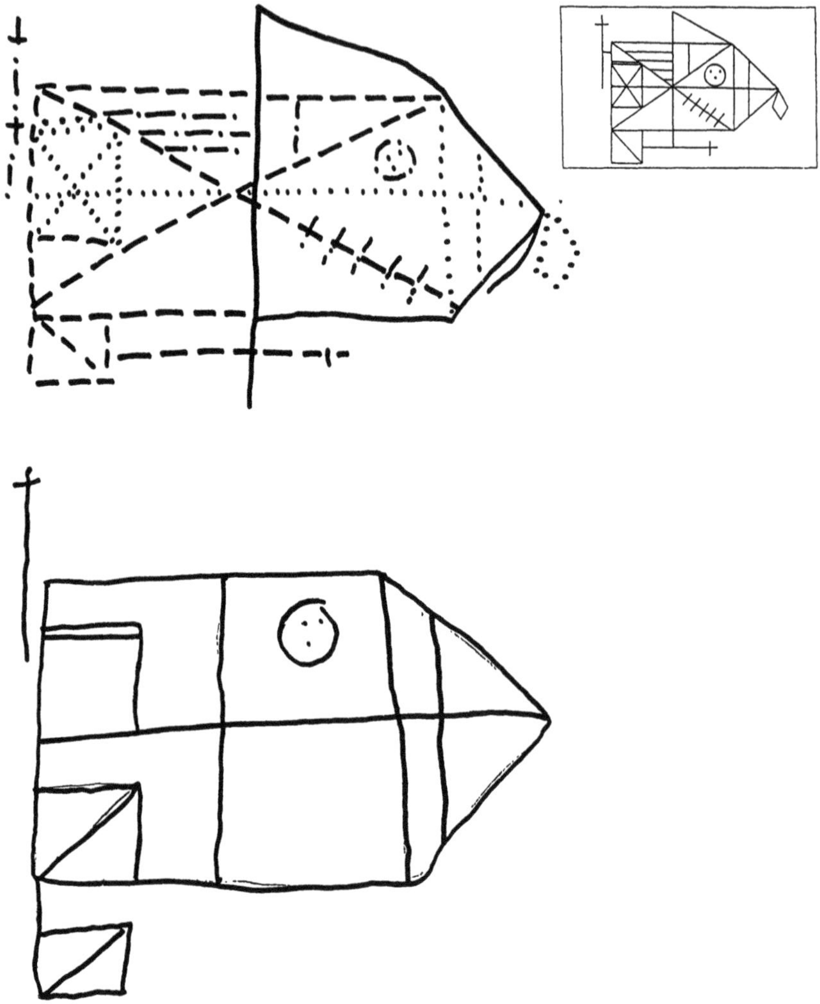

FIG. 2.1 Copying (a) and recall (b) of the Rey Figure (see insert) by patient J.B. (see Chapter 7). Copying illustration indicates the order in which various parts of the figure were copied: solid line first, broken line second, dotted line third, broken/dotted line fourth. Note how J.B. makes little use of the overall organisation of the picture when copying.

Rey Complex Figure appears more difficult than Taylor's alternative (Strauss & Spreen, 1990).

Adult Memory and Information-processing Battery (AMIPB)

This battery, devised by Coughlan and Hollows (1985), comprises a number of sub-tests, including story recall and figure recall, verbal and non-verbal learning, and two tests based on letter cancellation. The age range extends to 75 years, parallel versions are available and delayed retention is also included. However, the control and "cerebral dysfunction" standardisation samples are rather small. The AMIPB has not been validated against other memory tests but it correlates quite highly with intelligence. Reliability of the sub-tests varies, with story recall and figure recall being especially low. There are no recognition tests, nor are there tests of remote memory, memory span or procedural learning. The rationale to the test selection is not wholly clear, but the authors claim to have selected tests which are familiar to clinicians and which they hope will correlate rather better with everyday memory ability.

OTHER PSYCHOMETRIC MEMORY TESTS

There are several other memory tests which are used in clinical practice. Rey's (1964) Auditory Verbal Learning Test (AVLT) is a serial learning task involving two lists of concrete nouns. The subjects are read list A five times with recall tests after each presentation. Following one presentation and immediate recall of list B, delayed recall of list A is required followed by an optional recognition test for both list A and B items. An advantage of the test is the richness of information it provides, including serial position effects, sensitivity to interference and organisational factors. Re-administration of Rey's original procedure can be contaminated by practice effects and investigators should use the alternative version devised by Crawford, Stewart and Moore (1989) for retesting.

The Buschke (1973) Selective Reminding (SR) Test has been used in a number of clinical and experimental studies. A limitation of the test is that it measures only verbal recall, retest reliabilites are low, and practice effects are also encountered (Hannay & Levin, 1985). However, a recent study by Masur et al. (1990) indicates that performance on the SR test has good predictive value for the subsequent development of dementia, and Ruff, Light and Evans (1987) have provided age-related norms for test performance. An evaluation of SR is provided by Loring and Papanicolaou (1987).

Randt, Brown and Osbourne (1980) report a new memory scale for examining mild to moderate impairments of memory. The procedures are motivated more by theoretical considerations than are other available tests. For example, they include distractor tasks between learning trials to remove contamination from recency effects. The test has five versions, making it ideal for monitoring change. Memory is tested in several ways and the test has much in common with the WMS. An important difference, however, is that memory is assessed in different ways including recall, recognition and savings in learning. The patient first receives a general information test which serves as a screen for dementia. Next, the subject must learn five high-frequency words to a criterion of all correct on one trial using the Buschke SR procedure. Retention is tested immediately and by means of a savings measure 24 hours later. Forward and backward digit span is also tested, as is paired-associate learning. The latter contrasts learning of strongly and weakly associated pairs and unrelated pairs using both the selective reminding procedure and a delayed savings measure. Story recall is also assessed and there is a picture learning test in which the subject must identify seven previously exposed items from a larger array. Finally, an incidental recall task is given in which the patient recalls the items and titles of the preceding sub-tests. The battery was found to be sensitive to age-related decline in memory and to distinguish between this and clinical memory impairments. Retest reliability is between 0.79 and 0.93.

Concern about face validity led Crook, Youngjohn and Larrabee (1990) to develop the Misplaced Objects Test. In this test, the subjects are required to place 20 computer-simulated objects in different rooms of a schematic house. At test, 40 min later, the examiner names the objects and the subject indicates its location by touching the appropriate point on a screen. The authors stress the test's face validity but, in this respect, one must note the close correlation between test performance and the much more quickly administered WMS paired-associate learning test.

Finally, we must mention the memory battery recommended by Butters et al. (1990) as part of a basis for assessing cognitive deficits in AIDS patients. It comprises the California Verbal Learning Test, which enables the assessment of recall, recognition, serial position effects, learning rate, vulnerability to interference, learning strategies and qualitative error analysis. A test of working memory is also included, which measures performance on a pursuit tracking task while carrying out a concurrent digit span task. The third component is a visual reproduction test similar to that of the WMS. The test, which takes about 75 min to administer, tests a wide variety of functions. It seems particularly useful for characterising more subtle memory deficits and has the added advantage of a theoretical basis, but it is fairly lengthy to administer and requires a considerable amount of equipment.

Rivermead Behavioural Memory Test

Wilson and co-workers (Wilson, Cockburn & Halligan, 1987; Wilson, Cockburn, Baddeley & Hiorns, 1989) argued that existing memory tests were not representative of the everyday memory demands made on brain-injured people and this led them to develop the Rivermead Behavioural Memory Test (RBMT). Construction of the test was strongly influenced by clinical observations and patients' own reports of their memory difficulties. The test has many similarities with other tests, but it is novel in its inclusion of a prospective memory test (remembering to do something). The test is also considered to have greater face validity in that the sub-tests bear far more resemblance to everyday memory activities than other tests (e.g. the WMS).

There are 12 test items: recalling a name; spontaneously remembering where a belonging has been hidden; asking a specified question when an alarm rings; recognising previously presented pictures; immediate and delayed story recall; recognising unfamiliar faces; immediate and delayed recall of a route; remembering a message; and being able to answer questions about orientation in time, place and person. From this either a screening score or a more detailed profile score is calculated. Wilson et al. (1989) report high correlations for test–retest and inter-rater reliabilities and there are several alternative forms of some test items. As one might expect, the correlation with everyday memory complaints is high. The RBMT was originally found not to correlate with IQ, but more recent reports suggest that the correlation with IQ is in fact significant although not highly so (Wilson et al., 1989). The RBMT correlates better with the observations of relatives, staff and patients than psychometric tests and appears to show some promise in the early detection of dementia (Beardsall & Huppert, 1989).

Recently, the RBMT has been adapted for use with children (Aldrich & Wilson, 1991; Wilson, Ivani-Chalian & Aldrich, 1991), and Wilson, Forester, Bryant and Cockburn (1990) have also demonstrated that RBMT is a particularly good indicator of whether or not an amnesic patient had returned to some form of gainful employment. This finding is substantiated by Schwartz and McMillan (1989), who also found that RBMT related better to the recovery status of closed-head injury patients compared with other measures.

MEMORY QUESTIONNAIRES

Concern that cognitive tests may not predict or evaluate performance in real-life settings has led to various attempts at developing memory questionnaires. Herrman and Neisser (1978) developed a questionnaire which they called the Inventory of Memory Experiences (IME). The questionnaire was arranged in two main sections. The first section, comprising 48 questions, asks the subject to rate frequency of forgetting on a 7-point scale; the second section includes 24 questions concerning how well the subject remembers certain past events. Test–retest reliability (0.68) was good, and comparable to many psychometric tests. However, the study was carried out on normal subjects and the questionnaire would not be suitable for memory-impaired patients because many of them lack insight, memory ability or both, and therefore would be unable to report back accurately on their memory problems (Parkin, Bell & Leng, 1988a).

Other researchers have also examined everyday memory by using questionnaires (e.g. Bennett-Levy & Powell, 1980; Broadbent, Cooper, Fitzgerald & Parkes, 1982; Sunderland, Harris & Baddeley, 1983). It has been argued that the correlation between questionnaire responses and memory tests may not be reliable. Zelinski, Gilewski and Thompson (1980), for example, gave young college students memory tests and an everyday memory questionnaire but found no relationship between the two measures. However, because studies such as these have often used normal subjects, it is likely that lack of variability in memory test scores has reduced the scope for a significant correlation to emerge. This conclusion was strengthened by Sunderland et al. (1983), who found good correlations between the questionnaire and some memory test scores in stable head-injured subjects. Similarly, Knight and Godfrey (1985) examined the relationship between laboratory-based tests, questionnaires and observational rating scales in the assessment of alcoholic amnesics and found a high degree of positive correlation between all three procedures. One should also note that questionnaires provide an assessment of patients' insight into their memory disorder, which can be extremely valuable from a management point of view.

REMOTE MEMORY TESTS

There are no widely available psychometric tests of remote memory. This is surprising given the frequent occurrence of remote memory loss in many organic disorders, but it is probably due to the difficulties in constructing a valid test, and with the tendency for patients to be more concerned with their anterograde deficits. Remote memory can be assessed by compiling a personal history from a close relative and then testing the patient on this information. Unfortunately, few clinicians can justify the time necessary to do this, and comparison across patients is very difficult. A related but less time-consuming procedure for assessing memory is the "autobiographical cueing" or "Crovitz" technique (Crovitz & Schiffman, 1974; Robinson, 1976). Derived from the introspective methodology of Francis Galton, the subject is given a single word as a cue to recall an actual past event and subsequently required to date it. Recall can be "unconstrained" in that the subject is free to recall events from any time period with dating only required when the memory has been produced. An alternative "constrained" method requires the subject to restrict recall from a particular time period. Cueing may also be constrained by requesting a particular type of memory, e.g. memories related to emotions as opposed to actions.

Autobiographical cueing is a useful procedure for gaining an impression of a patient's remote memory, but it has some notable disadvantages. First, it is difficult to establish the truth of a patient's recall, a particular problem in patients with confabulatory tendencies. Secondly, self-dating of memory can be generally inaccurate and notably impaired by the frontal lobe impairments that often accompany memory disorder. Finally, one has to ensure that the events recalled are "specific" (i.e. relating to a particular time point) rather than generalisations based solely on the patient's general knowledge of their past—this judgement can have a high degree of subjectivity.

Recently, Borrini et al. (1989) produced a structured approach to measuring autobiographical memory. Their questionnaire covered the life-span by asking a subject if he or she could remember various life events. Validity was measured by comparing the subjects' responses on initial and subsequent testing or by obtaining confirmation from a witness. Inter-rater reliability between scorers was found to be high. The questionnaire was given to normal controls only in this study, but amnesic subjects were assessed in a subsequent study (Dall'Ora, Della Sala & Spinnler, 1989). These patients showed considerable variation in their performance, a result consistent with earlier studies (Baddeley & Wilson, 1986).

The problems that arise when attempting to assess an individual's autobiographical memory have led to tests which attempt to measure "public" remote memory, i.e. past memories that can be reasonably assumed to be represented in most people from a given culture. The most well-known is the Boston Remote Memory Battery (BRMB: Albert, Butters & Levin, 1979), which comprises a verbal test of past events and a recognition test for famous faces. All components of the test sample events and people equally from all decades, and the degree of success on items from different decades, can provide information about any temporal gradient that might be present. This test, and others derived from it (e.g. Parkin, Montaldi, Leng & Hunkin, 1990b), acknowledge that the ability of a patient to recall information about a particular event or person may not, necessarily, reflect recall of memories laid down during that time period. Many events and people (e.g. the Falklands War, Marilyn Monroe) continue to be talked about long after the time period in which they occurred. As a result, accurate recall of this type of information is not indicative of preserved memory for a particular time period. The solution to this difficult problem is to assume that the more difficult a piece of information is to recall, the more likely it reflects recall from a specific time period. In the case of faces, for example, Douglas Bader (the Second World War fighter ace) would be considered "decade-specific"—known primarily to people alive during the 1940s—whereas Winston Churchill would be known by most adults. In the BRMB, the above distinction is represented by the "hard–easy" dichotomy. However, it is noticeable that, despite poorer performance on the "hard" items, the pattern of deficits shown across time did not vary with item type—a point also noted by Parkin et al. (1990b).

Typically, remote memory tests assess performance using a recall measure (an exception being the recognition component of BRMB). Chapters 7 and 8 highlight recent findings indicating that anterograde recall deficits can be found when recognition memory is normal. A similar possibility needs to be acknowledged in the assessment of remote memory but, as yet, no standardised test other than the BRMT provides this contrast and this test is only available for U.S. populations. However, in two recent papers (Parkin, Dunn, Lee et al., in press a; Parkin & Stampfer, in press), data are presented from a "Famous Personalities Test", in which the patients had first to identify the famous persons in a group of four names and then explain why that person was famous. In both the above studies, the patients performed normally on recognition but were impaired on explanation.

Kapur, Young, Bateman and Kennedy (1989) report an alternative remote memory test known as the "Dead-or-Alive" test. The patient is given the name of a famous person and first asked if they are alive or dead. If the answer is "dead", the patient must further recall the mode of death (natural causes or killed) and attempt to date the time of death. Famous people are drawn from the 1960s up to the 1990s and our own use of the test indicates that it is an effective means of demonstrating temporal gradients in amnesic subjects (Parkin & Hunkin, in press). The dating component is of interest because it may dissociate from performance on the other two components, reflecting heterogeneity in remote memory impairment.

Kopelman, Wilson and Baddeley (1989) describe a number of remote memory tests employed in a study of temporal context memory in Korsakoff and Alzheimer patients. The first of these is a news events test, which comprises 50 pictures of memorable news events (10 for each of the decades between 1935 and 1984) which the subject has to describe. The second is a famous personalities test originally reported by Stevens (1979). Of the 160 names, 20 are excluded from the score because they are rated as being very famous, 60 are fictitious and the remaining 80 were well known at some point from 1930 onwards (although note that this test needs updating). The third test is the Personal Semantic Memory Schedule, developed in collaboration with Baddeley and Wilson. There are four sections covering background information, childhood, young adulthood and recent periods, and each section is scored out of 21. Subjects are tested for their knowledge of a number of personal facts, such as schools attended, friends, addresses, place and date of marriage and facts about a journey made during the last year. The patients' responses are then checked against information provided by someone who knows them well, such as next of kin. Finally, the Autobiographical Incidents Schedule, based on the autobiographical cueing technique (see above), is also administered. The latter two tests are now available commercially as the Autobiographical Memory Interview (AMI: Kopelman, 1990).

IMPLICIT MEMORY TESTS

Clinical memory assessments are almost exclusively concerned with tests of explicit memory. However, with recent interest in implicit memory phenomena and the implications these may have for rehabilitation (e.g. Glisky, Schacter & Tulving, 1986), clinicians will increasingly be including some measure of implicit function in their assessments. The most straightforward implicit tasks are those unambiguously tapping procedural memory. Among the most common of these are the pursuit rotor test and the mirror-drawing task (e.g. Corkin, 1968), but these may be least useful prognostically because they have little bearing on residual skills that may be harnessed for rehabilitation (see Chapter 9). Perceptual learning can be measured using such tasks as picture completion (e.g. Parkin & Streete, 1988) or perceptual closure (Crovitz, Harvey & McClanahan, 1981). In picture completion, subjects are shown a fragmented picture of an object. If they fail to identify it, more informative versions of the picture are shown until the subject identifies it correctly. To test learning, the sequence is re-presented and any savings in identification measured. Snodgrass, Bradford, Feenan and Corvin (1987) have produced sets of fragmented pictures suitable for use with patients and available on software.

Within the experimental literature, implicit memory in amnesia has been most frequently evaluated using verbal learning tasks. One example is *word stem completion*. In this task, the subject is first presented with a series of target words (e.g. METAL). After a retention interval, the subject is given a series of incomplete word stems (e.g. MET__?) and asked to say the first word that they can think of beginning with that stem. If target word completions exceed the chance rate, *priming* is said to have occurred—the implication being that some aspect of the prior learning episode has influenced learning even though that episode was not referred to. Stem completion allows a neat comparison of implicit and explicit performance because the same word stems can be used as explicit recall cues (e.g. what word did you see beginning with MET?). Experiments using this comparison have shown that amnesic patients show much better remembering under implicit than explicit instructions. At present, there are no "off the shelf" tests of stem completion or related procedures such as fragment completion (Tulving, Schacter & Stark, 1982). Researchers attempting to use these measures must therefore construct their own stimuli or, more advisedly, contact authors of papers and ask to have copies of their materials.

ADDITIONAL NEUROPSYCHOLOGICAL TESTING

Amnesia is rarely found as an isolated symptom, and therefore any assessment of memory impairment must consider other neuropsychological deficits that may also be contributing to the patient's overall performance. If this broader assessment is overlooked, the nature and severity of a patient's memory disorder may be wrongly evaluated. Some deficits can, on *a priori* grounds, be excluded from assessment. Anosmia (loss of smell), for example, is common in amnesic patients (see Chapter 3), but it is unlikely that this olfactory deficit has any bearing on the interpretation of memory performance (although one should acknowledge the Proustian quality of olfactory cues under some circumstances!). Apraxia (impaired movement), if present, is also likely to have little bearing on memory loss. However, there are other cognitive functions which, if not evaluated, can significantly distort interpretation of memory deficits.

In the following sections, we consider the most prominent of these deficits and how they might best be examined.

Other Cognitive Deficits

If possible, all patients should be administered either WAIS or WAIS-R (Wechsler, 1955; 1981). Aside from giving a measure of intelligence *per se*, administration of these tests gives a lot of additional information. Discrepancies between verbal and performance IQ provides some indication of asymmetry in a patient's lesion, and the extensive literature on the various sub-tests allows additional interpretation of specific sub-test failure (Lezak, 1983). Also, just the time spent observing the patient doing the various tests provides scope for the patient's deficits to emerge.

Administration of WAIS is quite time-consuming and may not be possible in a number of cases because of time constraints. However, it is possible to undertake a few tests that can screen out some of the more likely impairments that can confound interpretation of impaired memory performance. Post-encephalitic patients, for example, frequently exhibit a degree of anomia (e.g. Stewart, Parkin & Hunkin, 1992), but this can be easily checked for by giving the patient the Graded Naming Test (McKenna & Warrington, 1983) or simply selecting a range of line drawings and asking the subject to name them—a range of animals is often useful in this respect because these patients often have particular difficulty with these stimuli.

Perceptual deficits are often a problem. The Rivermead Perceptual Assessment Battery (Whiting, Lincoln, Bhavnani & Cockburn, 1985) provides a range of quickly administered sub-tests and a useful index of more subtle agnosia can be obtained by asking patients to name objects photographed from an unusual angle (Warrington & Taylor, 1978). There is also the newly developed Visual Object and Space Perception Battery (Warrington & James, 1991).

Frontal Symptoms

The most common and most problematic of impairments associated with amnesia are those due to frontal lobe damage. A detailed assessment of frontal function is essential because (1) frontal deficits such as perseveration (see below) can contaminate estimates of memory performance (e.g. forced choice recognition) and because (2) the frontal lobes are associated with specific memory abilities (see Chapters 7 and 8), and therefore detection of frontal impairments should alert the investigator to the possibility of memory deficits in addition to those expected from limbic system pathology.

The frontal lobes are somewhat enigmatic structures with a heterogeneity of function. The most widely used means of assessing frontal dysfunction is the Wisconsin Card Sorting Test (WCST), which is an essential adjunct to memory assessment in some amnesic patients since performance on WCST has often been shown to correlate with memory measures and therefore implicate frontal deficits in the interpretation of amnesic performance. Neuroanatomical and regional blood flow studies have suggested that WCST particularly engages the dorso-lateral pre-frontal cortex (Berman, Zec & Weinberger, 1986; Milner, 1971), but others have cautioned against its localising value (Bigler, 1988). Of the four measures possible with WCST, preservative errors are considered the most indicative of frontal involvement. The FAS word fluency test or its equivalents (e.g. the version described by Kolb & Whishaw, 1990), which measures the ability to generate words according to category headings, are also valuable, although their interrelation with IQ must not be overlooked (Miller, 1984). Design-fluency (Jones-Gotman & Milner, 1977) is a non-verbal equivalent of verbal fluency, although some may prefer Ruff et al.'s (1987) design fluency test which is both easier to administer and to score.

Cognitive estimation (Shallice & Evans, 1978) measures a patient's ability to estimate sizes, distances, etc., and it is noticeable that performance on cognitive estimation can dissociate from the impairment measured by WCST (Leng & Parkin, 1988a; Shoqeirat et al., 1990). One problem is that the test, as published, is for U.K. populations, although modifications for other countries would be straightforward. Trail Making (A & B) from the Halstead-Reitan battery is another test thought to be a good measure of frontal dysfunction.

The Stroop Test is also included in many "frontal batteries". The basic procedure involves measuring subjects' speed when naming colour patches, colour words and the ink colour of colour words in which the ink colour and name are always incongruent (e.g. RED written in blue ink). By subtracting performance on the former two measures from the latter, a measure of attentional selectivity can be derived. A published version of this test with norms is available (Trenerry, Crosson, DeBoe & Leber, 1989).

Attention

Attentional deficits can take a number of forms but within clinical practice the most important aspect of attention involves the patient's ability to concentrate and his or her susceptibility to distraction. Formal evaluation of attention can be carried out in a number of ways. The WMS-R provides an index of attention and concentration and the Stroop Test (described above) is also considered a test of attention. The Rivermead Inattention Test can be used if a broader assessment of attentional ability is used.

Pre-morbid Intelligence

Estimates of a patient's pre-morbid intelligence are valuable in any clinical setting. At present, the only widespread test for pre-morbid IQ is the National Adult Reading Test (NART: Nelson, 1985; 1991). The NART is based on the assumption that language abilities are less vulnerable to organic brain dysfunction than other cognitive abilities (Nelson & O'Connell, 1978), and it comprises a long list of irregularly spelled words ranging from the simple (e.g. CHORD) to the difficult (e.g. BEATIFY). The patient is simply asked to read each word aloud, and the error score, which has been standardised against WAIS, can be used to estimate pre-morbid IQ. (Note that a new version is now available which includes standardisation against WAIS-R: Nelson, 1991.) Apart from obvious problems, such as its use with patients with focal left hemisphere damage in which acquired dyslexias can contaminate performance, the test appears to provide a reasonable estimate of pre-morbid IQ, although no age correction is available. Its results should therefore always be combined with other pre-clinical indicators such as schooling and previous employment. Linked with this is the problem of knowing whether a patient's NART performance is itself impaired. In an attempt to overcome this problem, Crawford, Allan, Cochrane and Parker (1990) have devised a regression equation whereby NART scores can be predicted from demographic variables. NART may also fail to discriminate effectively between people of lower intelligence, and NART can be embarrassing for these subjects and therefore the Schonell (1942) Reading Test is a useful alternative. Baddeley's (in prep.) prototype "spot the word" test may be a useful alternative for subjects of lower IQ, because here the patient merely looks through a random list of words and nonwords and indicates only those which he or she considers to be a word.

Malingering

Generally, neurological patients try to perform as well as possible on neuropsychological tests. There will be instances, however, when patients may deliberately underperform (dissimulate), particularly if compensation issues are involved. For this reason, there has been growing interest in the detection of malingering, a development reinforced by Bernard's (1990) demonstration that impaired performance on three commonly used tests—the WMS-R, AVLT and the Rey Figure—can all be easily faked.

Malingerers can be detected by showing that they perform abnormally poorly on memory tests, i.e. worse than patients with genuine memory disorders. Rey (1964) devised a simple test for malingering now known as the Rey Memory Test. The test comprises a target array of five rows of characters each of which is designed to aid recall (e.g. A B C). In contrast, the instructions emphasise task difficulty by stressng that there are 15 items to remember and that the array will only be shown for 10 sec, thus suggesting that it is rather difficult. Evaluation of this test in brain-damaged and psychiatric populations suggests that recall of less than eight items should be viewed with suspicion (Bernard & Fowler, 1990; Lezak, 1983).

Malingerers also tend to exhibit disproportionately poor recognition memory (Bernard, 1990). Using a forced-choice recognition procedure, a number of studies have exposed malingerers by showing that their hit rates were significantly less than chance (e.g Binder & Pankratz, 1987). More recently, Hiscock and Hiscock (1989) have described a more subtle procedure for assessing malingering. They investigated a 45-year-old man who claimed to be unable to work as a result of neurological impairment, a fact suggested by his poor performance on a wide range of neuropsychological tests. A forced-choice recognition procedure was designed in which the demands on recognition memory appeared greater than was actually the case. In addition, the time between learning and test was increased throughout the procedure with the instruction that it would get "harder" as a result. The patient's performance started at chance and then fell significantly below chance as the retention intervals increased. This compared with continual chance performance by a demented patient and above-chance performance by a 5-year-old. The patient's malingering was clearly revealed by this procedure but, given time constraints, it is notable that his performance on the Rey Memory Test initially aroused "doubts".

OVERVIEW

Clinical and experimental investigators are confronted with a large array of test procedures and questionnaires concerned with memory function. This chapter has given some indication of the range of tests available and their advantages and disadvantages. For this reason, it is difficult even to attempt a set of recommendations as to which combination of procedures to use. However, it would seem wise to use either the re-standardised Russell variant of the WMS or the WMS-R simply because its wide usage makes comparison of patients between clinics and laboratories that much easier. We also note that the Warrington Recognition Tests are increasing in usage and this, along with the need to include a measure of recognition memory, leads one to recommend inclusion of these tests in any battery. After that, we feel it is really up to individual investigators, who must be guided by their goals and hypotheses concerning patient evaluation and the body of literature to which they wish to relate their studies.

3 Wernicke-Korsakoff Syndrome

In 1881, Carl Wernicke described a form of encephalopathy caused by various forms of poisioning, including ingestion of sulphuric acid and alcoholism. He noted several focal neurological signs, including an acute confusional state, ocular disturbance and gait apraxia. Around the same time, Sergei Korsakoff (1889; see Victor & Yakolev, 1955) was studying the long-term features of patients who had suffered the acute encephalopathy identified by Wernicke. Although a number of symptoms were noted, the primary disorder was a severe amnesic syndrome. Patients suffering from this disorder are now described as having the Wernicke-Korsakoff Syndrome (WKS) and they have provided the majority of experimental findings concerning the amnesic syndrome. Talland's (1965) extensive account *Deranged memory*, for example, was based entirely on observations of WKS patients. Similarly, Butters and Cermak (1980) devoted most of their book to descriptions of the WKS memory deficit—an honour not accorded to any other memory disorder. This results in a much more extensive chapter on WKS than those devoted to other aetiologies of amnesia.

Neuropathology

WKS most commonly arises from chronic alcoholism (Victor, Adams & Collins, 1989; Victor et al., 1971), but it can have other aetiologies (Reuler, Girard & Cooney, 1985; and see below). Both animal and human studies (Witt, 1985) indicate that thiamine deficiency is the primary cause of WKS. The particular association of WKS with chronic alcoholism is not fully understood, but it is known that alcohol interferes with the gastrointestinal transport of thiamine (e.g. Hoyumpa, Nichols, Henderson & Schenker, 1978) and that chronic liver disease diminishes the ability of the liver to store thiamine. There may also be a genetic disposition towards developing the disorder (Blass & Gibson, 1979).

Onset of WKS is usually associated with an identifiable episode of Wernicke's encephalopathy. Classically, this is characterised by a triad of neurological symptoms—ataxia, opthalmoplegia and confusion (Victor et al., 1989). However, it is clear that this defining triad is neither consistently nor frequently encountered. In addition, onset of the disorder may be sudden or evolve slowly over a number of days (Reuler et al., 1985). The variable characteristics of Wernicke's encephalopathy, both in the nature and extent of its presentation, make for considerable diagnostic difficulties. Indeed, these difficulties may result in many WKS patients remaining undiagnosed until autopsy (e.g. Harper, Giles & Finlay-Jones, 1986).

Thiamine is known to have a complex relationship with various aspects of cerebral metabolism. Derivatives of thiamine are involved in the function of excitable membranes, several biosynthetic reactions involved in glucose metabolism, and the synthesis of neurotransmitters, particularly acetylcholine and γ-amino-butyric-acid (for a detailed review of these issues, see Witt, 1985). But, despite this knowledge, it is still unclear why Wernicke's encephalopathy produces such a distinctive and consistent neuropathy.

From an early stage, bilateral damage to the diencephalon was reported to underlie WKS. Gamper (1928) noted a number of pathological abnormalities but emphasised the mamillary bodies as the critical area, and later investigations upheld this view (e.g. Malamud & Skillicorn, 1956). More recent studies have questioned whether the minimal lesion does in fact have to be in the mamillary bodies. From their extensive autopsy study, Victor et al. (1989) concluded that the dorso-medial thalamic nucleus (DMTN) was critically involved in WKS, but their data are also consistent with a joint lesion involving both the DMTN and an additional structure, most probably the mamillary bodies (see Fig. 3.1).

Mair, Warrington and Weiskrantz (1979) reported detailed autopsy findings from two WKS patients. Both patients had marked gliosis, shrinkage and unusual colouration in the mamillary bodies, which was disproportionate to that observed elsewhere. Also, a thin, bilateral band of gliosis was noted between the wall of the third ventricle and the dorsal medial thalamic nucleus. The DMTN is not specifically referred to as a critical structure, but the study would be consistent with a mamillary body and mid-line thalamic lesion as being the minimal requirement for WKS. Mayes et al. (1988) also report detailed neuropathological findings on two

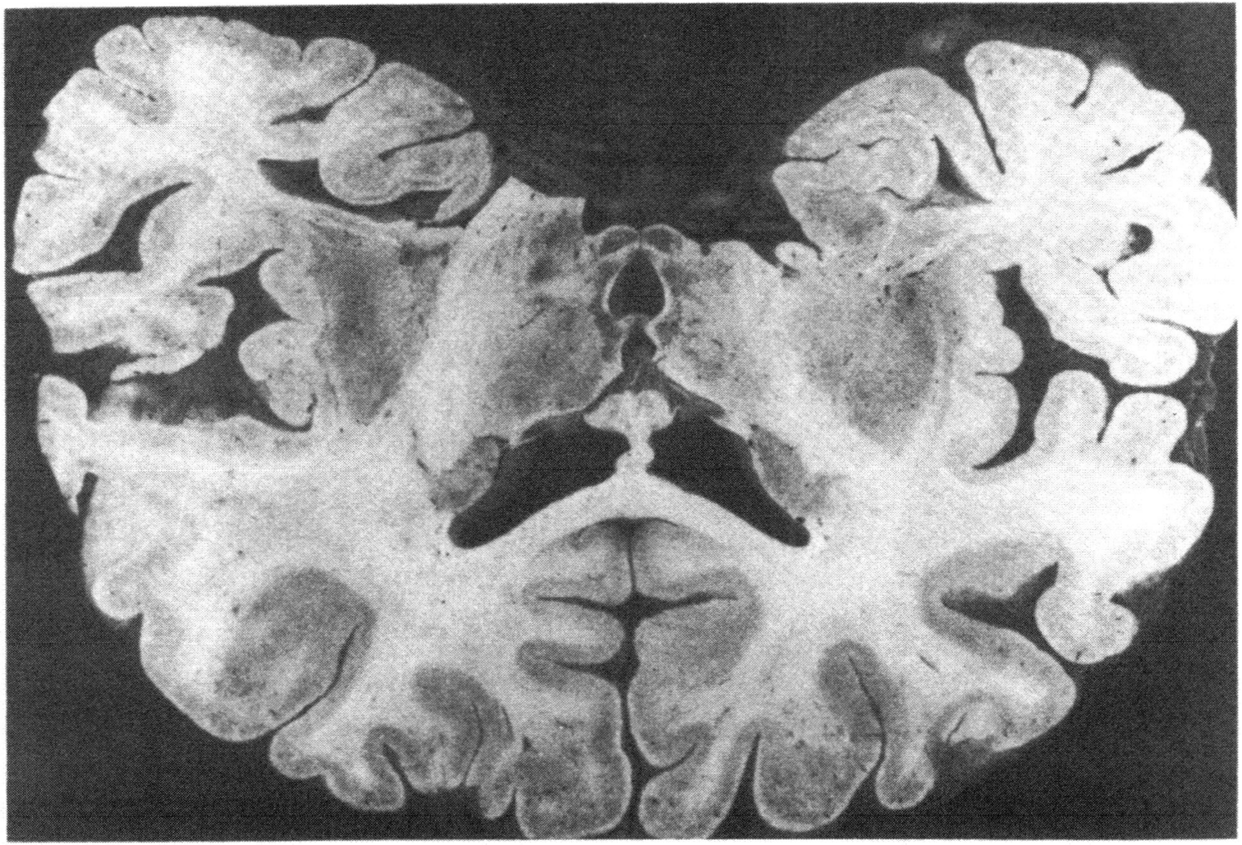

FIG. 3.1 Section of a WKS patient's brain indicating lesions in the mamillary bodies and grey matter surrounding the third ventricle. This pattern of damage is typical in this patient group. Reproduced from Victor et al. (1989) with the permission of the publisher and authors.

Korsakoff patients. Again, lesions were apparent in the mamillary bodies and the DMTN of both subjects. In a study of 45 WKS patients brought to autopsy, Torvik (1987) confirms the consistent involvement of both the mamillary bodies and DMTN. However, the author notes three patients in which significant memory impairments were present with lesions restricted to the mamillary bodies. However, this latter finding must be treated with caution as no neuropsychological assessment of these patients is presented.

Jernigan, Schafer, Butters and Cermak (1991) compared WKS patients, non-amnesic alcoholics and controls using magnetic resonance imaging (MRI). WKS patients exhibited widespread reductions in grey matter and increased cerebrospinal fluid (CSF), whereas non-amnesic alcoholics only showed increased CSF. Grey matter volumes were most reduced in the anterior diencephalic structures, orbito-frontal cortex and the medial temporal lobe. This latter impairment may indicate some medial temporal involvement—especially the hippocampus—in the WKS memory deficit. Mayes, Meudell, Mann and Pickering (1987b) have also raised the possibility of hippocampal damage in WKS and it must be noted that Hata et al. (1987) found reduced blood flow in the temporal limbic structures of WKS patients. Victor et al. (1989) also noted hippocampal damage in a small percentage of their WKS sample, but its relation to memory loss was not clear.

Despite numerous pathological investigations, the critical lesion for the appearance of WKS has still to be determined. Both the mamillary bodies and the DMTN feature heavily in neuropathological accounts, but damage to either structure alone appears to be insufficient for the appearance of the syndrome. Furthermore, recent research has now raised the possibility of hippocampal involvement in WKS, although the implication of this for understanding the memory loss of this patient group is not clear.

Selecting Korsakoff Patients for Study: The Problems of Severity and Global Intellectual Deterioration

As we have seen, identification of an amnesic syndrome requires that the patient be reasonably free of associated impairments that might confound interpretation of their memory performance. The selection of WKS patients provides a good example of the problems that can arise. Because of its prominently alcoholic aetiology, some patients diagnosed as WKS may have a level of intellectual deterioration more closely resembling cases of alcoholic dementia (Cutting, 1978; Jacobson & Lishman, 1987). An additional problem is that from our experience, diagnosis of WKS may sometimes be made rather loosely and may be made in patients with a

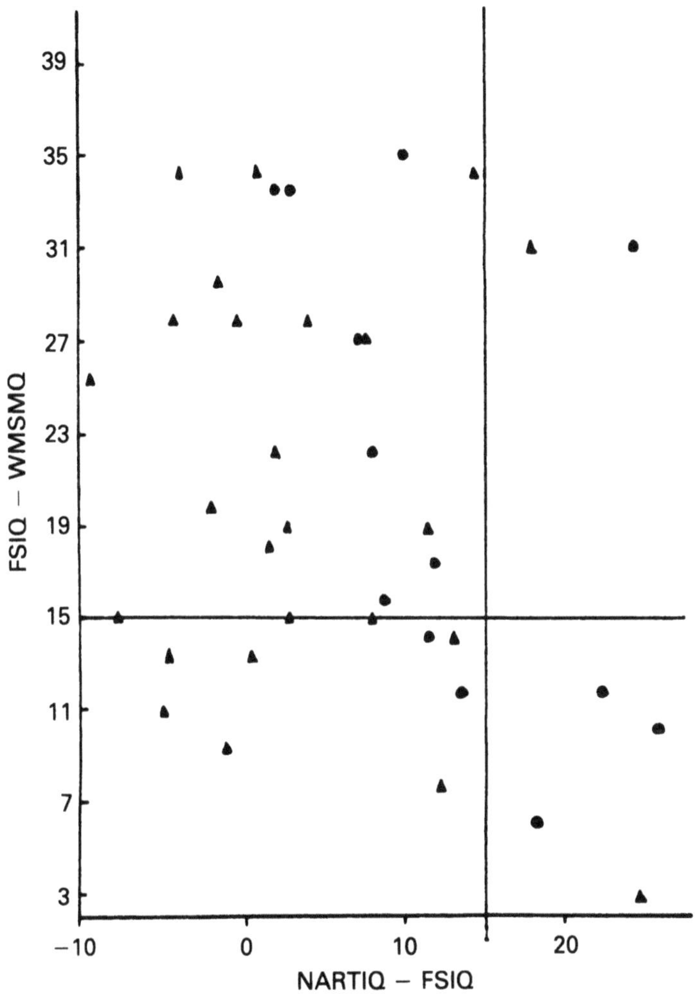

FIG. 3.2 Jacobson and Lishman's (1987) data showing their classification of "pure" WKS. Reproduced with the permission of Cambridge University Press and the authors.

drinking history who are just depressed, suffering some other form of mental illness, or with clear evidence of dementia.

Jacobson and Lishman (1987) employed a systematic approach to the problem of distinguishing "pure" WKS patients from patients with more global intellectual deficits and those whose memory disorder was too mild to warrant the diagnosis. They devised two discrepancy scores for their patients: FSIQ–WMSMQ and NARTIQ–FSIQ (see Chapter 2). Figure 3.2 shows the scattergram of their findings, which is divided into quadrants arrived at by assuming a 15-point cut-off. This measure places the bulk of the patients in the upper left quadrant which corresponds to the pure deficit, whereas the patients in the other three quadrants are considered to have either general intellectual deterioration or too mild a level of impairment.

In practice, researchers have restricted themselves to the FSIQ–MQ discrepancy. Butters and Cermak (1980) suggested that a minimum FSIQ–MQ discrepancy of 20 points should be used in the classifiction of WKS. However, Jacobson and Lishman point out that adoption of this criterion would have excluded eight patients from the pure WKS group in their patient study. Table 3.1 summarises the FSIQ–MQ discrepancies in 12 studies of WKS, and indicates a typical discrepancy score for WKS patients of 25. Thus, although restrictive, it appears that most researchers accept the 20-point discrepancy cut-off. Furthermore, this criterion is generally met in studies of other instances of the amnesic syndrome. However, as we shall see later in this chapter, unqualified adoption of this criterion can be misleading.

TABLE 3.1
WAIS FSIQ–WMSMQ Discrepancies in WKS Amnesia

	FSIQ	*WMSMQ*	*Difference*
Cohen and Squire (1981)	101.1	76.2	24.9
Corkin et al. (1985)	76.0	63.0	7.0
Hunkin (1991)	95.5	76.6	19.9
Leng and Parkin (1988b)	100.9	77.4	23.5
Mayes and Gooding (1989)	103.3	85.2	18.1
Mayes et al. (1988)	106.0	77.5	28.5
Parkinson (1979)	105.9	77.1	28.8
Squire and Shimamura (1986)	102.8	80.0	22.8
Victor et al. (1959)	95.9	78.8	17.1

Long-term Features of WKS

Following initial diagnosis of Wernicke's encephalopathy, patients are treated with thiamine supplements (e.g. "Parentrovite") in an attempt to reverse the symptoms. Many factors determine the prognosis at this stage but, more often than not, the outcome is a patient with multiple neuropsychological impairments, the most pronounced of which is amnesia. It is this chronic neuropsychological impairment that is properly termed WKS.

Example Case Histories

Case 1 is a 60-year-old former transport worker. During his career, he experienced several stressful incidents involving fatal accidents. The stress caused by these incidents led to a gradually worsening alcohol problem which resulted in his eventual transfer to cleaning duties. His heavy drinking continued and this culminated in an acute confusional episode with subsequent admission to a psychiatric hospital.

He exhibited a degree of ataxia but his primary disturbance was acute confusion and severe memory loss. When interviewed in hospital, he thought he was in the social club and that the year was 1955. He had normal immediate memory function but performed very poorly on tests requiring longer-term retention of both verbal and non-verbal information. He also exhibited severe retrograde amnesia when questioned about past events and when asked to identify famous people. An assesment of frontal lobe function also indicated a range of impairments including reduced word fluency and poor WCST performance. He was treated with thiamine supplements but these have been ineffective in restoring his memory function. He now receives permanent 24-hour care in a home for the elderly.

Case 2 is a 53-year-old publican with a history of chronic alcoholism (consuming between 10 and 20 pints of beer a day). Following separation from his wife, he had developed a nomadic lifestyle in motels and this led to increasingly poor diet without any reduction in his drinking. Finally, he suffered an acute Wernicke's episode which was treated with thiamine therapy.

Little recovery has so far been observed. He is disoriented in time, gives little account of his immediate past life, and cannot recall recent major events such as the Gulf War or Mrs Thatcher's resignation. He expresses genuine concern about the health of his chronically ill daughter even though she died several months previously. His anterograde memory is grossly impaired, being unable to remember virtually any paired associates or the content of logical memory passages. He asks the same questions repeatedly and these perseverative tendencies are reflected in his poor performance on frontal lobe tasks such as WCST, where he failed to achieve a single category, and word fluency.

Immediate Memory

There is agreement that all WKS patients show normal memory span (e.g. Baddeley & Warrington, 1970; Butters & Cermak, 1980) and an intact recency effect on the free recall task at immediate recall (Baddeley & Warrington, 1970).

Short-term Memory

Discrepant findings have been reported concerning the performance of WKS patients on the Brown-Peterson (BP) test (Brown, 1958; Peterson & Peterson, 1959). In this task, the subject is briefly presented with between one and three items, distracted for a variable interval, and then asked to recall the items. Mair et al. (1979) reported that their two WKS patients peformed normally on the BP test, as did those in Kopelman's (1985) series, although it should be noted that performance by the latter tended to diverge from normal at longer retention intervals. In contrast, all other studies involving the BP task report impaired performance by WKS patients (e.g. Butters & Cermak, 1980; Kessler, Markowitsch & Bast-Kessler, 1987; Leng & Parkin, 1989; Mayes et al., 1988; Starr & Phillips, 1970). Cermak (1976) gave WKS patients blocks of BP trials using a 9-sec retention interval and an inter-trial interval of either 6 or 60 sec. Compared with controls, the WKS patients benefited disproportionately under the 60-sec condition suggesting greater sensitivity to proactive interference. However, Leng and Parkin (1989) failed to observe this effect in a similar experiment.

Anterograde Amnesia

In his extensive study, Talland (1965) examined many aspects of learning and memory in WKS patients. He concluded that:

> . . . like other men and women, they too are more likely to succeed in recognition than in unaided recall, but in all tests of memory their capacity and reliability are abnormally small. (Talland, 1965, p. 231).

Although Talland's conclusions about recognition memory may need qualification in the light of more recent findings, his general conclusions are borne out by more recent investigations. Cermak (1975), for example, reported that WKS patients were impaired on paired-associate learning, taking 25 trials to reach criterion as compared with 5 trials for controls. Leng and Parkin (1988b) gave patients 10 learning trials of hard paired associates and found that WKS patients made a mean of 36.9 errors compared with only 4.49 errors for controls. Free recall tests also indicate marked impairments in WKS patients, as shown by the poor performance on the logical memory component of the WMS.

Other studies indicate that the WKS anterograde deficit is a more complex phenomenon because the deficit may vary with the type of retention test used. Lhermitte and Signoret (1972) found that WKS patients needed more learning trials than controls to learn a 3 × 3 picture array, performed very poorly on free recall of the array, but showed normal retention under cued recall conditions. Researchers have also reported a normal rate of forgetting among WKS patients. By using longer initial exposure times, Huppert and Piercy (1978a) and later Kopelman (1985) brought WKS patients up to the same level of acquisition as controls. Recognition testing 24 hours and 7 days later showed similar performance by controls and WKS patients (see Squire, 1981, for a similar finding).

However, WKS patients do not show such good recognition under all conditions. Huppert and Piercy (1978b) gave WKS patients 80 pictures on one day followed by a further 80 the next day. On each occasion, half the pictures were shown three times and the other half once. After presentation on day 2, the patients were given a recognition test for previously exposed pictures and asked whether the identified targets had been presented on day 1 or day 2. The WKS patients were reasonably accurate at discriminating pictures seen three times on day 2 from those seen once on day 1, but were poor at discriminating pictures seen once on day 2 from those seen three times on day 1. In contrast, the control group performed both tasks quite accurately (for further confirmation and clarification of this result, see Meudell, Mayes, Ostergaard & Pickering, 1985).

A study by Mattis, Kovner and Goldmeier (1978) also shows that WKS patients' recognition is differentially impaired under certain conditions. They required WKS and post-encephalitic patients (see Chapter 6) to learn four types of 20-word list: "categorised", "mixed", nonsense hexagrams (e.g. PUFMAX) and Persian words (e.g. TAH-ZEE). Two tasks were used, modified free recall (Buschke, 1973) and yes–no recognition. Modified free recall involves patients learning a list across a succession of trials. After trials 4, 8 and 12, a recognition test is given for the words being learned. Both percentage correct recall and recognition accuracy in the probe task as measured by d' were measured. No differences in free recall were found, although both patient groups performed much worse than the controls. Performance on the recognition probe task differed in the two groups, with the WKS patients producing d' levels significantly above chance with most recognition probes, whereas post-encephalitic patients responded at chance at all times. Yes–no recognition testing involved learning a 20-word list and a recognition test comprising 20 targets and 20 distractors. The procedure was repeated 12 times. Here the d' values for both the amnesic groups were uniformly below chance, whereas the control group responded significantly above chance. The discrepancy between yes–no recognition and recognition probe performance by the WKS group is attributed to methodological differences. The two tasks differed in the ratio of presenting targets and distractors prior to the point at which discrimination between them was required. In the recognition probe task, each target was presented four times (i.e. four recall trials) prior to experiencing the distractor items in the probe task. In contrast, the yes–no test involved presenting the 20 targets and 20 distractors on all 12 trials. Thus in the recognition probe condition, the subjects saw the distractor items only 3 times compared with 12 times in the yes–no condition. To examine recognition performance equated for distractor familiarity, Mattis et al. compared the d' values at recognition probe 3 with those at yes–no recognition test 3. This analysis showed no difference between the WKS and control groups on all lists except "categorised" English. This finding suggested that WKS and control subjects process novel information in a similar manner, and that overall poor performance in the yes–no recognition task by the WKS patients arose from their inability to discriminate between targets and distractors of equal familiarity. This explanation could also apply to the study of Huppert and Piercy (1978b). On the assumption that familiarity fades with time, the performance of the WKS subjects suggests that their decisions about which day a picture was shown on, were determined largely by just how familiar a stimulus was, rather than actually recalling its presentation on a specific day. Thus pictures presented three times on day 1 seemed as recent as those presented once on day 2, because these items evoked similar amounts of familiarity. In contrast, those presented once on day 1 and three times on day 3 had discriminably different degrees of familiarity, thus allowing an apparent ability to remember which day they had been presented on. In Chapter 8, we will see that this reliance on familiarity in WKS recognition peformance may be of critical importance in explanations of the WKS memory deficit.

Retrograde Amnesia

A consistent and impressive feature of WKS patients is their extensive and temporally graded retrograde amnesia. In an early study, Seltzer and Benson (1974) found that WKS patients could recall events which occurred in the 1930s and 1940s more easily than those which had occurred in the 1960s and 1970s. This study was extended by Albert et al. (1979) using the Boston Remote Memory Test (see Chapter 2). Marked temporal gradients were found on all the recall measures, but on the recognition measures no temporal gradients were observed despite generally impaired performance.

Parkin et al. (1990b) examined the performance of 20 WKS patients on a prototype famous faces test for U.K. populations. The test comprises two versions: a "no-context" version in which each face is presented with minimal cues as to the depicted person's identity (e.g. Mrs Thatcher in a flak jacket), and a "context" version in which some feature of the picture provides a clue to the person's identity (e.g. Mrs Thatcher outside 10 Downing Street). The test addresses the five decades from 1935 to 1985 and for each decade there are three decade-specific faces and three publicly rehearsed faces. The results are shown in Fig. 3.3 and demonstrate that

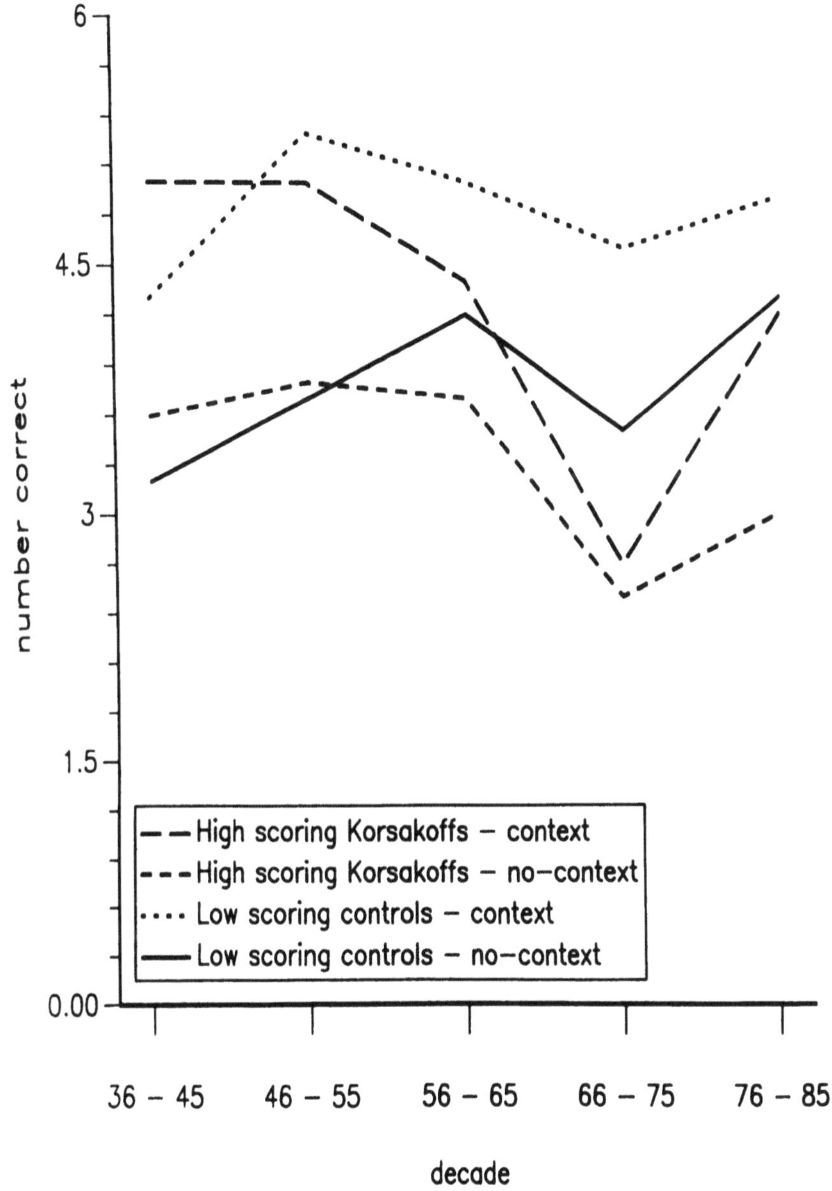

FIG. 3.3 Data from Parkin et al. (1990b).

the WKS patients performed more poorly than the controls, and that the WKS patients also showed a marked temporal gradient which was not evident in the control data. The provision of context enhanced control performance consistently across all decades, but in the WKS group the beneficial effects of context declined systematically as more recent decades were tested.

Kopelman (1989) compared WKS patients and controls on four different measures of retrograde amnesia—a news events test, a famous personalities test, a personal semantic memory schedule and an autobiographical incidents schedule (see Chapter 2). All four measures showed significant temporal gradients but, despite these similarities, correlations indicated that these tests were addressing two relatively independent forms of remote memory, one involving the famous personality test and both the recall and recognition measures of the news events test, and the other the personal semantic memory and autobiographical incidents schedules.

Using six different tests of remote memory, Squire, Haist and Shimamura (1989b) showed a consistent temporally graded retrograde deficit over a period of about 15 years in WKS patients. Memory for more remote periods did not appear to differ from controls. The authors also explored the consistency of patients' remote memory impairments by means of repeated testing. WKS patients were as consistent in their responses as the control subjects, indicating that retrograde amnesia in WKS patients reflects a genuine loss of memory as opposed to random access difficulties, which can be overcome given sufficient retrieval opportunities.

Implicit Memory

Korsakoff himself noted the ability of his patients to learn their way around the hospital despite severely impaired memory. Claparede (1911), in an often cited anecdote, reports shaking hands with a female WKS patient while concealing a pin in his hand. Returning some minutes later and offering his hand again, the patient refused commenting "pins are sometimes hidden in hands". This suggests "one trial learning" in WKS patients, but one should note Barbizet's (1970) lack of success in replicating this result with his patient Mr Pa. More recently, Johnson, Kim and Risse (1985) explored the possibility of experimentally induced affective reactions in WKS patients. In their first experiment, unfamiliar melodies were played to the patients and matched controls. After a retention interval, the subjects heard the original tunes intermixed with novel unfamiliar tunes and were asked to indicate their preference. The WKS patients showed similar preferences to the controls for previously heard memory but were inferior to the controls in recognising which melodies had been played before. In a second experiment, the subjects saw photographs of two men, one depicted as a "good guy" and the other as a "bad guy". After 20 days, the patients were asked to give their impressions of the two men. These were less favourable for the "bad guy" even though the patients could not recall having heard information about the men in a previous episode. The data of Johnston et al. show the acquisition of preferences in amnesics but one should note that another study, in which attempts were made to induce preferences merely by varying frequency of presentation, was unsuccessful (Redington, Bruce & Gazzaniga, 1984).

Studies of WKS patients indicate reasonably intact classical conditioning (e.g. Talland, 1965; Warrington & Weiskrantz, 1979). Gantt and Muncie (1942) tried to train WKS patients on a conditioned avoidance procedure. The patients learned successfully to press a switch in the presence of a red light to avoid shock (somewhat fiendishly adminstered by electrodes placed inside the fingertips of the rubber gloves worn by the patients), but became confused when safety trials involving a white light were interpolated in the sequence. WKS patients have also been shown to perform normally on a broad range of motor learning, maze learning and perceptual learning tasks (Brooks & Baddeley, 1976), including near-normal performance in terms of learning and retention on a pursuit rotor task (Cermak et al., 1973) and savings on performance sub-tests of the Wechsler Bellevue Intelligence Scales (Victor, Hermann & White, 1959). In an overlooked study, Meissner (1967) demonstrated the ability of WKS patients to learn and retain a spatio-motor sequence providing the sequence did not exceed the capacity of immediate memory.

Using a technique known as "Heilbronner's Method", Schneider (1912) provided an early demonstration of perceptual learning in WKS patients. The method involved showing the patients gradually more informative fragments of a picture (e.g. a pram) until identification was achieved. After a retention interval, the same sequences were re-presented and any savings in learning measured. Schneider found evidence of savings on this task and several others that would today be classified as implicit memory (see Fig. 3.4).

Warrington and Weiskrantz (1970) presented three WKS patients and one temporal lobectomy amnesic with degraded words and provided increasingly informative versions until identification was achieved. In line with Schneider's earlier findings, substantial savings were found on retesting. A report by Meudell and Mayes (1981) can also be interpreted as preserved perceptual learning. Their Korsakoff patients were shown cartoons containing a hidden object and the time taken to find the object was measured. On re-presentation, location times were significantly reduced, even though the patients failed to distinguish between new and old cartoons at subsequent testing.

Warrington and Weiskrantz (1970) also provided an early demonstration of another implicit memory phenomenon which has now become of considerable theoretical and practical interest. Their patients, a mixed group in which two suffered from WKS, were first read aloud 16 target

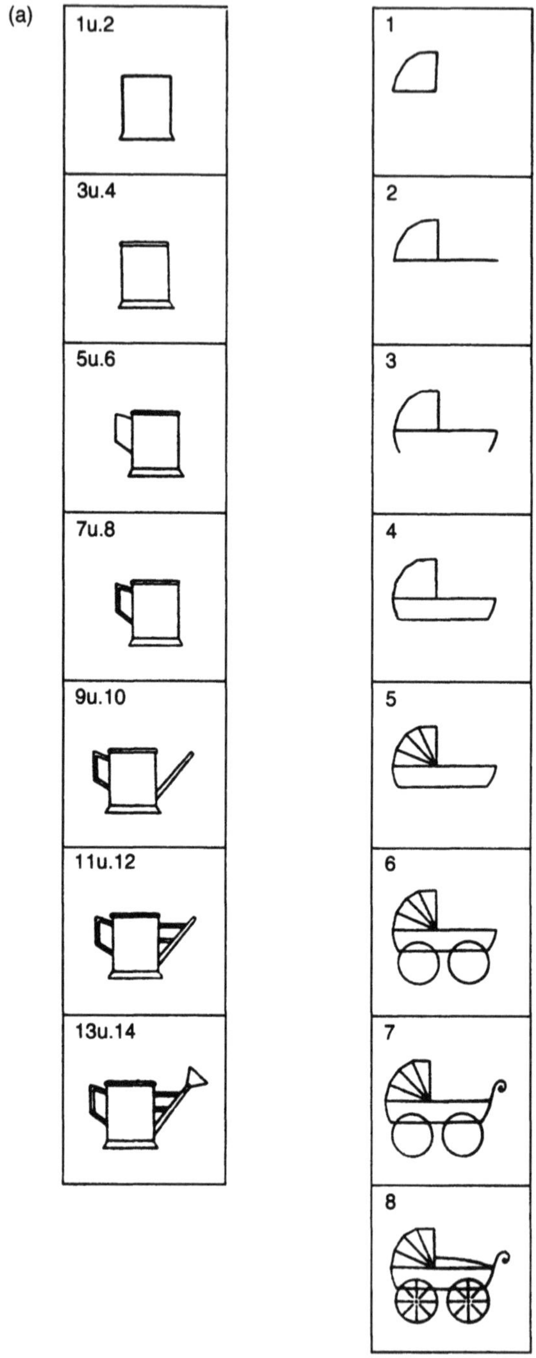

FIG. 3.4 Stimuli used by Schneider (1912) (a) and Meudell and Mayes (1981) (b) to demonstrate preserved implicit memory in WKS patients.

(b)

words. Retention was tested either by cued recall or by means of a yes–no recognition task. The cued recall test involved presentation of the first three letters of the target word and the subject was invited to state what the word was. The probability of guessing the target word was very low, in that at least 10 words began with the first three letters of each target word. The results showed that amnesics performed better on the cued recall test than the yes–no recognition task.

This result can now be considered as an early demonstration of stem completion priming (see Chapter 2). Other studies have also shown substantial stem completion priming in WKS patients (Graf, Shimamura & Squire, 1985; Graf, Squire & Mandler, 1984; Longmore & Knight, 1988). However, when the stems are used as recall cues for the original learning episode, WKS patients do very badly. Cermak, Talbot, Chandler and Wolbarst (1985) have shown that WKS patients exhibit lowered tachistoscopic recognition thresholds for words exposed on a previous learning task, but no such effect was observed with pseudowords. In a further study, Cermak, O'Connor and Talbot (1986) demonstrated that WKS patients exhibit bias in their spelling of ambiguous words as a function of the context in which those words were experienced in a prior learning episode.

In a study involving patients of mixed aetiology, Graf and Schacter (1985) used a modified stem completion procedure to examine whether amnesics could learn novel associations. The subjects viewed word pairs such as WINDOW–REASON. Stem completion for the second word was then tested, either by re-presentation of the same pairing (i.e. WINDOW–REA___?) or by a different pairing (e.g. GARDEN–REA___?). Graf and Schacter found what has been termed a *word enhancement effect*—the correct stem completions for same pairings being greater than those for different pairings. On the basis of these results, Graf and Schacter concluded that amnesic patients could learn novel associations via priming mechanisms. However, the authors later modified this view to suggest that this only occurred in patients with less severe amnesia.

Cermak, Bleich and Blackford (1988) attempted to demonstrate word enhancement effects in a group of eight WKS patients, but failed to find any effect across two experiments. Interestingly, they also found no evidence of word enhancement in the alcoholic control groups, who in fact showed better completion for word stems paired with a different stimulus. One other puzzling result was that the WKS patients produced much higher levels of stem completion *per se*. Mayes and Gooding (1989) looked for word enhancement effects in a mixed group of 17 amnesics. Significant word enhancement effects were found in four WKS patients (although for one of these this was due to particularly poor performance in the same context condition) and one post-encephalitic patient. The ability of the patients to show word enhancement effects correlated positively with word fluency and cued recall but not with amnesic severity or general intelligence.

The ability of WKS patients to learn novel information has recently been addresed by Cermak et al. (1991). They examined whether their earlier failure to show priming with pseudowords (Cermak et al., 1985) arose because these stimuli are both orthographically and semantically unfamiliar—the argument being that priming may depend critically on some pre-existing representation of a priming stimulus being available. Patients were presented with separate lists of words, pseudowords (e.g. SPIRK) and pseudohomonyms (pseudowords with a phonology corresponding to a real word and therefore capable of eliciting some semantic activation, e.g. PHAIRE), and priming was measured by examining the effect of repetition on verbal identification latency. WKS patients again showed impaired priming of pseudowords but normal priming of words and pseudohomonyms. Cermak et al. (1991) concluded that normal priming in WKS required the prior availability of a semantic representation, but this conclusion was complicated by a second experiment in which pseudohomonyms produced impaired priming when presented intermixed with real words. This led to the conclusion that pseudohomonym priming depends on both a pre-existing semantic representation and an ability to realise the "conceptual salience" of novel stimuli.

In a further study of WKS priming, Verafaellie, Cermak, Letourneau and Zuffante (1991) found that repetition priming in lexical decision was comparable to non-amnesic alcoholics at lags of up to 15 intervening items. However, recognition of those same items under similar presentation conditions was impaired in the WKS group. Verafaellie et al. concluded that priming in WKS is based on the perceptual fluency (see Chapter 8) engendered by a re-presented stimulus as opposed to any explicit recognition memory.

The importance of a pre-existing semantic representation in determining WKS learning is exemplified by Grossman (1987), who attempted to teach WKS patients the low-frequency adjective "bice"—meaning a dark green colour. The meaning of the word was initially conveyed by associating the word with a pen of that colour. The patients were reasonably good at learning which pen was the "bice-pen" but, on subsequent testing, they appeared to have assimilated little of the factual knowledge represented by the word. They could not distinguish reliably between sentences in which bice was used in its correct grammatical form and those in which it was used incorrectly. Thus WKS patients appeared able to learn the arbitrary association between "bice" and a pen of particular colour, but unable to abstract the meaning represented by that association.

Nissen and Bullemer (1987) tested six WKS patients on a sequence learning task. On each trial, a light appeared in one of four locations and the subjects had to press a key below that light. In one condition the same sequence of lights was repeated across 10 trials, whereas in the other condition the sequence was random. The WKS patients, like the control subjects, showed decreasing response latencies in the repeated sequence condition which exceeded the small practice effect evident from the random condition. However, unlike the control subjects, none of the WKS patients appeared to be aware that a repeated sequence had been presented. Nissen, Willingham and Hartman (1989) report that two WKS patients successfully learnt an embedded repeated sequence in a visual reaction time task similar to that used by Nissen and Bullemer (1987). However, the same two patients performed very poorly on learning a tactile maze. Nissen et al. explain this discrepancy by arguing that the two tasks differ in the extent to which the task characteristics can restrain potential responses. In the reaction time task, the various response alternatives are all present, whereas the various options are not so readily constrained in a maze, and this may make the patient more reliant on explicitly remembering the outcome of previous learning attempts.

Semantic Memory

It has often been held that WKS patients have normal semantic memory. Both Talland (1965) and Baddeley and Warrington (1970) found that WKS patients generated category exemplars at the same rate as control subjects. More recently, the nature of semantic memory abilities in WKS has been investigated extensively by Cermak and his colleagues. Cermak, Beale and Baker (1978) investigated the speed at which WKS patients could search semantic memory. Their subjects were shown a category name followed by a letter (e.g. fruit B____?) and asked to provide an exemplar as quickly as possible. This procedure was assumed to test lexical semantic memory and performance was compared with a second procedure involving more conceptual processing—here the subject was shown a response category paired with a descriptive adjective (e.g. fruit–red?) and asked to provide an exemplar. The WKS patients were slower on both tasks, but this only reached significance in the conceptual processing task. Because only the rate of conceptual search was affected in the WKS patients, and not the ability to come up with the right answer, the authors suggested that semantic memory might retain its organisation but that there is some impairment in access. Verfaellie, Cermak, Blackford and Weiss (1990) examined this directly by comparing WKS and non-amnesic alcoholics on semantic memory tasks which did not require active search. In all three experiments, no difference between the groups was found and the authors concluded that semantic memory retained its normal organisation in WKS and that deficits reflected access problems.

The idea that access as opposed to organisational deficits underlie semantic memory deficits in WKS is also consistent with the study of Mattis, Kovner, Gartner and Goldmeier (1981), who found that WKS patients generated category exemplars more slowly than controls, and the study of Butters, Wolfe, Granholm and Martone (1986), in which perseveration with high-probability exemplars impeded access to exemplars lower in the response hierarchy. However, it is probably unwise to conclude that sematic memory is intact in WKS. The above studies all examined aspects of semantic memory that were presumably intact at a relatively early age, and therefore the normal organisation evident in performance might merely reflect the greater robustness of early pre-morbid memory *per se*, rather than specific preservation of semantic memory (note also that this objection undermines use of normal performance on WAIS VIQ because information assessed here is also acquired relatively early in life).

A better test of the intactness of semantic memory in WKS patients, therefore, is to examine the nature of semantic memory formed in later parts of the pre-morbid period. This was done in a little known study by Nyssen (1956), who reported that WKS patients exhibited significant loss of vocabulary acquired towards the end of the pre-morbid period. We have similar unpublished data from the Sussex WKS population using a test devised by Gill Banks and Frances Cooper. The patients were asked to define words known to have come into use at specific time periods. They were good at defining words such as RADAR and BOFFIN, but generally poor at defining words such as FILOFAX and KISSOGRAM, which were introduced at later stages of the pre-morbid period. Patient P.Z. (Butters, 1985) also shows evidence of impaired semantic memory in that he was dramatically impaired in his ability to identify important figures in his own scientific discipline.

Frontal Symptoms

Early accounts of the neuropathology of WKS emphasised subcortical origins, but more recent studies indicate that frontal pathology is a prominent feature of WKS. Mayes et al. (1988) reported macroscopic evidence of frontal atrophy in their patient B.C. and morphometric analysis revealed reduced nucleolar volumes in layers II and V of the frontal cortex of both their patients. Shimamura, Jernigan and Squire (1988) carried out detailed CAT scans on seven WKS patients and cortical atrophy was detected in the frontal sulcal and peri-sylvian areas of all the patients. Furthermore, high fluid values in the frontal sulci correlated significantly with the patients' behavioural measures of cognitive impairment.

There is abundant evidence that WKS patients are impaired on psychometric tests of frontal lobe function. Poor performance on WCST has been reported by Jacobson (1989), Hunkin (1991), Leng and Parkin (1988a), Shoqeirat et al. (1990) and Squire (1982) among others. Perseverative tendencies evident in poor WCST performance have also been found in other tasks. Lhermitte and Signoret (1972) required their patients to learn a logical arrangement, followed by a code learning task and an attempt at learning an ordered word sequence. Their WKS patients performed far worse compared with post-encephalitic amnesics, to some extent due to their perseverative responding. Similarly, Oscar-Berman (1971) reported that Korsakoff patients scored poorly on the Levine concept formation test because they tended to perseverate with an incorrect response. Oscar-Berman, Sahakian and Wikmark (1976) noted perseverative errors by their patients on a two-choice spatial probability task. Talland (1965) reported poor performance on the Embedded Figures Test, which he attributed to the patients' inability to change perceptual set and a number of studies have also indicated reduced word fluency in WKS patients (Butters et al., 1987; Hunkin, 1991; Shoqeirat et al., 1990; Squire, 1982).

Another task, once considered sensitive to frontal dysfunction, is a variant of the BP test—"release from proactive interference (PI)" (Wickens, 1970). Here, the subject is given a series of trials, typically five, involving presentation of three items, a distractor task and then recall. Succeeding trials follow on immediately and for the first four the target items are all drawn from the same category. On trial five, the items are again from the same category (the non-shift condition) or from a new one (the shift condition). The targets can be letters, numbers or words from a taxonomic category or some other semantic group such as affective status. Normal subjects demonstrate a build-up of proactive interference across successive trials but, in the shift condition, recall recovers to near the level of the first trial (release from PI). In contrast, recall remains poor or deteriorates further in the non-shift condition. For controls, this pattern of performance holds whether the shift involves alphanumeric or taxonomic change, but WKS patients only show release from PI with alphanumeric shifts (Butters & Cermak, 1980).

Linkage of release from PI to frontal function derives from Squire (1982), who found that the extent to which WKS patients showed release from PI was inversely related to pyschometric estimates of frontal dysfunction. However, it is important to note that Squire combined his release from the PI index with another assumed frontal measure (temporal discrimination—see below) to achieve this result. More recent studies indicate that frontal disturbance is not a sufficient condition for showing a failure to release from P1 and that a subcortical lesion must also be present (Freedman & Cermak, 1986; Kopelman, 1991; Parkin & Stampfer, in press).

There is, however, evidence that at least part of the poor performance of WKS patients on BP can be attributed to a frontal deficit. Leng and Parkin (1989) found that errors by WKS patients on the BP task correlated with WCST errors but not with "a composite memory score" derived from patients' performance on several standard memory tests. A frontal component to BP performance is supported by Parkin and Walter (1991). They replicated the well-known age-related decrement on the BP task and showed that at least two independent factors contributed to the deficit—a frontal component, which they suggested was primarily affecting retrieval processes, and an acquisition/storage factor. This suggests that Leng and Parkin should have obtained correlations between BP performance and both frontal and memory measures. Failure to observe the latter, however, may be due to floor effects stemming from low levels of memory performance.

As noted above, Squire (1982) also claimed that poor temporal discrimination in WKS has a frontal origin. Squire used the list discrimination paradigm reported by Squire, Nadel and Slater (1981). Here, subjects are shown two lists of unrelated sentences separated by an interval of several minutes. A yes–no recognition test for the target sentences is then given and, when a "yes" response is made, the subject is required to state whether the sentence occurred in the first or second list. Squire claimed that performance on the list discrimination component was influenced by frontal dysfunction, whereas the recognition component was not, a conclusion consistent with the research of Milner, Corsi and Leonard (1991).

Squire's argument was based on a correlation between a mean rank score of frontal measures and a combination score of temporal discrimination plus a measure of release from PI (see above). However, along with doubts already raised about this measure, the WKS group also appeared, overall, to be performing at chance on the discrimination measure. In addition, other studies of WKS have failed to show a relation between temporal discrimination and frontal impairments (Hunkin & Parkin, in press; Kopelman, 1991; Shimamura, Janowsky & Squire, 1990) and in others patients with no frontal pathology have shown marked temporal discrimination problems (Bowers, Verafaellie, Valenstein & Heilman, 1988; Parkin & Hunkin, in press).

Confabulation

Confabulation may be defined as the replacement of "the gaps left by a disorder of memory with imaginary experiences consistently believed to be true" (*Collins English Dictionary*) or, more succinctly, "honest lying" (Moscovitch, 1989). As a descriptive term, confabulation has been used rather loosely in much of the clinical literature. However, Berlyne (1972) introduced a distinction between "momentary" and "fantastic" confabulation. Momentary confabulations were defined as false memories provoked by probing the patient's memory and that these memories consisted of real experiences transposed in time; in contrast, fantastic confabulations were described as spontaneous, often grandiose, and implausible.

WKS patients are often described as "confabulatory" but this conclusion needs to be modified in the light of the above distinction. In our experience, fantastic confabulation is a rare occurrence in WKS patients and it is more properly considered as a symptom of certain focal lobe lesions (e.g. Baddeley & Wilson, 1986; Kapur & Coughlan, 1980; Moscovitch, 1989; Parkin, Leng, Stanhope & Smith, 1988b; Stuss, Alexander, Lieberman & Levine, 1978; see also Chapter 7). This point was demonstrated formally by Kopelman (1987b), who examined the pattern of momentary and fantastic confabulation—Kopelman calls these "provoked" and "spontaneous" confabulations—in WKS patients and normal subjects in a story recall task. Neither the WKS patients nor the controls produced significant numbers of fantastic confabulations and it was also shown that momentary confabulations produced by the WKS patients were similar to those produced by normal subjects after a long delay. Kopelman concluded that most confabulation in WKS is similar to that which occurs when normal subjects attempt to compensate for poor memory (for an interesting example of extensive momentary confabulation, see Warrington & Weiskrantz, 1979).

Perceptual Deficits

Although perceptual impairments in WKS have been noted since the turn of the century, Talland (1965) was the first researcher to comment extensively on this aspect of the WKS deficit. Talland's group of Korsakoffs exhibited a range of perceptual impairments including failures on the Embedded Figures Test and marked difficulties in achieving reversals of the Necker Cube. More recent studies have added to the range of perceptual difficulties experienced by WKS patients. Dricker et al. (1978) found that WKS patients are more affected than normals by the presence of distracting stimuli in a visual array. Similarly, Glosser, Butters and Samuels (1976) found that WKS patients performed poorly on a test of dichotic listening. These findings suggest that there may be a generalised attentional deficit in WKS. Consistent with this is the demonstration of decreased noradrenergic activity in WKS which, when produced in animals, causes attentional impairments (e.g. McEntee & Mair, 1979).

Butters and Cermak (1980) found that WKS patients performed very poorly on the digit–symbol task. This task, a form of which constitutes part of WAIS and WAIS-R, requires the subject to pair numbers with specified abstract symbols. Performance can be affected by motor impairments and by visuo-perceptive factors. Analysis of the WKS data showed that when speed of responding was partialled out, a significant deficit still remained—a finding that indicated visuo-perceptive difficulties in the patients. The ability of WKS patients to match pictures of the same face was also examined using a task designed to assess facial recognition in young children. The subjects were shown a target face alongside two alternatives and were required to select the one that matched the target. One alternative, the distractor, shared some paraphernalia or expression with the target, whereas the face matching the target differed along these dimensions. WKS patients found this task difficult, tending to match in terms of paraphernalia and expression rather than overall configuration.

In our discussion of the neuropathology of WKS, we note the frequency of DMTN lesions and the consistent presence of cortical atrophy, particularly in the frontal lobes. Animal studies involving ablation of these structures have consistently produced olfactory deficits (e.g. Eichenbaum, Morton, Potter & Corkin, 1983) and it is therefore predictable that WKS patients may also show similar kinds of impairment. Butters and Cermak (1980) report that WKS patients are poor at discriminating between odours and estimating their intensity. Mair, Capra, McEntee and Engen (1980) confirm that WKS patients have poor odour discrimination but, unlike Butters and Cermak, they failed to find evidence for impaired judgement of intensity—a discrepancy which they attribute to more refined methodology and analysis in their own study. Despite this difference, both groups of researchers attribute the observed WKS deficit as one specific to the olfactory sense as opposed to one that is a consequence of some more generalised deficit.

Wernicke's Encephalopathy in a Young Person

Studies of WKS usually involve subjects who have developed the disorder in middle to old age. It is notable, however, that Victor et al. (1989) did report instances of Wernicke's encephalopathy (WE) in women as young as 20. However, detailed information about the neuropsychological status of young people surviving WE has been non-existent with only the anecdotal account of Turner, Daniels and Greer (1989) available. Recently, however, Parkin et al. (in press a) have presented a detailed case report of a 20-year-old woman who survived WE.

Example Case History

Case 3 (L.E.) is a 20-year-old woman who was admitted following an 18-month period during which she drank the equivalent of a bottle of whisky a day. She also had a 6-year history of bingeing and vomiting. Neurological examination revealed the classic triad of WE which ameliorated following therapy. Neuroradiological examination indicated grade 4 cortical atrophy but there was no sign of any subcortical damage (see Fig. 3.5). Neuropsychological testing revealed a profound deficit in recall, although she did pass Rey's malingering test (see Chapter 2). In contrast, her recognition performance matched that of her controls. Recognition performance relating to remote memory was also normal, but some recall problems were noted. Performance on WAIS indicated a markedly poorer verbal than non-verbal IQ. On tests of frontal lobe function, she generally performed well, although there were some suggestions of a mild deficit.

Her memory deficit caused considerable problems for her but was not sufficiently disabling to warrant permanent care. Her preserved recognition memory, for example, enabled her to recognise familiar people and she would then use situational cues to work out who they might be. Her preserved intellect also meant that she was quite good at covering up her memory lapses.

Parkin et al. (in press) point out that, using the IQ–MQ criterion, L.E. meets the criterion of an amnesic syndrome because her discrepancy score is greater than 20 points (see pp. 38–40 and Chapter 2). However, her normal recognition memory rules out an amnesic syndrome because this is characterised by both defective recall and recognition. The authors conclude that the patient is suffering from a frontal system memory impairment (see Chapters 7 and 8) but are unclear whether experience of WE has been instrumental in determining the deficit. According to Lishman (1990), alcoholics are at risk from two sources of brain insult: cortical and subcortical damage arising from alcohol neurotoxicity, and subcortical damage arising from thiamine deficiency. Parkin et al. concede that cortical damage could be entirely responsible for L.E.'s deficits, but note that these are far more severe than typically found in young female alcoholics. An alternative possibility is that WE has been instrumental in determining the pattern of deficit producing a "prodromal" WKS in which recall deficits stemming from an impaired frontal system have been established in the absence of more substantial damage needed for a full-blown WKS to develop.

Wernicke-Korsakoff Syndrome in Non-alcoholics

We noted earlier that Wernicke (1881) did not consider alcoholism a necessary condition for WE and many of his cases had other aetiologies. It is therefore curious that for at least 50 years following that report, Wernicke's encephalopathy was regarded as purely a condition associated with alcoholism (Lindboe & Lobert, 1989). However, Neuberger (1937) described a case of non-alcoholic WE and, since then, a steady stream of papers has reported WE due to diet (de Wardener & Lennox, 1947), hyperemesis gravidarum (Wood, Murray, Sinha, Godley & Goldsmith, 1983), hunger strike (Beaufils, Ramirez & Feline, 1988; Pentland & Maudsley, 1982), anorexia nervosa (Handler & Perkin, 1982), dialysis (Jagadha, Deck, Halliday & Smyth, 1987), prolonged intravenous therapy (Nadel & Burger, 1976), renal insufficiency (Faris, 1972), subtotal gastrectomy (Ferla, Giometto, Meneghetti & Schergna, 1981) and gastric partitioning (Villar & Ranne, 1984).

Despite the extensive investigations of memory and associated intellectual impairments in alcoholic WKS, there are few neuropsychological investigations of non-alcoholic WKS. As we have noted, interpretation of alcoholic WKS deficits is made problematic by difficulties in estimating the influence of prior chronic alcoholism on the patient's pattern of impairment (see Chapter 8). For this reason alone, the study of non-alcoholic WKS is of considerable scientific interest.

Example Case History

Case 4 (C.M.) was admitted to hospital in April 1947 aged 44 years. She had a 9-year history of Crohn's disease (a malabsorptive gut illness). A Crohn's abscess was diagnosed and two operations separated by a period of intravenous feeding were carried out. Recovery seemed uneventful, but 2–3 days post-operation her relatives noticed that she appeared disoriented and that her memory was poor. Subsequently, she was referred to the psychiatric services with a history of memory impairment and an apparent inability "to take charge of her life". She neglected the house and her three dogs, could not feed herself, and became increasingly reliant on neighbours for help. She was also in debt because of unpaid bills and unnecessary repetitive spending. On admission, she exhibited marked problems with her memory, needing reminders and reassurance in the performance of most tasks. An MRI scan performed 15 months post-operation was normal apart from the presence of small subcortical lesions, probably vascular in origin. C.M. lives with her daughter and is currently unable to work.

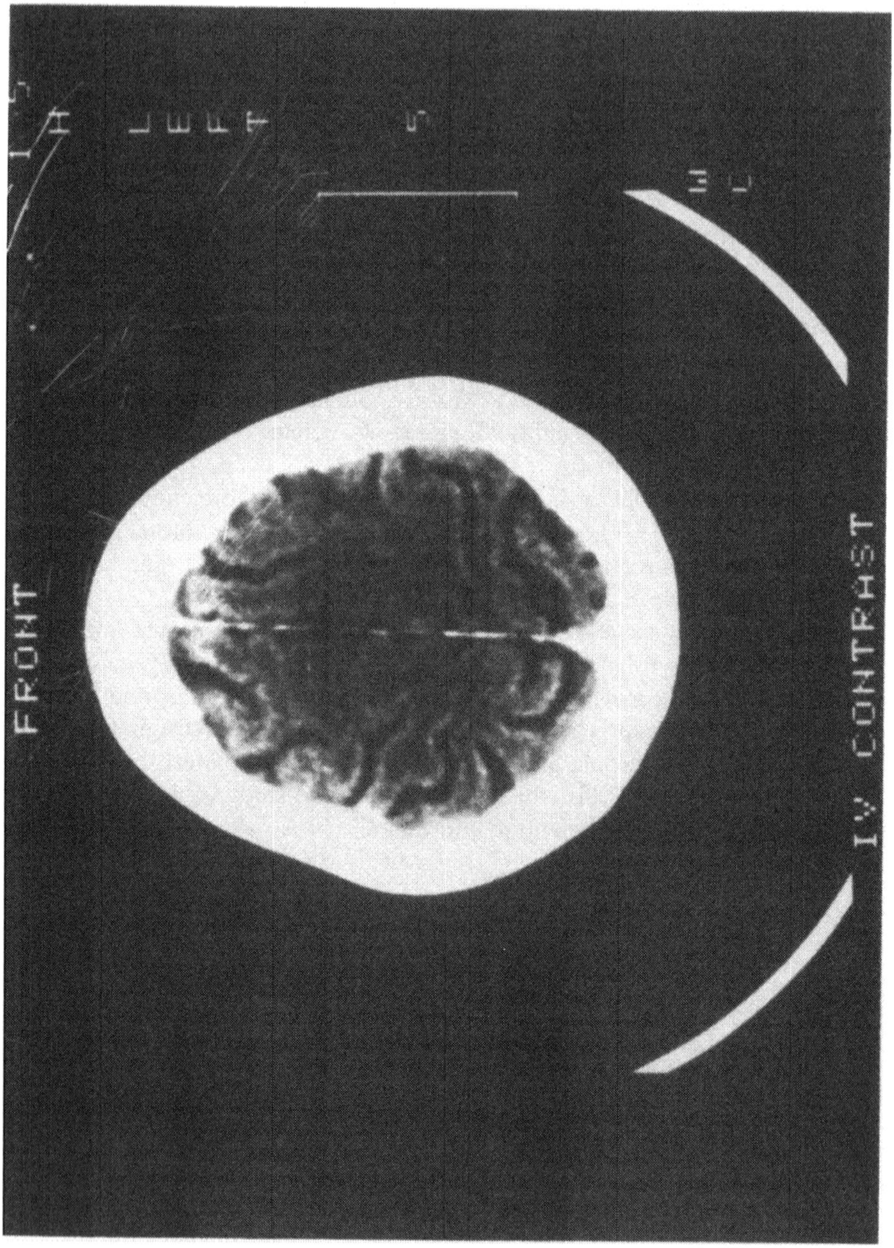

(a)

(b)

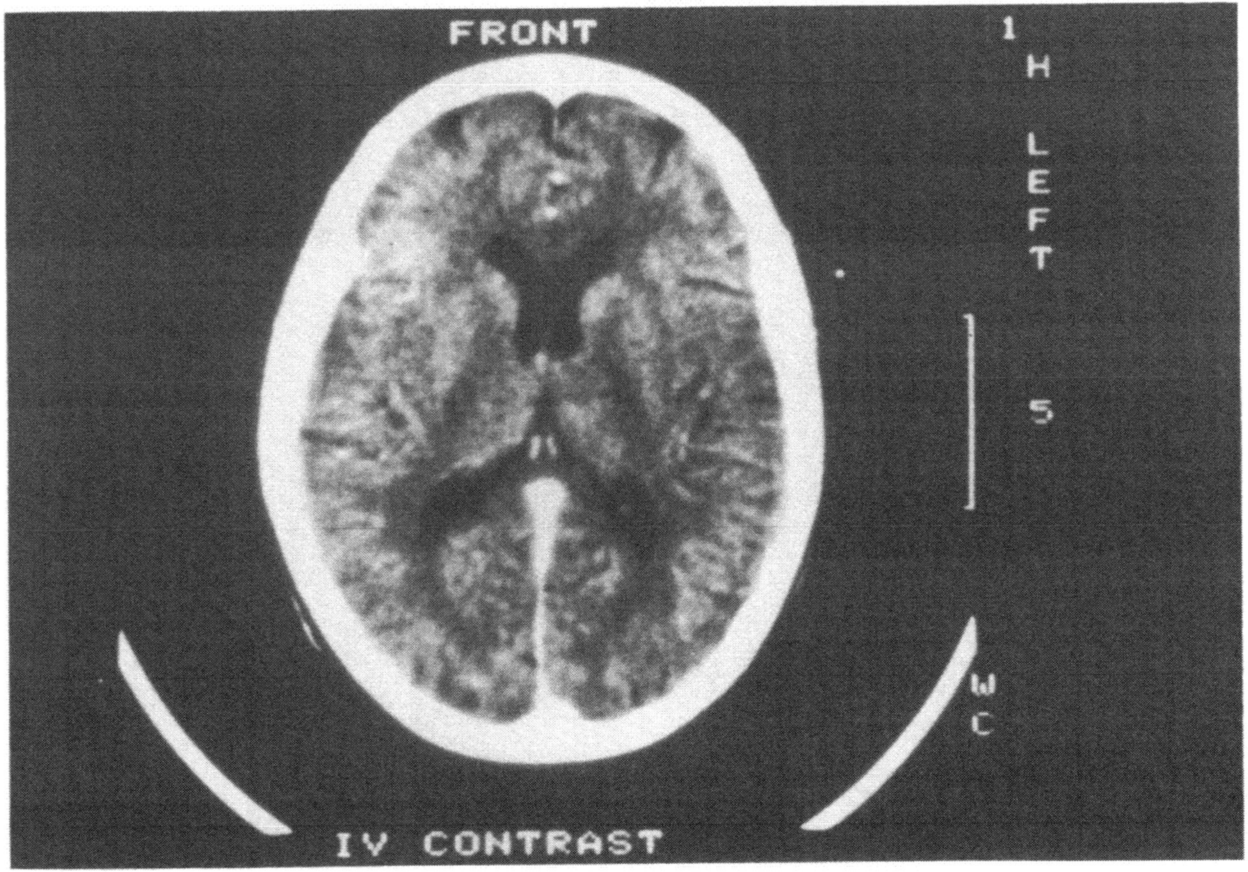

FIG. 3.5 CAT scans of patient L.E showing (a) severe cortical atrophy and (b) absence of subcortical pathology.

C.M. has been studied in detail by Parkin, Blunden, Rees and Hunkin (1991). On tests of anterograde memory, her performance is poor and comparable in all dimensions with alcoholic WKS patients. She also exhibits a marked retrograde amnesia, performing badly on a test of famous faces and one concerned with public events. On both tasks, there is evidence of a temporal gradient and autobiographical cueing procedures elicited few memories from the 10-year period preceding her operation. A further interesting finding was that C.M. showed frontal impairment.

Beatty, Bailly and Fisher (1988) report a temporary WKS in a patient suffering from anorexia and vomiting. Like C.M., this patient (L.B.) had severe anterograde deficit and a mild, but temporally graded retrograde amnesia. In contrast to C.M., L.B. performed normally on the WCST. However, it should be noted that L.B. was not free of frontal symptoms in that she showed some increase in perseverative responding.

Patient B.C. (Becker, Furman, Panisset & Smith, 1990) suffered systemic sclerosis complicated by inflammatory myopathy and small bowel malabsorption. Prior to admission, the patient began vomiting, lost weight dramatically and became confused. Testing on the WMS-R revealed a profound anterograde amnesia as did other tests of new learning. On the Boston Remote Memory Test, B.C. showed a marked deficit that was temporally graded. B.C. also performed poorly on the Brown-Peterson Task at a level comparable with Korsakoff patients. Performance on frontal lobe tests was, however, normal.

The three case studies just described show a degree of uniformity. Following nutritional disorders of some kind, all three developed confusional states followed by a dense anterograde amnesia and temporally graded retrograde amnesia. In addition, two of the patients showed evidence of frontal impairments. Given that the anterograde and retrograde impairments constitute the "hallmark" of WKS, and that frontal symptoms do vary in their severity across alcoholic WKS patients, the characteristics of these non-alcoholic WKS patients do not distinguish them, behaviourally, from WKS patients with an alcoholic aetiology. More cases of this kind may, therefore, provide a good opportunity to study the acute onset aspects of WKS uncontaminated by the influence of prior alcoholism.

Neuropsychology of Wernicke-Korsakoff Syndrome: A Summary

WKS is encountered primarily but not exclusively in patients with an aetiology of chronic alcoholism. The neurological events surrounding the onset of the disorder may well be defined or insidious in origin. The critical brain lesion for WKS is generally considered to lie in the midline diencephalon, but its exact location has yet to be determined. WKS patients exhibit a marked anterograde amnesia in the presence of largely preserved intellect, the typical WMS–WAIS-R discrepancy being 25 points. Retrograde amnesia is invariably present and always exhibits a marked temporal gradient. The most significant additional cognitive impairments are those associated with frontal lobe dysfunction and these must be taken fully into account when assessing the patient. Other impairments are also likely to be present, most notably olfactory and visuoperceptive deficits. WKS patients show a variety of residual learning abilites. From the limited data available, it appears that WKS arising from a non-alcoholic origin has similar characteristics to the alcoholically generated variety.

4 Thalamic and Other Diencephalic Amnesias

Chapter 4 emphasised the important role that diencephalic structures play in memory function. However, our knowledge of this fact does not just stem from patients who have suffered Wernicke's encephalopathy. Diencephalic structures can become damaged in a number of different ways, all leading to memory impairments of comparable severity to Wernicke-Korsakoff Syndrome (WKS).

Thalamic Infarction and Haemorrhage

Primary thalamic haemorrhage is relatively frequent, accounting for over 10% of all intracranial haemorrhages (Choi et al., 1983), and within this patient group there have been numerous reports of amnesia as a primary chronic symptom (e.g. Bogousslavsky, Regli & Uske, 1987; Brown, Kieran & Patel, 1989; Choi et al., 1983; Cramon, Hebel & Schuri, 1985; Gentilini, De Renzi & Crisi, 1987; Ghidoni, Pattacini, Galimberti & Aguzzoli, 1989; Graff-Radford, Tranel, Van Hoesen & Brandt, 1990; Guberman & Stuss, 1983; Meissner, Sapir, Kokmen & Stein, 1987; Nichelli, Bahmanian-Behbahani, Gentilini & Vecchi, 1988; Parkin, Rees, Hunkin & Rose, in press b; Rousseaux et al., 1986; Signoret & Goldenberg, 1986; Speedie & Heilman, 1982; Stuss, Guberman, Nelson & La Rochelle, 1988; Winocur et al., 1984). One should note, however, that non-haemorrhagic infarction is also associated with persistent amnesia (Graff-Radford, Eslinger, Damasio & Yamada, 1984). The occurrence of thalamic amnesia appears dependent on infarction occurring in a particular region of the thalamus. Following earlier descriptions, Bogousslavsky et al. (1987) delineated four main

(a)

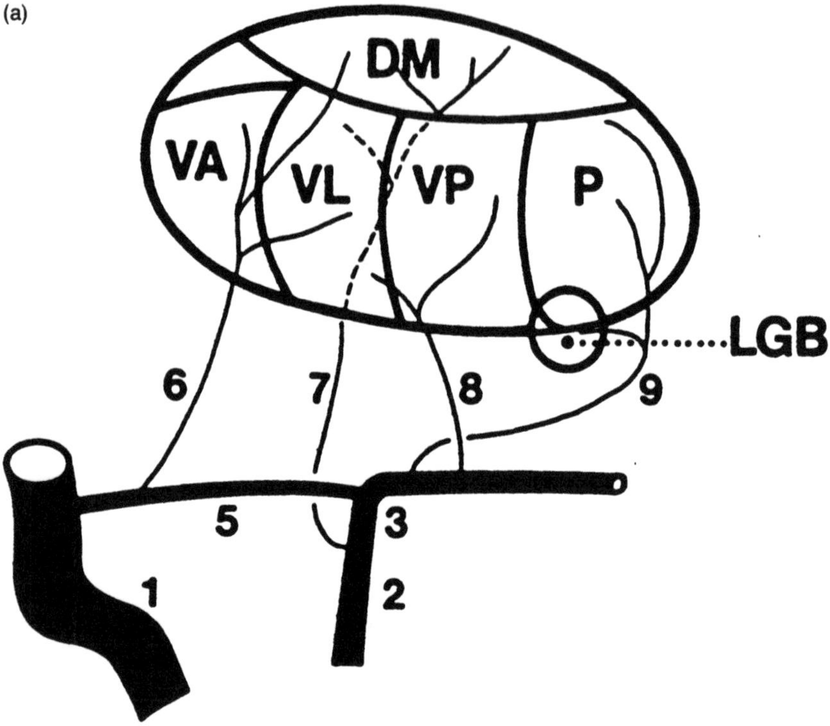

FIG. 4.1 (a) Arterial supply to the thalamus. (b) Region of the thalamus in which infarction is most commonly associated with amnesia. Key: Arterial supply: 1, carotid syphon; 2, basilar artery; 3, basilar communicating artery; 4, posterior cerebral artery; 5, posterior communicating artery; 6, tubero-thalamic artery; 7, paramedian pedicle; 8, infero-lateral pedicle; 9, posterior choroidal arteries. Thalamic nuclei: VA, ventral anterior; VL, ventral lateral; VP, ventral posterior; P, pulvinar; IL, intralaminar; DM, dorsomedial; LGB, lateral geniculate body. Reproduced from Bogousslavsky et al. (1988) with the permission of Edgell Communications and authors.

arterial territories within the thalamus: *inferolateral, tuberothalamic, posterior choroidal* and *paramedian*. Their investigations revealed that infarcts in each of these territories were associated with a distinct neurological syndrome and that memory impairment was only associated significantly with infarction of the paramedian territory (see Fig. 4.1).

Other studies of thalamic amnesia have also identified it with infarction of the paramedian territory (e.g. Gentilini et al., 1987; Guberman & Stuss, 1983; Graff-Radford et al., 1990; Speedie & Heilman, 1982; Stuss et al., 1988; Winocur, Oxbury, Roberts et al., 1984). Indeed, Meissner et al. (1987) described a "paramedian diencephalic syndrome" characterised by a clinical triad of hypersomnolent apathy, amnesic syndrome and impaired vertical gaze (sometimes referred to as Parinaud's Syndrome). Although

(b)

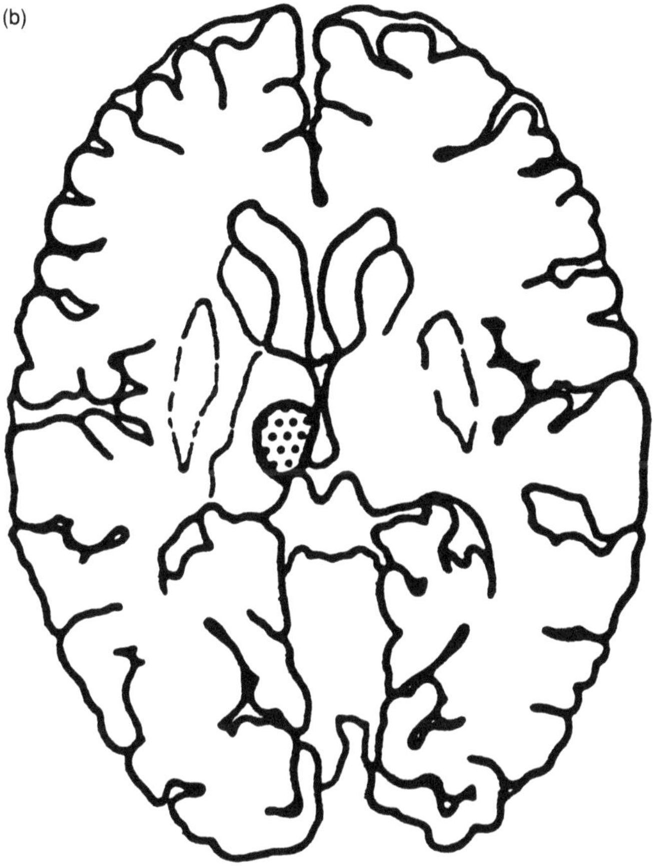

not present in all patients with thalamic amnesia, this triad has been identified in a number of cases (e.g. Gentilini et al., 1987; Stuss et al., 1988; Swanson & Schmidley, 1985), and its presence was also noted in patient N.A. (Weiskrantz, 1985; see below). The neuroanatomical basis of thalamic amnesia has formed part of the more general debate concerning the anatomy of memory, and a more detailed discussion of this topic is postponed until Chapter 8.

Example Case History

Case 5 (J.R.) is a 48-year-old engineer who experienced a "funny turn" at work during which his eyes became briefly unfocused. Subsequently, he experienced difficulty remembering people's names and, briefly, also had problems remembering the names of some objects. A magnetic resonance imaging (MRI) scan has subsequently revealed an infarction in the left thalamus (see Fig. 4.2).

On the WMS, J.R. had an MQ of 98, but a detailed breakdown showed very poor verbal memory in comparison with near-normal visual memory. Further testing revealed that he had particular problems remembering the temporal order of novel information, but this temporal ordering deficit was not apparent in his retrograde memory ability. His WAIS also reflects greater linguistic impairment with his verbal IQ (100) being 12 points below his performance IQ (112). He does not show any marked retrograde amnesia except on tasks which require him to name famous people. In this situation, he shows clear knowledge of who the person is but is incapable of providing their name. On tests of frontal lobe function, he performs within normal limits. He is still at work but unable to carry out his former responsibilities.

Severity of Amnesia

Table 4.1 summarises available FSIQ–WMSMQ discrepancy scores in examples of thalamic amnesia. In a number of instances, the discrepancies are compatible with those encountered in other aetiologies of amnesia, but there are also a number of smaller discrepancies associated with reduced FSIQ. This observation is relevant to our discussion concerning the distinction between thalamic amnesia and thalamic dementia (see below).

TABLE 4.1
WAIS FSIQ–WMSMQ Discrepancies in Thalamic Amnesia

	FSIQ	*WMSMQ*	*Difference*
Brown et al. (1989)	95	86	9
Graff-Radford et al. (1984)	76	61	15
Meissner et al. (1987)	79	60	19
Mori et al. (1986)	105	90	15
Parkin et al. (in press b)	113	98	15
Speedie and Heilman (1982)	88	64	22
Stuss et al. (1988)	98	86	12
Tsoi et al. (1987)	66	62	4

Immediate Memory

Performance on digit span appears variable in thalamic amnesia. Several studies (Brown et al., 1989; Cramon et al., 1985; Dusoir et al., 1990; Teuber, Milner & Vaughan, 1968; Winocur et al., 1984) have all reported normal digit span performance among their patients. However, others (Fensore, Lazzarino, Nappo & Nicolai, 1988; Rousseaux et al., 1986; Stuss et al., 1988) report significant reductions in the digit span of their patients. This variability may have clinical significance in the categorisation of patients exhibiting memory impairments following thalamic lesions.

Short-term Memory

Although the extent of impairments varies, most patients show impaired Brown-Peterson performance (e.g. case A.V. of Butters, 1984; case J.R. of Parkin et al., in press b). The performance of B.Y. improved with target exposure time, but he was still showing impairment at longer distraction intervals (Winocur et al., 1984). He also failed to show release from PI following a semantic shift. Speedie and Heilman (1982) administered the BP procedure to their patient using consonant trigrams presented either auditorily, visually and sequentially, or visually simultaneously. Performance under different distraction intervals was compared with distraction-free periods of the same length. Performance was strikingly better without distraction. An exception to this pattern of poor performance is J.E. (Brown et al., 1989), who showed normal performance on both BP and release from PI.

Anterograde Amnesia

Graff-Radford et al. (1984) report that recall of the Rey figure, WMS logical memory and paired-associate learning were impaired in all five cases. Patients with left-sided lesions had both verbal and visual memory impairment, whereas the right-sided case presented only with visual memory loss. In the second study of thalamic amnesia by Graff-Radford et al. (1990), two cases had severe anterograde deficits, but in the other two memory impairments were only evident at delayed testing. The patients of Akiguchi et al. (1987) were similar in this respect, with left lesions producing verbal memory deficits and right lesions visual memory problems. Of the six cases of thalamic infarction studied by Cramon et al. (1985), four were considered to have "chronic amnesia", performing significantly below a control group on tests such as paired associates, face–name paired associates, and the AVLT. The three left-sided thalamic lesion cases described by Fensore et al. (1988) were found to have persistent verbal memory impairments, but relatively preserved visual memory. J.E. (Brown et al., 1989) had a left thalamic infarction and this gave rise to severe verbal learning problems with much better visual memory performance.

In patient B.Y. (Winocur et al., 1984), the primacy effect was limited to the first item, the recency effect was normal and delayed recall was poor at all word list positions. B.Y. was also severely impaired on hard paired

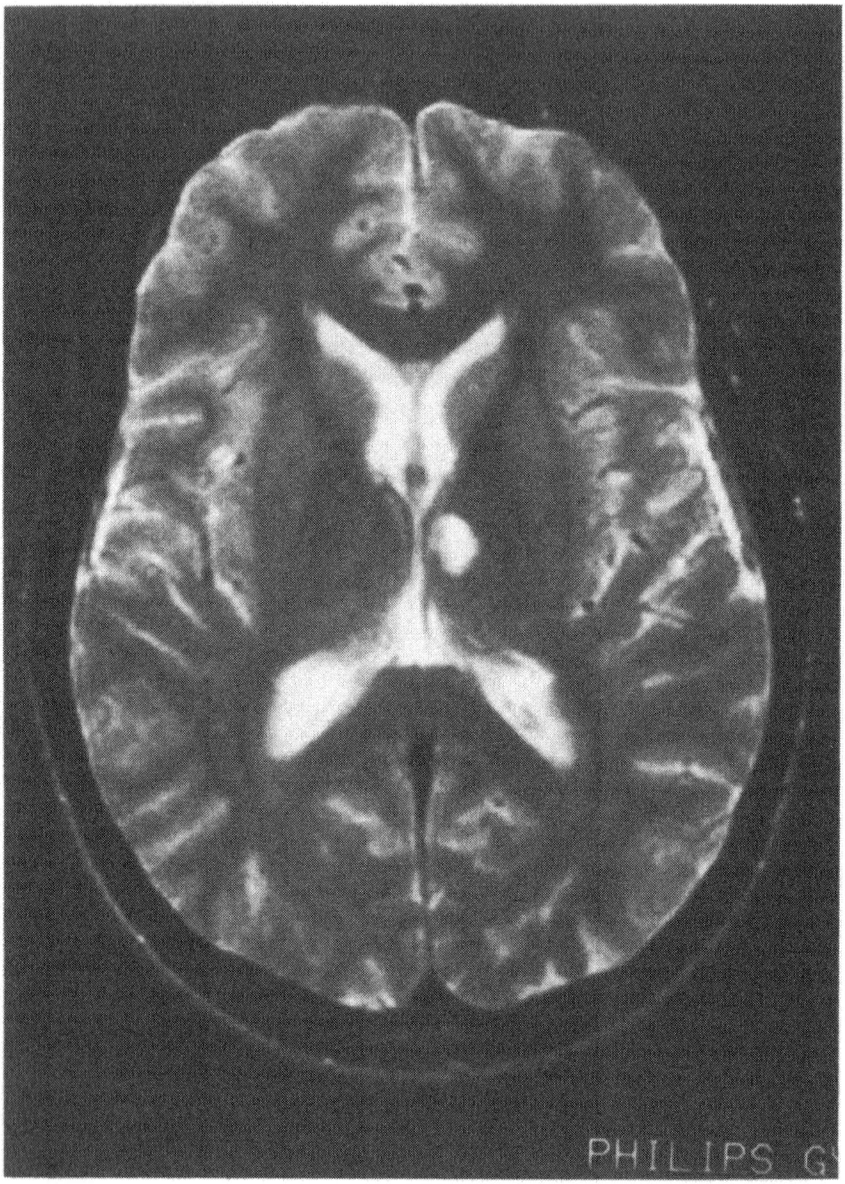

FIG 4.2 MRI scans of patient J.R. showing left anterior thalamic infarction. Reproduced with the permission of Dr J.E. Rees.

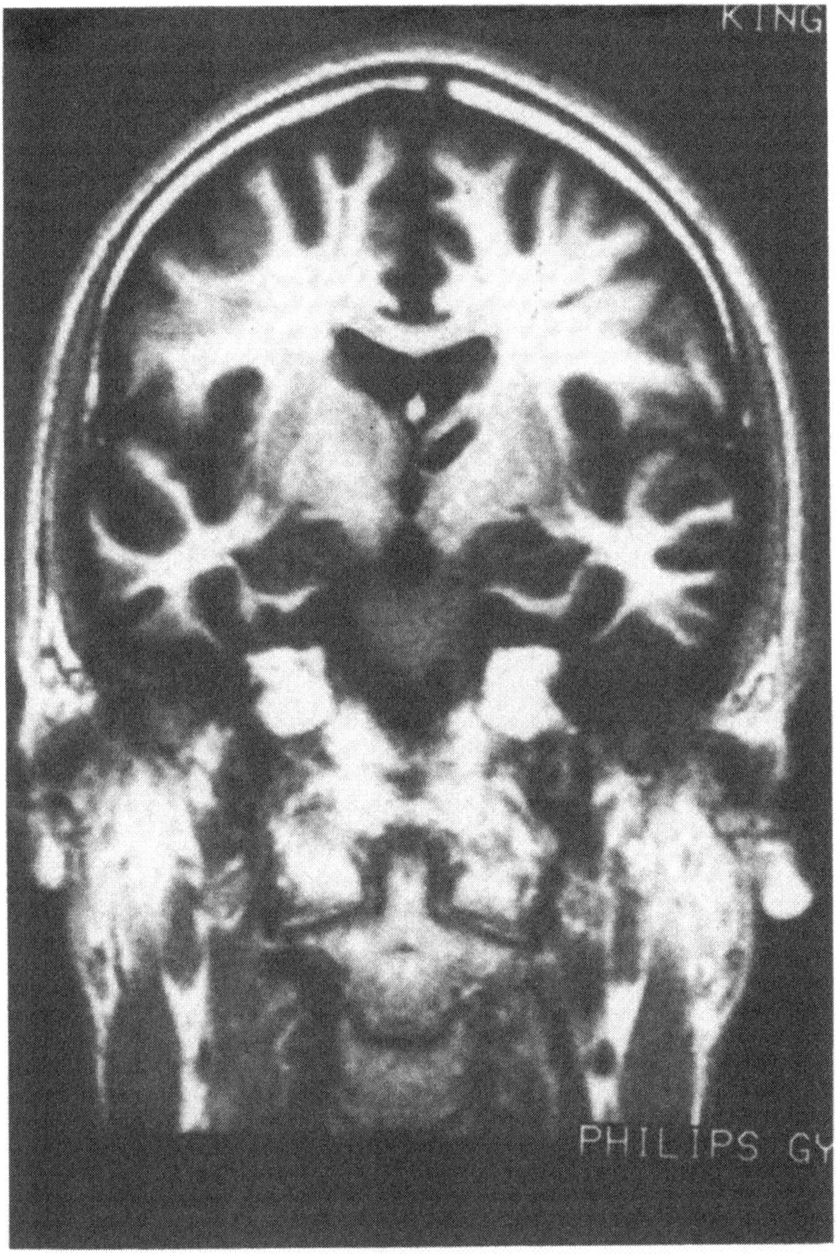
KING
PHILIPS GY

associates, and on the negative transfer paradigm he had problems learning list 2, but unlike WKS patients (Winocur & Weiskrantz, 1976) this latter finding was due to omission rather than intrusion errors. B.Y. was able to copy the Rey Figure correctly but showed severely impaired recall 40 min later. On the Warrington Recognition Test, B.Y. performed below the controls but did better than typical amnesic patients. Speedie and Heilman's (1982) patient had poor WMS logical memory and could not learn hard paired associates. His Rey Figure copying was reasonable but subsequent reproduction was poor.

Retrograde Amnesia

B.Y. has been assessed on two remote memory tests (Winocur et al., 1984). On the Stevens (1979) famous personality test and on Newcombe's (unpublished) test of photographs of famous people, B.Y. performed as well as controls. However, the Stevens test is very easy and good performance does not exclude retrograde amnesia. J.E. (Brown et al., 1989) was examined on two sub-tests of the Boston Remote Memory Battery (BRMB). His scores were better than the controls on both easy and hard famous faces and similar to controls on verbal recall. Some evidence of a temporal gradient was also present.

R.C. (Stuss et al., 1988) had persisting retrograde amnesia with some evidence of a temporal gradient. On the BRMB, Graff-Radford et al.'s patients averaged 5 out of 48 correct and this increased to 6.5 with cues. Performance on the recall component of the BRMB was also very poor and not temporally graded. Recall of recent presidents was also poor, averaging only 1.5 out of 6. Recall and recognition of events measured by both Squire et al.'s test and the BRMB also showed marked impairment, but again no evidence of a temporal gradient was found. Cramon et al. (1985) report two tests of remote memory—"famous faces" and "life events". Only one patient was considered to be impaired on both tests. However, evaluation of this result is problematic because no description of the test procedures is given. Fensore et al. (1988) evaluated autobiographic memory in their three patients and all showed a "good" level of performance. In contrast, Barbizet et al. (1981) report an extensive retrograde amnesia following ischaemic lesions in the thalamic region.

J.R. (Parkin et al., in press b) was given Kapur's "Dead or Alive Test" (see Chapter 2), which tests knowledge of whether famous people are still alive and, if not, how and when they died. J.R. performed similarly to controls on all components of this task despite showing gross impairments on anterograde measures of temporal memory. This finding indicates that the ability to derive temporal knowledge from remote memory may dissociate from the ability to form new temporal memory—see the case of Bowers et al., (1988), Parkin and Hunkin (in press) and Chapter 8.

Implicit Memory

Nichelli et al. (1988) examined the performance of a single patient on a mirror drawing task. Normal acquisition was demonstrated despite the patient consistently denying that he had done the task before. On mirror reading (see below), learning was observed for both repeated and non-repeated words, although in the latter his learning curve was more erratic than controls. Using the procedure outlined by Woods, Schoene and Kneisley (1982), the patient was also able to acquire the Fibonacci rule. Graff-Radford et al. (1990) found that all four of their patients maintained improvements in mirror drawing after a 1-hour delay but only three showed learning on pursuit rotor.

Frontal Symptoms

Patient I.G. (Stuss et al., 1988), despite her high IQ, was severely impaired on the Wisconsin Card Sorting Test (WCST). Patient R.C., from the same study, perseverated on a simpler colour form sorting task. This was not thought attributable to IQ because another patient, R.M., of lower IQ, completed it successfully. Speedie and Heilman (1982) found that their patient performed poorly on the WCST, but Parkin et al. (in press b) report minimal frontal disturbance in their patient J.R., and patient J.E. (Brown et al., 1989) performed within normal limits on the WCST.

Confabulation

Stuss et al. (1988) report the presence of confabulation during the acute stage in all three of their patients. They also noted apathy, personality change and lack of insight. These changes, which have been noted in other studies of thalamic infarction (e.g. Graff-Radford et al., 1984; Mills & Swanson, 1978), are most evident in the early stages of recovery.

Other Deficits

Damage to the thalamus can result in a range of additional cognitive deficits, some of which may confound interpretation of memory test performance. In this account, we will restrict ourselves to patients with thalamic damage who present memory impairment as a significant chronic symptom. Graff-Radford et al. (1984) report the presence of constructional apraxia in four of their five thalamic patients (two left- and two right-sided lesions). All of the patients had visuoperceptive deficits and impaired spatial discrimination. On right–left discrimination, patients with left thalamic lesions were impaired on both self and confrontation sub-tests, whereas right thalamic patients only failed on the confrontation sub-test. Patients with left thalamic lesions were also described as aphasic, being particularly impaired on naming, aural comprehension and reading. However, sentence and digit repetition were not affected. Patients with right thalamic lesions did not appear aphasic.

Stuss et al. (1988, p. 19) report language deficits in three of their thalamic cases, which they described as:

> . . . poor initiation of speech with a general poverty of output that occasionally was contaminated by confabulation and lack of monitoring of output; fluctuation and variability in performance; relatively intact repetition and comprehension; and naming problems, apparently characterized more by perceptual errors, nonaphasic misnaming, intrusions, perseverations, and confabulation than by phonemic and semantic paraphasias.

Language impairments also characterise the additional deficits found in the patients reported by Meissner et al. (1987) and Fensore et al. (1988). Bogousslavsky et al. (1987) report dysphasia in 2 of their 14 patients with paramedian territory infarcts. Visuospatial deficits are reported in two of this sample and five demonstrated hemi-neglect.

Overview of Thalamic Amnesia

This form of amnesia can arise in a number of ways, the most common being infarction following primary thalamic haemorrhage. Infarcts involving the paramedian territory are most likely to cause permanent memory loss. Most patients evaluated on the BP task have shown impairments. On tests of anterograde memory, there is abundant evidence of severe amnesia in this patient group. Lesions are often unilateral with left-sided deficits most common. In these instances, verbal memory is more affected. The majority of patients appear to show retrograde impairments without a temporal gradient, but there are notable exceptions to this.

On tests of frontal lobe function, some patients show significant deficits whereas others perform normally. The presence of other cognitive deficits also seems variable, although evidence relating to this is almost entirely restricted to cases of memory loss involving thalamic infarction. In this group, associated linguistic impairments predominate, but visuoperceptive difficulties, constructional apraxia and hemi-neglect have also been described.

Thalamic Dementia

The foregoing account indicates the range of impairments that can arise following focal damage to the thalamic region. This raises the issue that, when incorporating thalamic patients into studies of the amnesic syndrome, care must be taken to exclude those who are more properly described as suffering from dementia. Two likely criteria arise as a means of distinguishing thalamic amnesia from thalamic dementia. First, as was the case with alcoholic WKS, amnesic patients could be accepted on the basis of a substantially higher WAIS FSIQ compared with WMSMQ. Secondly, performance on digit span might provide a sufficient guide. It is certainly notable that those thalamic patients presenting the purest amnesic deficits are those in which digit span is normal (e.g. B.Y. of Winocur et al., 1984; Cramon et al., 1985), whereas those studies describing memory loss alongside other significant impairments report significant impairments in digit span.

Penetrating Paranasal Head Injury

Cases of low-velocity penetrating head injury are a rare but interesting source of information about brain function. The famous case of Phineas Gage, for example, is often used to focus attention on the role of the frontal lobes in cognition. Within memory research, penetrating head injuries have provided several instances of amnesia and one of these patients, N.A., has been the subject of much investigation and not a little controversy.

Case N.A.

In 1968, Teuber et al. reported an extraordinary instance of an amnesic syndrome. Their patient, N.A., was a young U.S. airman who suffered what, in cold medical terms, would be described as a "low-velocity penetrating head injury". Remarkably, N.A. is able to recount the circumstances of his injury:

> I was working at my desk. . . . My room-mate had come in [and] he had taken one of my small fencing foils off the wall and I guess he was making like Cerano de Bergerac behind me . . . I just felt a tap on the back . . . I swung around . . . at the same time he was making the lunge. I took it right in the left nostril, went up and punctured the cribiform area of my brain (cited by Parkin, 1987).

It is not clear if N.A. is inaccurately reporting what he has been told by others or whether he has a patchy pre-traumatic memory for the incident, but apparently the foil entered his right nostril.

Following an initial period of confusion, N.A.'s symptoms ameliorated leaving only a marked amnesic syndrome and ocular disturbance. When first seen, N.A.'s retrograde amnesia extended back at least 2 years but, as his general post-traumatic state improved, this deficit "shrank" to an estimated 2-week period prior to the accident. However, despite a considerable level of recovery some 3 years after the accident, N.A. still has a marked amnesic deficit.

The exact nature of N.A.'s brain lesion has been a matter of considerable controversy. Initially, N.A. was thought to have a circumscribed dorso-medial thalamic nucleus (DMTN) lesion (Squire & Moore, 1979). However, this view was forcefully challenged by Weiskrantz (1985), who argued that, logically, it was impossible for the fencing foil to reach the DMTN without passing through other critical sub-cortical structures en route. In a somewhat heroic attempt to settle the issue, Squire and Zola-Morgan (1985) tried to replicate N.A.'s injury on a cadaver but the results were inconclusive. These efforts have now been superceded by a more sophisticated approach, MRI neuroimaging, which shows, in line with Weiskrantz's view, that N.A. has lesions in the left thalamus, left mamillo-thalmic tract, mamillary bodies, hypothalamus and the anterior temporal lobe (Squire et al., 1989a). One cannot therefore describe N.A.'s deficit as primarily diencephalic and inclusion of his case details in this chapter is somewhat arbitrary.

On initial testing, N.A. (Teuber et al., 1968) had a WMSMQ of 64 and full scale WAIS FSIQ of 99, which subsequently improved: MQ = 97, IQ = 124. Digit span was within normal limits, but on the Brown-Peterson task he performed more poorly than controls when distraction intervals were greater than 9 sec. However, he did show normal release from PI. Because of this left-sided injury, his memory was worse for verbal material. His delayed logical memory score was 0 (Squire & Slater, 1978) and he could not learn hard paired associates. On the continuous recognition task, his deficit was far worse for verbal material. Short-term tests of visual memory were within normal limits, but delayed recall of the Rey Figure was impaired.

N.A. has been tested for public events and television programmes (Squire & Slater, 1978). In both cases, recall was worse than controls for the period 1960 onwards, whereas testing under multiple-choice conditions revealed normal performance throughout the whole time period covered by the test (1950–1975). However, since N.A. became amnesic in 1960, the former results reflect recall of information acquired post-morbidly. According to these assessments, therefore, pre-morbid memory appears largely intact. Finally, N.A. showed no evidence of frontal impairment as assessed by WCST, word fluency and the embedded figures test (Teuber et al., 1968; Squire, 1982).

The injury sustained by N.A. might seem highly improbable but perusal of the penetrating head injury literature indicates a number of transnasal penetrating injuries involving items such as paint brushes and chopsticks. Interestingly, two of these studies report memory deficits following the injury (Czechmanek, 1954; Dusoir et al., 1990). Dusoir et al.'s (1990) patient, B.J., had a snooker cue pushed up his left nostril into the base of the brain during a pub brawl. Neuroimaging failed to indicate any thalamic damage, but lesions were identified in the mamillary bodies. Neuropsychological testing was carried out on B.J. while he was attending a day centre. B.J. was managing to do quite complex woodwork which he himself designed despite his impaired memory. On a variety of verbal memory tests, including components of the WMS-R and Rivermead Behavioural Memory Test (RBMT), and word list learning, B.J. was impaired, particularly when delayed testing was given. In contrast, non-verbal memory performance was, at worst, only mildly impaired.

B.J.'s retrograde amnesia appeared mild, extending back around 18 months prior to his injury. On Kopelman's (1990) public events test, B.J. performed normally except for a slight impairment on the dating component. On the "Dead-or-Alive" test, B.J. showed no evidence of impairment. B.J. also showed no impairments on tests of frontal dysfunction. The deficits shown by B.J. were, therefore, consistent with those encountered in N.A., except that there was no evidence of vertical gaze paralysis.

Tumours

Tumours can arise in the diencephalon, most notably in the third ventricle and, when this occurs, compression of thalamic and hypothalamic structures may result in an amnesic syndrome which, following removal or destruction of the tumour, will often ameliorate. This factor, along with the rather poor prognosis associated with deep brain tumours, has resulted in few detailed case reports of memory loss in this patient group.

Example Case History

Case 6 (R.K.) was 34 years old when a hypothalmic glioma was detected. In order to relieve hydrocephalus, his ventricles were shunted but some hours later a spontaneous haemorrhage into his tumour occurred. Because of its inoperable nature, radiotherapy was used to reduce the tumour and this has proven effective.

On initial testing, he presented a marked anterograde amenesia with a WAIS FSIQ–WMSMQ discrepancy of 23 points. On the WMS, his logical memory score was only 6 and he could not learn any of the hard paired associates. On continuous recognition, he learned the items quite quickly but, on delayed testing, his performance was significantly poorer than a group of Korsakoff patients. He showed good recognition

> of previously exposed sentences, but performed at chance when asked to decide in which of two lists they had been presented. However, he showed no evidence of retrograde amnesia, performing well above average on a famous faces test. He also showed no evidence of impairment on tests of frontal lobe dysfunction.
>
> Subsequent testing has shown a marked improvement in his anterograde deficit—a fact that has been attributed to the reduction of his tumour. On recognition tasks, R.K. now performs within normal limits but there has been no parallel improvement in tasks that demand memory for temporal order. Delayed recall is also extremely poor. These improvements in his memory have enabled him to return to work although, because of his residual memory problems, he has been unable to take up his previous responsibilities. (For a detailed account of this case, see Parkin and Hunkin, in press.)

Williams and Pennybacker (1954) report severe anterograde deficits and variable retrograde amnesia in a series of third ventricle patients. Palmai, Taylor and Falconer (1967) describe marked memory problems in subject C.R., who was found to have an inoperable craniopharyngioma. Ignelzi and Squire (1976) provided a more detailed study of a patient with a cystic craniopharyngioma involving the third ventricle. A pneumoencephalogram showed a mass in the suprasellar region which extended into the third ventricle. Part of the tumour was removed by sub-frontal craniotomy, and post mortem study showed that the rest of the tumour was adjacent to the mamillary bodies and that the cyst was in the third ventricle. The thalamic nuclei were intact and no other abnormalities in the diencephalic area were found. Before drainage of the cyst, the patient had severe anterograde and retrograde amnesia. His memory improved post-operatively, but remained below the control mean. Ignelzi and Squire presumed that the amnesia arose from pressure exerted by the cyst on the thalamus, possibly the mamillary bodies.

Kahn and Crosby (1972) reported five patients with craniopharyngiomas that compressed the mamillary bodies. Three of the four surviving patients exhibited both anterograde and retrograde deficits which were reduced significantly following tumour removal. Rizzo (1955) reports a comparable case of a patient with a cyst pressing on the mamillary bodies. However, as the cyst shrank, the memory and endocrine deficits appeared to ameliorate in parallel. A patient with a bilateral mamillary body tumour is also described by Assal, Probst, Zander and Rabinowicz (1976), who had severe anterograde deficits, minimal remote memory loss and some evidence of savings on the picture completion task.

Williams, Medwedeff and Haban (1989) describe a patient, B.W., who developed a dermoid cyst near the third ventricle which was removed without complications. Neuropsychological evaluation revealed a severe memory deficit in the presence of reasonably intact intellect. Williams et al. were particularly interested in B.W.'s temporal awareness and compared her with normal subjects on various measures of time estimation. B.W. was found to be markedly impaired in that she grossly underestimated intervals (e.g. 60 sec judged as 11.6 sec, 120 sec judged as 25.8 sec).

A few cases of amnesia as a result of tumours directly infiltrating the thalamus have also been reported. McEntee, Biber, Perl and Benson (1976) describe a patient with severe anterograde and retrograde deficits subsequently attributed to a tumour which invaded the medial and posterior thalamus bilaterally. Ziegler, Kaufman and Marshall (1977) report both anterograde and retrograde memory impairments in a patient with a bilateral thalamic tumour. However, interpretation of this case is complicated because the tumour also invaded the medial temporal lobes. Butters (1984) described the case of an amnesic syndrome with an astrocytoma in the paramedian thalamic area (patient A.V.). CT scan showed the tumour to be restricted to the right medial thalamic area, although it was considered that due to compression of the third ventricle the left medial thalamic region was also affected. Anterograde and retrograde amnesia was extensive in this patient.

Thalamotomy

Before moving on, some mention must be made of patients who underwent thalamotomy—electrolytic ablation of one or more thalamic nuclei for the relief of Parkinson's disease or intractable pain. Among the target nuclei for this therapy is the DMTN which, as we saw in Chapter 3, has been repeatedly associated with memory deficits. As a result, one might expect, given the relative imprecision of this treatment, some evidence of memory impairment in this patient group.

Orchinik (1960) studied the effects of stereotactic lesions placed bilaterally in the DMTN in psychiatric patients. The patients tended to show significant reduction in WMSMQ post-operatively. However, this was due largely to poorer performance on the information and orientation subtests, and to a lesser extent on those components of the WMS thought to be most sensitive to the presence of amnesia. In an earlier study, Spiegel, Wycis, Orchinik and Freed (1955) had reported loss of both recent and remote memory following thalamotomy centred on the dorsomedical nucleus. An interesting observation was that patients treated in this way had "a rather elementary disturbance of orientation in time" (p. 771), which the authors termed "chronotaraxis". This deficit was, however, short-lived, lasting at most 6 months. It is likely that the deficit observed here may have the same origin as that observed by Williams et al. (1989; see above).

5 Temporal Lobe Amnesia

The medial aspects of the temporal lobes are vulnerable to many forms of brain insult, including ischaemia, anoxia, metabolic abnormality, epileptic seizure, viral infection and dementing illness. It has also been known for a long time that memory disturbance is a major consequence of damage to this brain region (Sommer, 1880; Uchimura, 1928). An early account of amnesia following temporal lobe damage is that of Kohnstamm (1917), who described a relatively pure amnesic syndrome in a soldier who suffered probable carbon monoxide poisoning after being buried in rubble for 2 weeks. Kohnstamm noted several phenomena one would now identify as typical of a "pure" amnesia. Intelligence testing suggested preserved intellect and knowledge of foreign languages was preserved. He had major problems learning new information such as his way around the hospital and failed to recall various social activities he had engaged in. Recall of pre-morbid information was also impaired, although he did show savings in relearning poetry he had known before. He could still play familiar pieces of music on the piano, despite forgetting their name, and retained his ability to converse in foreign languages.

Kohnstamm's case is one of a number of early studies indicating a link between the temporal lobes and memory but, for most scientists and clinicians, this association is known through the characteristics of one famous case, H.M.

Case H.M.

In 1953, H.M., aged 23, was operated on by the neurosurgeon William Scoville (Scoville & Milner, 1957). H.M. was suffering from intractable epileptic seizures and temporal lobectomy was considered the only treatment option available. The resection carried out on H.M. included portions of the hippocampus, hippocampal gyrus, uncus and amygdala, all bilaterally. A consequence of this "frankly experimental" (p. 11) surgery was a significant improvement in H.M.'s epileptic condition, although he has remained on anti-convulsant medication. However, as an unexpected consequence, H.M. had one of the most dense and pure amnesic syndromes ever recorded. H.M. was one of a series of temporal lobectomy patients and examination of the specific removals in each case led Scoville and Milner to conclude that hippocampal removal was the critical factor producing amnesia. However, these data are equally compatible with the view that joint bilateral removal of the hippocampus and amygdala is required for amnesia to develop (see Chapter 8).

In her overview of H.M.'s clinical and experimental history, Corkin (1984, p. 251) notes that one of his "most striking characteristics is that he rarely complains about anything . . . is always agreeable and co-operative to the point that if, for example, he is asked to sit in a particular place, he will do so indefinitely". H.M.'s placid disposition and his continuing good health have undoubtedly contributed to the fact that probably more data are available about his case than any other account of an amnesic syndrome. Indeed, at the time of writing, investigations of H.M. are still being published.

A pre-operative assessment of H.M. found his WAIS FSIQ to be 104 (Fisher, cited by Corkin, 1984). Post-operatively, there appeared to be some improvement in FSIQ, although practice effects confound an exact interpretation. More recently, he has been found to have a FSIQ of 108 and WMSMQ of 64. The severity of H.M.'s amnesia is supported by considerable anecdotal evidence. Although able to retain some isolated facts (e.g. that the T.V. character Archie Bunker calls his son "Meathead"), H.M. retains little of ongoing events. He cannot identify Watergate, name the President, or properly explain what Skylab is, even though he watches T.V. every night. It is not without reason that H.M. comments "Every day is alone, whatever enjoyment I've had, and whatever sorrow I've had" (Milner, Corkin & Teuber, 1968, p. 217). Data on H.M. will be considered at various points in the following account, but before doing this, it is necessary to consider other causes of *temporal lobe amnesia*, which we will define as any amnesic state arising from a primary lesion or dysfunction in the medial temporal lobes.

Other Causes of Temporal Lobe Amnesia

Aside from the extensive investigations of H.M., temporal lobectomy patients have provided only a few additional cases of amnesic syndrome (e.g. Penfield & Mathieson, 1974). Our broader understanding of temporal lobe amnesia has been derived from other aetiologies and we consider all these in the present chapter except herpes simplex encephalitis, to which we devote the whole of the next chapter.

Anoxia giving rise to cerebral ischaemia is the most common cause of temporal lobe amnesia. It arises frequently in two clinical situations, cardiac arrest and atherosclerosis, and also as a sequel to near-drowning, carbon monoxide poisoning, anaesthetic accidents and failed suicide-by-hanging (e.g. Berlyne & Strachan, 1968; Medalia, Merriam & Ehrenreich, 1991; Spinnler, Sterzi & Vallar, 1980). Instances of cerebral ischaemia selectively affecting the temporal lobes and causing amnesia have been reported in a number of studies (e.g. Cummings, Tomiyasu, Read & Benson, 1984; Muramoto, Kuru, Sugishita & Toyokura, 1979; Trillet, Fischer, Serclerat & Schott, 1980; Volpe & Hirst, 1983a; Woods et al., 1982; Zola-Morgan, Squire & Amaral, 1986). Autopsy findings on these patients have often indicated damage restricted to the hippocampal region. However, anoxia can often produce a far more extensive pattern of cognitive impairment more comparable with dementia (Bigler & Alfano, 1988; Parkin, Miller & Vincent, 1987), and it is encouraging to note that hypothermia and barbiturate "protection" can produce remarkable preservation of memory and other cognitive functions in ischaemic patients (Newman et al., 1989).

Both clinical and experimental studies have indicated that a particular region of the hippocampus, CA1 (otherwise known as Sommer's sector, the vulnerable sector, H1), is most prone to ischaemic damage (e.g. Auer, Jensen & Whishaw, 1989; Zola-Morgan et al., 1986). Selective necrosis of CA1 following ischaemia has been linked to release of glutamate, which may cause neuronal death by acting at *N*-methyl-D-aspartate (NMDA) receptors. These receptors are thought to play a central role in *long-term potentiation*, a process considered to be involved centrally in memory consolidation. CA1 has a high concentration of NMDA receptors and this may explain the selective vulnerability of this sector to ischaemic injury (Auer et al., 1989).

The distribution of the posterior cerebral artery (PCA) covers occipital, parietal and posterior/medial regions of the temporal lobe and occlusions of this artery can cause amnesia. One anecdotal account (De Jong, Itabashi & Olson, 1969) reports a patient with dense amnesic syndrome, attributed at autopsy to bilateral hippocampal lesions. Two studies (Benson, Marsden & Meadows, 1974; Trillet et al., 1980) present substantial series of patients with impaired memory following PCA occlusion, but both studies give only brief neuropsychological details. A severe amnesic syndrome associated with PCA occlusion is also reported by Victor, Angevine, Mancall and Fisher (1961), and two of the temporal lobe amnesics reported by Parkin et al. (1990a) also suffered PCA disruption.

A potential, and largely under-investigated, cause of temporal lobe amnesia can occur in patients who have received radiotherapy for nasopharyngeal cancer (NPC). When radiotherapy for NPC is carried out, the radiation beams often pass through the temporal lobes and can cause delayed brain damage which has been termed *late temporal lobe necrosis* (A. Lee, Ng, Ho et al., 1987). P. Lee et al. (1989) reported mild to moderate degrees of memory impairment in 16 irradiated NPC patients. Parkin and Hunkin (1991), however, have provided the first instance of a severe amnesic deficit following NPC radiotherpay (see example case history below) with confirmed temporal lobe pathology.

Recently, Duyckaerts, Derousne, Signoret et al. (1985) described another unusual cause of temporal lobe amnesia. They describe a young man who demonstrated a severe amnesia which persisted until his death 20 months later. At autopsy, Hodgkin's disease was diagnosed and microscopic examination showed "almost complete" neuronal loss in the hippocampus and the amygdala. Interestingly, Carr (1982) also reports an association between Hodgkin's disease and amnesia but, following treatment, the memory disorder in his patient ameliorated leaving only an amnesia for the period of illness. Tumours can also invade the temporal lobe region. Shimauchi, Wakisaka and Kinoshita (1989) describe a 57-year-old woman who became severely amnesic due to a bilateral glioblastoma limited to the hippocampal formation. However, cases such as this have not contributed much to the study of temporal lobe amnesia.

Two final examples further illustrate the selective vulnerability of the medial temporal region. Mumenthaler, Kaeser, Meyer and Hess (1979) noted instances of transient global amnesia (TGA) in a number of patients who had taken clioquinol to combat diarrhoea while on holiday. Subsequent research indicated that clioquinol had adverse effects on the hippocampus and the drug was withdrawn. Teitelbaum et al. (1990) examined a number of patients who developed neurological and gasterointestinal symptoms after eating mussels contaminated with domoic acid. Severe anterograde memory deficits were found in a number of cases and autopsy again revealed necrosis in the amygdala and hippocampus.

Example Case Histories

Case 7 (T.J.) was 32 years old when NPC was diagnosed and then successfully treated with radiotherapy. No neuropsychological sequelae were noted. Seven years later, NPC was again detected and a second course of radiotherapy undertaken. Initially, no neuropsychological sequelae were detected but, 2 years later, a significant and disabling memory deficit emerged which was worsened somewhat in the ensuing 7 years.

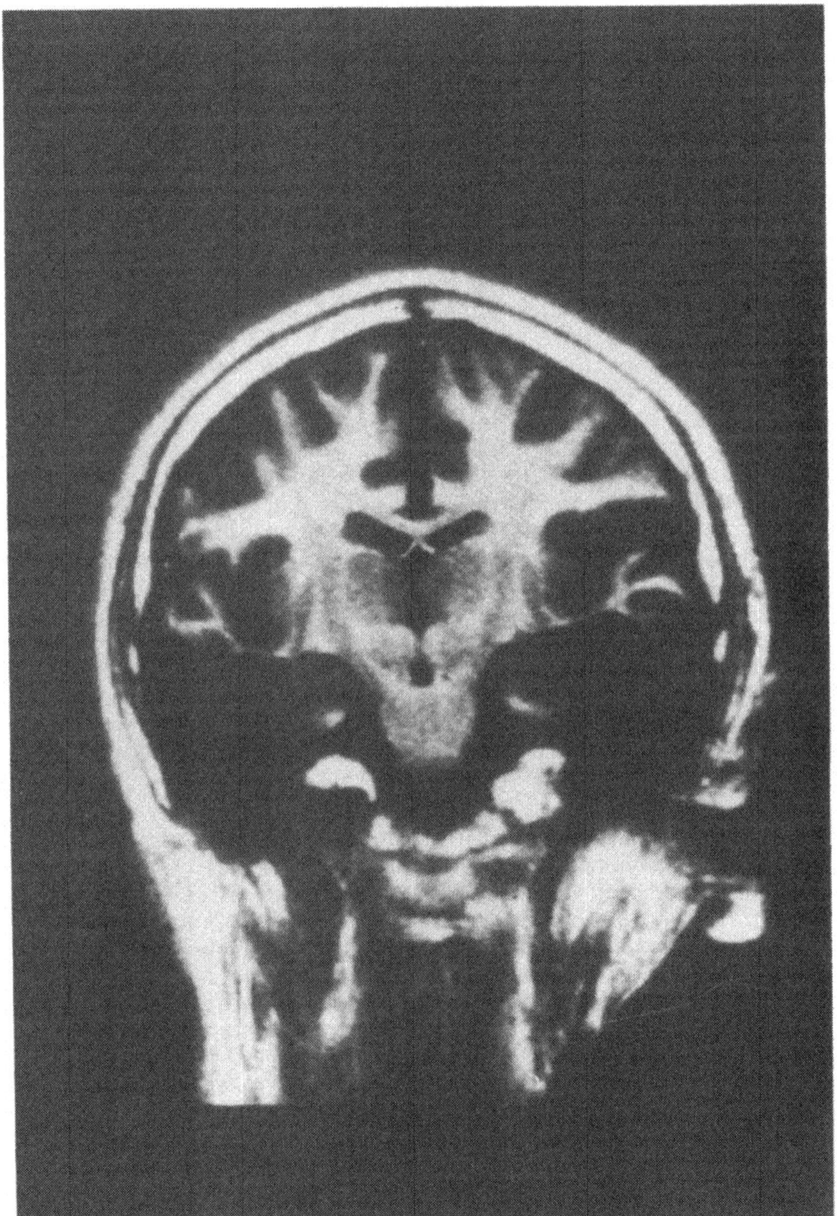

FIG. 5.1 MRI scans of patient T.J. showing massive temporal lobe necrosis due to radiotherapy. Reproduced with the permission of Dr N. Kapur.

Examination of treatment procedures showed that both temporal lobes received full levels of irradiation and MRI scanning had indicated bilateral temporal lobe necrosis (Fig. 5.1). He presents a marked memory impairment which is somewhat more pronounced for verbal information. He can, for example, recall very little on the logical memory component of the WMS, and also has great difficulty with the hard paired associates. His retrograde amnesia is extensive, both for general knowledge and autobiographical memory, and this impairment might be considered more severe than his anterograde deficit, a relatively rare state of affairs. He has not suffered any loss of skills and is still able to pursue his major practical hobby.

Case 8, a college lecturer, suffered a cardiac arrest and, although successfully resuscitated, remained in a coma for 3 weeks. On regaining consciousness, a marked generalised cognitive impairment was noted, but this ameliorated to leave amnesia as the primary neurological deficit. Memory assessment revealed an anterograde deficit that was much worse for verbal than non-verbal material. On logical memory he remembered little initially and nothing when tested after a delay. A considerable retrograde amnesia was also present, he had only a vague idea about the Vietnam War and Watergate, but on more remote events (e.g. the Cuba and Suez crises) he appeared slightly more knowledgeable. Recognition of relatives' photographs was only good for pictures taken 15 or more years previously. He also experienced difficulty with price estimation and his wife reported difficulties taking him shopping because of his continual complaints about how expensive things were. Assumed ischaemia has resulted in other deficits, most notably a visual field defect and mild apraxia. Despite the latter, he was able to continue woodwork as his primary pastime even though, when questioned, he was unlikely to remember what he had been making.

Case 9 (B.S.) is a 52-year-old man who attempted suicide by carbon monoxide inhalation. Assessment revealed a full-scale IQ of 106 which was significantly below an estimated pre-morbid IQ of 115. On memory testing, he showed defective story recall on both immediate and delayed testing and he could not learn any hard paired associates. Visual recall was, however, quite good, although his recognition memory for faces, like that for words, was relatively poor. He showed considerable insight and concern about his memory disorder—so much so that he attempted to cheat on the logical memory test by secretly writing down key points! On tests of frontal lobe function, word fluency appeared normal but performance on the Wisconsin Card Sorting Task (WCST) was impaired. Following treatment for depression, he has left hospital, but it is doubtful that his cognitive impairments will remit sufficiently for him to regain his previous employment.

Severity of Amnesia

Table 5.1 presents FSIQ–WMSMQ discrepancies for cases of temporal lobe amnesia and it can be seen that consistently high discrepancies are observed.

TABLE 5.1
WAIS FSIQ–WMSMQ Discrepancies in Temporal Lobe Amnesia

	FSIQ	*WMSMQ*	*Difference*
Beatty et al. (1987a)	112.0	92.0	20.0
Corkin (1984)	109.6[a]	66.0	43.6
Corkin et al. (1985)	98.0	77.5	22.3
Duyckaerts et al. (1985)	113.0	74.0	29.0
Leng (1987)	112.0	86.0	26.0
Press et al. (1989)	113.3	77.0	36.3
Trillet et al. (1980)[b]	95.0	75.0	20.0
Volpe and Hirst (1983a)	117.0	82.3	34.7
Zola-Morgan et al. (1986)	112.0	91.0	21.0

[a] Average of six assessments. [b] Estimate based on equivalent French tests.

Immediate Memory

H.M.'s digit span increased post-operatively and since then has remained near-normal for both verbal and non-verbal material (Corkin, 1984). The studies of Volpe and Hirst (1983a), Muramoto et al. (1979), Benson et al. (1974) and Della Sala and Spinnler (1986) report normal or near-normal digit span. T.J. (Parkin & Hunkin, 1991) had an above average span as did De Jong et al.'s (1969) case. Corkin et al. (1985) reports somewhat reduced digit span in her anoxia cases.

Short-term Memory

Wickelgren (1968) reports that H.M. performs normally on the probe digit test of short-term recognition memory and Corkin (1982) demonstrated normal performance by H.M. on the Brown-Peterson (BP) task. Volpe and Hirst (1983a) found that free recall following 30 sec of distraction was above or within normal limits for two of their ischaemia cases but below normal in the third case. M.R.L. (Beatty, Salmon, Bernstein & Butters, 1987a) was considered normal on the Auditory Verbal Learning Test (AVLT) and a four-word STM task. Della Sala and Spinnler (1986) found C.G. to have normal recency but impaired recall from earlier list positions. Leng (1987) found normal BP performance in two cases of PCA occlusion.

Anterograde Amnesia

H.M.'s grasp of personal information and orientation in time are poor (Corkin, 1984) and a number of studies illustrate his global amnesia for a broad range of material including words, objects, songs and locations (Corkin, 1982; Corsi, 1972; Smith & Milner, 1981; Smith, 1988). H.M. is impaired on continuous recognition tests using words, designs, numbers and nonsense syllables (Penfield & Milner, 1958) as well as on forced-choice recognition of faces (Corkin, 1984). Recently, there has been some disagreement over H.M.'s rate of forgetting. Huppert and Piercy (1979) reported an experiment in which H.M. was compared with controls using recognition of pictures. Initial acquisition was equated at about 85% correct 10 min after learning by giving H.M. longer initial exposure to the items. Twenty hours later, H.M.'s performance was a little below the controls, but by 1 week he appeared to have forgotten more rapidly. Both Parkin (1984) and Weiskrantz (1985) have questioned the validity of these findings and Freed and co-workers (Freed, Corkin & Cohen, 1987; Freed & Corkin, 1988) have demonstrated normal rates of forgetting in H.M. in a variety of paradigms.

Sagar et al. (1990) assessed recognition and temporal context memory in H.M. and 10 matched controls. Temporal context was measured for both verbal and non-verbal material using a modified version of Volpe and Hirst's (1983a) verbal temporal ordering task, and a frequency discrimination task in which the subjects made discriminations between items repeated one, three or five times. Recognition memory was assessed under parallel conditions using a two-alternative forced-choice task. Compared with control data, H.M. showed above-chance and often normal temporal context memory at points where his equivalent measure of recognition memory was at chance. These findings led Sagar et al. to conclude that memory for temporal context does not require intact recognition memory.

R.B.'s (Zola-Morgan et al., 1986) WAIS FSIQ–WMSMQ discrepancy was only 21 points, less than H.M. and N.A. (Chapter 4) and somewhat less than the typical values found in alcoholic WKS. However, on two of the three components of WMS that we have suggested are most sensitive to amnesic deficits (paired associates, logical memory), R.B.'s deficit appears as great as N.A., a group of alcoholic WKS patients, and three other patients with memory loss due to hypoxic ischaemia. R.B.'s ability to recall a 10-word list was shown to be as poor as that of a group of alcoholic WKS patients and to have changed little across 4 years of the post-morbid period. R.B.'s recognition memory was tested eight times using several procedures and his performance at all times was very poor.

Volpe and Hirst's (1983a) anoxic patients averaged 8.8% on free recall, compared with 35% by the controls, but recognition measures were much closer to the controls (see also Volpe, Holtzman & Hirst, 1986). On cued recall, two patients performed better than the controls, the other two being clearly impaired. On serial list learning, the patients and the controls made approximately the same number of responses per trial but far fewer patients' responses were correct due in part to higher intrusion rates. In a second study, Volpe, et al. (1986) showed that forgetting rate, as assessed by free recall, was more rapid in a group of patients with amnesia following cardiac arrest, but group differences in recognition were minimal. C.G. (Della Sala & Spinnler, 1986) showed gross impairment on the Buschke-Fuld verbal learning task, Corsi's spatial learning task, and prose memory. C.L. and M.D., from the same study, also demonstrated severe anterograde deficits. T.J. (Parkin & Hunkin, 1991) showed a moderate degree of impairment on the Rey Figure following a retention interval of 15 min. R.B. (Zola-Morgan et al., 1986) showed poor retention of the Rey Figure after a relatively short retention interval, as did patient M.R.L. (Beatty et al., 1987a).

The patient reported by Duyckaerts et al. (1985) did not receive much formal testing, but the results presented are indicative of a severe anterograde deficit. They report, for example, that "recognition (in the visual, tactual or verbal modes) was impossible as soon as an interfering task (counting backward) was undertaken" (p. 315). Muramoto et al.'s (1979) patient also had a severe anterograde deficit with "grossly defective memory of his recent experiences" and could not recall what had happened in the "preceding few minutes" (p. 54).

Retrograde Amnesia

Anecdotal reports from the early post-operative period suggested that H.M.'s deficit extended back only 2 years, but subsequent reports have suggested a more substantial impairment. On a recognition test for famous faces and public events, H.M. performed normally for the 1940s and 1950s but, as one would expect from his anterograde deficit, very poorly for subsequent decades. On describing famous scenes, he was impaired for all decades except the 1940s, and on a tune naming test, he was impaired for all decades except the 1950s. Dating was, however, impaired in a similar manner on both tests. On autobiographical cueing without temporal constraints, H.M. failed to describe a single event happening after his 16th birthday. When constrained to the later pre-morbid period he complied but, in comparison with controls, he was impaired. Consistent with this was H.M.'s inability to remember major events from that period such as the end of the Second World War (Corkin, 1984).

Marslen-Wilson and Teuber (1975) tested H.M. and controls for their unprompted recognition of public figures who had become famous in each decade from 1920 to 1960. Unprompted, H.M. performed normally for the 1920s, 1930s and 1940s, but he was impaired on subsequent decades. Both H.M. and the controls were then given semantic and phonemic prompts for faces they failed to recognise. H.M.'s performance improved to 80% for non-recognised faces from the 1950s and 1960s, a finding that suggests that H.M. had acquired some post-morbid knowledge of famous people. Gabrieli, Cohen and Corkin (1988) re-evaluated H.M. on recognition of famous personalities and found a similar result to Marslen-Wilson and Teuber. However, with phonemic and semantic cueing, they found virtually no evidence of post-morbid memory for famous people.

Overall, the findings suggest a more extensive retrograde impairment in H.M. than the initial estimate of 2 years, but this conclusion must be tempered by two factors. First, H.M. was prescribed anticonvulsants from the age of 16 onwards and the decline in his remote memory after this point may be partly attributable to the anterograde effects of this medication. Also, much of the testing indicating more severe loss was carried out a long time after his operation and his performance may be confounded with natural ageing effects. This point is made by Corkin's (1984, p. 256) observations of H.M. at his high-school reunion:

> A number of his classmates remembered him and greeted him warmly: one woman even gave him a kiss. As far as we could determine, however, H.M. did not recognize anyone's face or name. But he was not alone in this respect. We met a woman who claimed that she too did not know anyone in the room. Clearly she and H.M. were the exceptions in this regard, but her comments remind us that as people age they also forget.

Parkin and Hunkin (1991) report that, on a test of public event memory, T.J. was severely impaired, being unable to answer questions about very prominent past events (e.g. What was "Ready, Steady, Go"?; What did Lord Lucan do?). He also performed poorly on Parkin and co-workers' (1990b) famous faces test but, when given a familiarity version of the test in which he merely had to decide which of two people was famous, he performed at ceiling.

R.B.'s (Zola-Morgan et al., 1986) event memory was tested by asking a series of short questions (e.g. What was the SLA?), repeating the test in a multiple-choice recognition format, and then repeating recall of as much detail as possible about each event. Overall, R.B. performed considerably better than matched control subjects but he did show some impairment in detailed recall of events occurring in the decade preceding his illness. On an updated famous faces component of the Boston Remote Memory Battery (BRMB), R.B. performed at the same level as controls but he was noticeably worse on a recognition test of television programmes broadcast in the decade before his illness. On autobiographical cueing, his performance is described as being "as good as the control subjects . . . [and] . . . In addition, the time periods from which the memories were drawn were similar for R.B. and his control subjects" (p. 2954). This latter conclusion must be treated with some caution given that only 10 cue words were used in the test and no breakdown supporting the conclusion is given.

M.R.L. (Beatty et al., 1987a) was tested on two versions of the BRMB and, on both occasions, exhibited a severe and temporally graded deficit. It is notable, however, that M.R.L. performed better than controls on the earliest decade. The autobiographical cueing also indicated temporally graded retrograde amnesia and recall of residential history also fitted this pattern. A problem with Beatty et al.'s case is the patient's previous history. The precipitating event of his amnesia was a series of generalised epileptic seizures, but M.R.L. also had an extensive history of severe chronic alcoholism which included an extraordinary number of alcoholic blackouts and a number of alcoholic convulsions. Beatty et al. consider a possible role for Wernicke's encephalopathy in the generation of M.R.L.'s deficits, but rule it out on the grounds that M.R.L. does not show any of the frontal signs that typify alcoholic WKS (see Chapter 3). Despite this, caution must be applied to the interpretation of M.R.L.'s deficits. First, alcoholic WKS patients can vary in the extent to which they exhibit frontal pathology and behavioural deficits indicative of that pathology. Secondly, chronic alcoholism may play some role in the exacerbation of retrograde deficits that arise acutely for other reasons (Parkin et al., 1990b). Retrograde amnesia in the three hypoxic ischaemia cases of Volpe and Hirst (1983a) is only reported anecdotally but, within this limitation, the findings suggest only moderate deficits. The large group of amnesics studied by Volpe et al. (1986) also had relatively moderate retrograde impairments extending back only for the years immediately preceding their hypoxic episode.

Other case reports emphasise variability in the retrograde deficit of temporal lobe amnesics. Milner (1959) provided some information about the extent of R.A. in other temporal lobectomy patients. In case 1, the deficit is described as 4 years, but in case 2 the deficit was only 3 months. Although not described in detail, case 4 appears to have had a more extensive deficit. Victor et al. (1961) report that their patient with hippocampal damage has a circumscribed retrograde amnesia but this is only anecdotal. The series of Trillet et al. (1980) had deficits ranging from 10 years to "retrograde lacunaire". Muramoto et al.'s (1979) patient is described as having "intact" memory for events preceding his illness and the case of Duyckaerts et al. (1985) "could comment on important political events that took place three years before his illness" (p. 315). The patient of De Jong et al. (1969) appeared to have more extensive retrograde amnesia. Della Sala and Spinnler (1986) report the outcome of autobiographical enquiries in patient C.G. Based on information supplied by his wife, it was concluded that his remote memory was "characterised by the same extreme scarcity of events" and the absence of any temporal gradient (p. 105). However, it is notable that the same patient performed perfectly on the "Popes Test". Here the patient was given the names of five recent popes, Italian, U.S. and Soviet presidents, and the names of five recent wars, and asked to put each set of names in the correct chronological order.

Implicit Memory

Milner (1966) reported that H.M. had a "completely normal" learning curve on a mirror drawing task extending over 3 days. Two other temporal lobectomy patients with severe memory disorders (F.C. and P.B.) also learned the mirror drawing task without difficulty. H.M. also showed very good levels of learning on bimanual tracking, tapping and pursuit rotor tasks. On the latter, like all motor tasks, H.M. denied having done the tasks before, yet showed clear "testing habits" (Corkin, 1968).

Ogden and Corkin (1991) recount many instances of implicit learning in their entertaining memoir of their investigations of H.M. In one instance, they relate how H.M., then aged 60, broke his ankle and was obliged to use a fold-up wheelchair to get around. He learned how to open it, the most efficient way of transferring into it from another chair, and was able to explain its use to fellow patients. This illustrates the therapeutic benefits of intact implicit memory function in amnesic patients, a point we return to in Chapter 9.

H.M. was also evaluated on the Gollin (1960) incomplete picture sequences. On this task, the patient is first shown a picture in its most degraded form. Successive, more informative versions are given until identification occurs. Learning is measured by re-presenting the sequence to see if identification occurs at an earlier point than that found initially. H.M. showed clear evidence of perceptual learning on this task. He was proficient at learning the Tower of Hanoi puzzle in which the subject's task is to move the blocks from the first peg to the third peg one at a time without ever placing a larger block on a smaller one. The optimal solution requires 31 moves and Cohen (1984) reports that H.M. achieved this, although more slowly than controls—after 16 trials H.M. had reduced his solution to 40 moves, whereas the controls needed only 34.1 moves. H.M. was also able to learn the Missionaries and Cannibals problem (Ogden & Corkin, 1991).

Gabrieli, Milberg, Keane and Corkin (1990) have carried out a further investigation of this residual learning ability using a novel procedure for assessing non-verbal priming. In the first session, H.M. and the controls were presented with six arrays of dots and asked to generate a pattern from each array by connecting up the dots in any way that suited them. In the second session, the dot arrays were re-presented and the subjects were instructed to copy a particular pattern on to each one. Following a distractor interval, the dot arrays were presented and the subjects were asked to construct any figure by connecting the dots. Session three repeated this procedure except that the subjects copied a different pattern on to the arrays in the initial phase. In the final session, a third set of different figures was copied on to the arrays but, following a retention interval, the subjects were presented with the arrays and asked to draw again the patterns they had copied at the beginning of that final session.

The data from session 1 served as a baseline measure, i.e. the probability that a given pattern would be drawn by chance. The extent to which the subjects drew copied patterns in the final phase of sessions 2 and 3 minus baseline probability served as a measure of priming. The data from the last part of the final session, in contrast, acted as a measure of cued recall. The data showed evidence of a reliable priming effect in both H.M. and controls. H.M. also showed no difference from the controls on cued recall. This might imply that H.M. has the same degree of explicit access to prior patterns as controls. Gabrieli et al. dismiss this view and argue instead that the controls, for some reason, under-performed on the cued recall test and that H.M.'s performance is simply a measure of priming. This argument is backed by a second experiment using a similar procedure in which priming in H.M. was shown to be present despite chance level recognition of previously copied patterns. Most recently, Savoy and Gabrieli (1991) have demonstrated normal retention of the McCullough Effect in H.M.

H.M. has been evaluated extensively on the mental rotation task in which the subject is presented with a letter in either its normal or mirror-reversed form in one of eight different orientations. The subject is required to decide as quickly as possible whether the letter is in its correct form or not. In normal subjects, correct reaction time is an increasing monotonic function of the target letter's angle of displacement, thus suggesting that the stimulus is mentally rotated prior to responding. H.M. has shown consistent learning on this task, as shown by reduced overall response time and error rates, but there is no conclusive evidence that he learns the mental rotation strategy typical of normal subjects (Ogden & Corkin, 1991).

Beatty et al. (1987a) tested patient M.R.L. on a slightly easier version of the Tower of Hanoi. He was given the puzzle eight times on each of 2 days. On day 1, M.R.L. learned as well as the controls, averaging 37 moves to a solution. At the beginning of day 2, however, M.R.L.'s intitial solutions required far more moves than the controls (47 *vs* 37), but by the end of the session M.R.L.'s moves to solution approximated those of the controls. M.R.L.'s poor performance at the beginning of day 2 indicates that memory for prior learning episodes (intact in controls but largely absent in M.R.L.) can play an important role in retention of the Tower of Hanoi solution, at least in the relatively early stages of acquisition.

M.R.L. was tested on two further measures of residual learning. In the transformed script task, he was required to read out words that had been written backwards. Some trials were repeated and others were presented only once. M.R.L.'s performance was comparable to controls, showing a 33% improvement for repeated trials and a 13% improvement for unique trials. On a mirror reading task similar to that used by Cohen and Squire (1980), M.R.L. showed evidence of normal learning within each daily session but, in line with his Tower of Hanoi findings, he showed less retention of the mirror reading skill across days. Graf et al. (1984) examined free recall, recognition, cued recall and stem completion in two anoxia amnesics and compared their performance with alcoholic WKS patients and controls. Both amnesic groups performed very poorly on the recall, recognition and cued recall tests, but the amnesics achieved normal performance on word completion.

Hirst, Phelps, Johnson and Volpe (1988) present a remarkable instance of residual learning in a post-cardiac arrest amnesic. This patient was able to learn a second language (French) at the same rate as a control subject—her husband. Mohr, Leicester, Stoddard and Sidman (1971) tested the ability of a severely amnesic PCA occlusion patient on a test of generalisation learning. The patient was first trained to select a circle from an array of elipses. Generalisation was then tested by presenting trials in which the elipses were more circle-like. After 9 days of exposure, the patient acquired the generalisation but 4 days later he had no idea what to do on the task and performed at chance.

Semantic Memory

Corkin (1984) reports that H.M. has a "minimal anomia" but performs normally on the Boston Naming Test. H.M. also experiences mild difficulty with the token test and on the reporter's test of language production. Spelling is also impaired in H.M. but this may be of pre-operative origin. However, H.M.'s mild verbal and symbolic dysfluency is attributed to post-operative cognitive changes. Parkin and Hunkin (1991) noted a significant disturbance in their patient's ability to define words correctly, although linguistic functions were, in general, unaffected. M.R.L. (Beatty et al., 1987a) performed normally on the Boston Naming Test, as did patient R.B. (Zola-Morgan et al., 1986). However, M.R.L.'s semantic memory cannot be considered normal because Beatty et al. found that his knowledge of surveying terms (M.R.L. was a surveyor) was significantly poorer than a group of surveyor's assistants who were less well educated and experienced as M.R.L. This indicates that more refined testing can reveal semantic memory deficits not apparent from standard clinical evaluation (see Chapter 8).

Gabrieli et al. (1988) have examined H.M.'s pre-morbid semantic memory and tested his ability to acquire new linguistic knowledge. H.M. performed normally on pre-1950 words, was borderline on words introduced in the 1950s and markedly impaired for words first used in the 1960s (e.g. charisma, jacuzzi, psychedelic). Similar results were obtained using recognition of definitions and basic work identification measures, and it was concluded that H.M. has learned very little indeed about vocabulary introduced since his operation but that his pre-morbid semantic memory is intact.

Frontal Lobe Symptoms

H.M. has been evaluated on a range of tests sensitive to frontal lobe dysfunction. He has repeatedly performed normally on the WCST, making relatively few perseverative errors. He also shows normal release from PI and his test quotient on the Porteus Maze has risen during the post-operative period. His attentional abilities are also thought to be normal, but there is a reduction in verbal fluency. However, given the absence of frontal symptoms on other tests, it has been suggested that this dysfluency is not indicative of frontal impairment.

The three hypoxic ischaemia cases of Volpe and Hirst (1983a) all performed well on the WCST. T.J. (Parkin & Hunkin, 1991) also performed normally on the WCST, as well as having normal verbal fluency and cognitive estimation. Distractability, as measured by the Stroop paradigm, was also within normal limits. Formal testing of frontal lobe dysfunction in case RB (Zola-Morgan et al., 1986) is not reported, but it is notable that the investigators considered that "RB showed no signs of significant cognitive impairment other than loss of memory" (p. 2954). Similarly, as noted above, patient M.R.L. (Beatty et al., 1987a) appeared largely free of frontal impairment.

Other Deficits

Many patients with temporal lobe amnesia complain of olfactory deficits. The most comprehensive investigation of this was carried out on case H.M. (Eichenbaum et al., 1983). In a series of experiments, they demonstrated that H.M. performed normally on tests of odour detection, intensity discrimination, and adaptation but, in striking contrast, he could not identify or discriminate odours in same–different or matching-to-sample tasks. Furthermore, he could not identify by smell objects that he was able to name from visual or tactile representations. Data from patient H.M., therefore, indicate that the mechanisms of odour detection and discrimination are dissociable.

Because of their distribution, occlusions of the PCA can often produce visual field defects in association with amnesia and their presence needs to be borne in mind when assessing these patients. Case 1 of Benson et al. (1974) had extensive visual field defects which may well have contributed substantially to his poor perceptual abilities. Mohr et al. (1971) report a range of visual impairments in a patient who became amnesic following PCA occlusion. Along with a right hemianopia, the patient also exhibited a colour-naming deficit, and failure on simultaneous and delayed matching of colours.

Although memory impairment is perhaps the primary cognitive deficit associated with carbon monoxide poisoning, other deficits are also common. Min (1986), for example, reports apathy, hypokinesis, distractability and bizzare behaviours (e.g. "silly smiles") as common features of CO poisoning cases. Bryer, Heck and Reams (1988) describe a case in which diffuse neuropsychological impairment included general intellectual and visual/spatial deficits. This patient, like many other cases, also showed delayed onset of serious psychiatric difficulties (e.g. Jaeckle & Nasrallah 1985).

Overview of Temporal Lobe Amnesia

Patients with primary bilateral lesions in the medial temporal regions from causes other than herpes simplex encephalitis (for this disorder, see Chapter 6) have consistently presented a dense amnesic syndrome. This syndrome is characterised by a uniformly severe anterograde deficit but a markedly variable retrograde deficit. Temporal lobe amnesics are, characteristically, normal on tests of immediate and short-term memory, and semantic memory impairments, where observed, are relatively minor. Asymmetry of lesions may also result in a degree of material specificity. Frontal impairments are not typically observed in temporal lobe amnesics. The most significant associated impairments in this group are loss of smell and perceptual impairment, the latter being most notable in instances of PCA occlusion.

6 Herpes Simplex Encephalitis

The central nervous system is vulnerable to attack from many different viruses, some of which can cause marked cognitive impairment. It is now widely recognised, for example, that the human immunodeficiency virus (HIV) exerts a direct neuropathogenic effect on the brain, resulting in widespread cognitive deficits. From the perspective of memory loss *per se*, the most damaging virus is herpes simplex. Infection with this virus can cause a rare neurological disease known as herpes simplex encephalitis (HSE). This disease was first identified in 1941, but interest in its neuropsychological sequelae has grown only recently. Illis and Gostling (1972), for example, did not discuss neuropsychological sequelae in their monograph on HSE.

Neuropathology

It has been recognised since the early 1970s that herpes simplex virus is the primary cause of sporadic and acute necrotising encephalitis in the Western world (Baringer, 1978). Herpes simplex virus exists as two strains: type 1, commonly recovered from oral lesions, and type 2, associated with genital lesions. Primary infection with type 1 usually occurs as a result of stomatitis in childhood and latent recurrences of viral activity characterised by "cold sores" are common in adult life. These latent infections occur primarily in the trigeminal ganglia and are present in a high proportion of adults (e.g. Croen et al., 1987; Stroop, 1986). Primary infection with type 2 occurs in the genital mucosa and has an increasing incidence with the onset of sexual maturity. The development of HSE in adults is usually associated with type 1 and HSE in childhood (see below) with type 2 virus.

The initial symptoms of HSE include fever, headache and vomiting. Diagnosis must be achieved rapidly, since untreated infections can cause severe brain damage in periods as short as 24 hours (Schlitt et al., 1986). Diagnosis may be definitively established by brain biopsy, although other methods of diagnosis, some recently discovered, do exist. Development of anti-viral drugs such as acyclovir has greatly improved the prognosis of HSE patients, but the resulting quality of life for many of these patients is still extremely poor (however, see Klapper, Cleator & Longson, 1984, for instances of good recovery following HSE).

Radiological and post-mortem studies have shown that HSE has a consistent neuropathology. Primary damage occurs in the lateral and medial temporal cortex after which viral necrosis can extend into the orbito-frontal cortex, and rearwards to the parietal lobe. Sub-cortical damage is relatively uncommon in HSE (e.g. Rumbach et al., 1988; see Fig. 6.1). The specificity of the damage induced by the herpes virus is at present

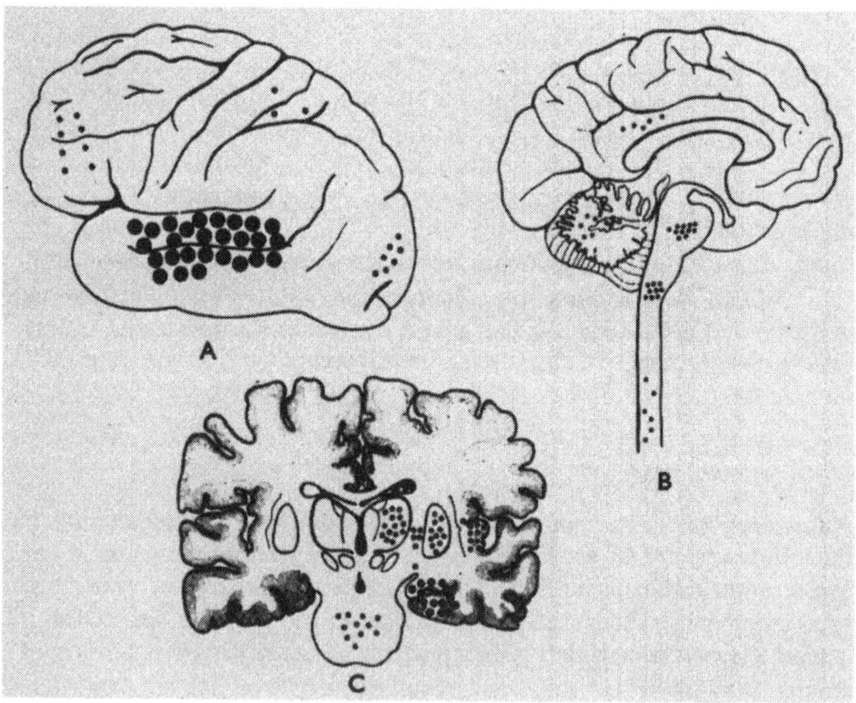

FIG. 6.1 Distribution of lesions in herpes simplex encephalitis. (A) Lateral aspect of the left cerebral hemisphere; (B) median sagittal section; (C) coronal section. Size of dots indicates frequency and intensity of infection. Note the predominance of lesions in the medial temporal lobe. Reproduced from Illis and Gostling (1972).

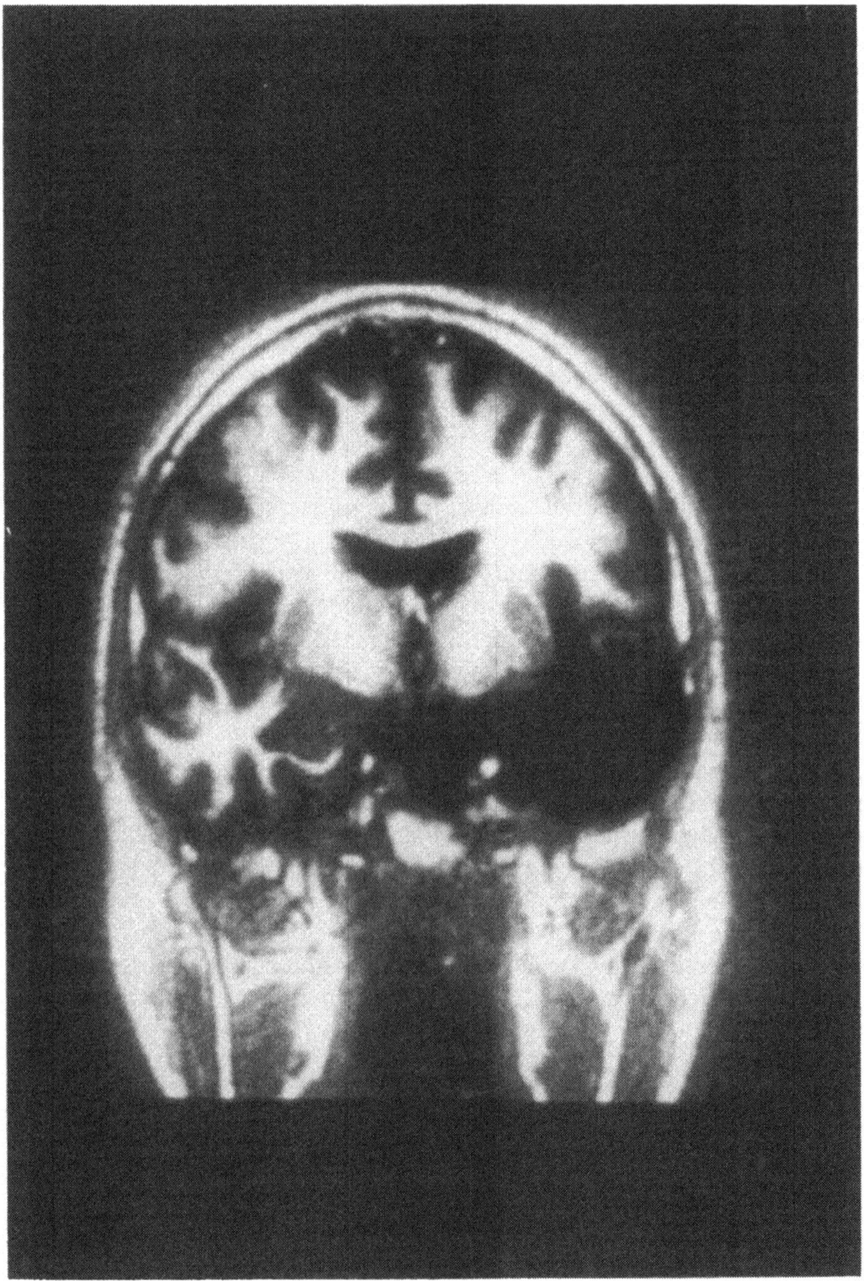

FIG. 6.2 MRI scan showing the extent of temporal lobe lesions following herpes simplex encephalitis. Note massive left temporal lobe lesion. Reproduced with the permission of Dr N. Kapur.

unresolved. One view is that primary temporal lobe damage arises because this cortical site is nearest the virus' entry point in the cranial cavity (e.g. Davis & Johnson, 1979). An alternative view, proposed by Damasio and Van Hoesen (1985), is that the herpes virus has a special neuroanatomical, neurochemical and neuroimmunological affinity for this brain region, in that the virus will exert its destructive influence there regardless of its point of entry into the brain.

Acute Phase

The immediate consequences of HSE are an acute confusional state and a severe amnesia. This primary disorder can be accompanied by other behavioural deficits (Greenwood, Bhalla, Gordon & Roberts, 1983) and may include one or more of the following: hyperphagia (indiscriminate eating and drinking of all solids and liquids), spasticity, aggressive behaviour, obscene language, obsessive spitting, fluent dysphasia with jargonaphasia, and hypersexuality. These acute symptoms tend to ameliorate across time, but residues may remain producing additional long-term management difficulties (e.g. Giles & Morgan, 1989).

The temporary behavioural disturbances associated with HSE resemble deficits found in the Kluver-Bucy Syndrome and, in severe cases, this syndrome can be a permanent feature. Alongside a severe memory impairment, patients with Kluver-Bucy Syndrome exhibit agnosia, hyperorality, increased sexual activity, and a loss of normal anger and fear responses. Lilly, Cummings, Benson and Frankel (1983) present one patient who, 13 years after developing HSE, still exhibited visual agnosia, compulsive manual and oral examination of objects, and emotional placidity. The link between HSE and the development of Kluver-Bucy Syndrome should always be borne in mind in the clinical assessment of HSE patients (for a review of this syndrome in HSE, see Greenwood et al., 1983).

Long-term Features of HSE

The major symptom of HSE survivors is a memory disorder involving both anterograde and retrograde amnesia which can vary considerably in its severity, although even in mild infections the memory impairment may be severe enough to preclude independent existence.

Example Case Histories

Case 10 developed HSE at the age of 19. Her primary deficit is a dense amnesic syndrome reflected in very poor WMS performance and other tests of anterograde amnesia. On tests of retrograde amnesia, she was unable to identify most famous people, even the present prime minister. Her spatial learning was exceptionally poor in that it took her about 6 months to learn the way from her living room to the bathroom. There were also linguistic difficulties, particularly in reading. Frontal impairments were much in evidence with both word fluency and cognitive estimation performance being quite poor. On the Wisconsin Card Sorting Test (WCST), however, she was close to normal performance.

Her non-verbal skills such as typing are preserved. She does make some errors, but these arise principally from keyboard characters that have changed position on typewriters since she developed her illness. She is cooperative in testing but is easily distracted. Her behaviour can at times seem childish with a relentless tendency to produce puns and puerile jokes ("Witzelsucht"). She exhibits some insight into her disorder in that she has learnt to make notes as an aid to her memory.

She lives at home with her parents, needs substantial supervision, but can be left alone for short periods of time. If the telephone rings she can take messages. She attends a day centre for the mentally handicapped and takes part in several activities including painting and dancing. She is a remarkably happy person given her deficits.

Case 11 (H.O.) is a 49-year-old housewife who suffered HSE in January 1988. Her recovery was exceptionally good and she is able to cope relatively independently. She can, for example, drive a car, but only along well-learnt local routes. She is also able to play golf but loses far more balls than the average golfer! Psychometric tests do reveal a substantial deficit. Visual memory is markedly impaired and she also does poorly on tests of verbal memory, being unable to learn any of the hard paired associates from the WMS or recall much of a short story. She also fails badly on the famous faces test, although her problem appears to be retrieving the name rather than recognising the faces as familiar. Often she is able to say quite a lot about a person while unable to give their name. She also exhibits a mild degree of anomia which, subjectively, she notices more for living than non-living things. She is relatively free of frontal impairments, although she does exhibit some difficulty with cognitive estimation.

Severity of Amnesia

Table 6.1 shows the FSIQ−WMSMQ discrepancy scores in studies of post-HSE amnesia. In general, the scores are close to the 20-point discrepancy, but several larger discrepancies can also be noted.

Immediate Memory

Data on immediate memory function in HSE are restricted to those derived from the digit span component of the WMS. To our knowledge, there are no indications of marked impairments of span performance in HSE patients.

TABLE 6.1
WAIS FISQ–WMSMQ Discrepancies in Herpes Simplex Encephalitis

	FSIQ	*WMSMQ*	*Difference*
Cermak and O'Connor (1983)	133.0	92.0	41.0
Corkin et al. (1985)	115.9	78.5	37.4
Damasio et al. (1985)	84.0	62.0	22.0
Glisky and Schacter (1988)	84.0	65.0	19.0
Hunkin (1991)	95.0	70.0	25.0
Kapur (1988b)	95.0	79.0	16.0
Leng and Parkin (1988b)	95.4	74.4	21.0
Mayes and Gooding (1989)	101.8	76.8	24.0
Starr and Phillips (1970)	126.0	85.0	41.0
Stewart et al. (1992)	102.0	87.0	15.0

Short-term Memory

Starr and Phillips (1970) reported that their patient, M.K., performed similarly to controls on the Brown-Peterson (BP) task with distractor intervals between 0 and 10 sec, showed poorer performance between 10 and 20 sec, but curiously did not differ from controls at 40 sec. In two other studies, S.S. (Cermak, 1976; Cermak & O'Connor, 1983) has performed within normal limits on the BP task in contrast to a WKS group who were severely impaired. Butters and Cermak (1980) also report good BP performance in three other post-HSE amnesics and good performance was also found in the 18-year-old HSE patient studied by Butters, Miliotis, Albert and Sax (1984). Leng and Parkin (1989) reported that a group of temporal lobe amnesics (comprising mainly post-HSE patients) performed better than alcoholic WKS patients on BP. However, this does not indicate normal performance in this group, because deficits were observed on a task where controls were at ceiling. Unlike WKS patients, the short-term memory performance of S.S. is also uninfluenced by the massing of trials or trial sequences involving items all drawn from the same conceptual category, and S.S. also shows normal release from PI following a taxonomic shift.

Anterograde Amnesia

Conrad (1953) provides the first report of amnesia following HSE and he describes his patient, J.K., as having a "Minuten-Gedachtnis"—a memory of minutes. This seems an apt description. J.K. was severely disorientated, asking repeatedly where he was but never able to retain the information. Taken out of a room and brought back a minute later, he could not remember being there, even when this was repeated many times. M.K.

(Starr & Phillips, 1970) showed profound learning difficulties on various tests of verbal learning including free recall and story recall.

Lhermitte and Signoret (1972) compared the learning capabilities of four HSE patients with 10 WKS patients on a test of spatial learning which involved learning the position of objects in a 3 × 3 array. Only one of the HSE patients reached criterion on this task, whereas the WKS group managed to learn the array reasonably well. Furthermore, comparison of the HSE patient who reached criterion with a sub-group of matched WKS patients, shows that this patient forgot the stimuli more rapidly (Parkin, 1984; see also Signoret, 1972, for an account of this study in English). The Lhermitte and Signoret study was the first of a number of studies suggesting more rapid forgetting in HSE patients, usually in comparison with WKS patients, but for now we will just consider the findings themselves. Mattis et al. (1978) compared recall and recognition performance in two HSE patients and three WKS patients. No differences were found on measures of free recall but on recognition the WKS group performed better. An important feature of this result is that the superiority of WKS patients only held up when the distractors used in the recognition test had not been presented at an earlier stage of the experiment (see Chapter 3 for a fuller account of this result).

S.S. (Cermak, 1976; Cermak & O'Connor, 1983) also exhibits marked anterograde memory loss with impaired performance on immediate and delayed free recall and recognition. Hunkin (1991) reports an experiment comparing HSE patients with WKS patients on the continuous recognition task (Kimura, 1963). This measures the ability to detect repetition of items in a learning sequence and is a good means of comparing memory deficits in different populations. Although no overall group difference was found, HSE patients were found to be worse than the WKS group at detecting repetitions of words, a finding that may be linked to their anomic difficulties (see below). However, interpretation is problematic because poorer performance could reflect either faster forgetting or slower learning. However, Leng (1987) has shown that HSE patients forget more rapidly than Korsakoff patients on a test of cued recall, despite showing no difference in trials to criterion during learning. Differences in forgetting rate between these groups have been used as evidence for different forms of amnesia and we shall return to this in Chapter 8.

Retrograde Amnesia

J.K. (Conrad, 1953) exhibited the dense retrograde amnesia typical of many HSE patients. He thought the Second World War was still going on and that Hitler was in power. Questions about personal events were most frequently answered "How should I know?" Rose and Symonds (1960) commented on the nature of retrograde amnesia in their series of post-encephalitic patients (note that these patients were not diagnosed as HSE specifically). Case 1 recalled in "adequate detail" events up to about 2 years before his illness, whereas cases 2 and 3 showed more extensive retrograde amnesia (RA). This variability in RA was also found in the 16 post-HSE cases reported by Foletti, Regli and Assal (1980), where RA estimates ranged from 3 months to 20 years.

S.S. (Cermak & O'Connor, 1983) was tested twice—1980 and 1981—on the battery devised by Albert et al. (1979). On the recall test, which involves giving one-word answers to questions about different decades, S.S. performed poorly on both occasions but there was little consistency across test sessions. Similar findings were also found in his performance on the famous faces component of the battery. A final test involved a recognition procedure in which a question was presented and the patient asked to select the answer from a series of alternatives. Under these conditions, S.S. showed substantial impairment but consistency across the two test sessions. The autobiographical recall of S.S. was also severely impaired. Although he attempted to answer many questions about his past, the answers were often generalisations and analysis showed that he had little access to specific experiences. Damasio and Van Hoesen (1985) present a detailed account of RA in their post-HSE patient D.R.B. This man scored 0 on all components of the Boston Remote Memory Battery (BRMB) and was able to recall only a few fragmentary personal experiences. More recently, Hunkin (1991) has explored RA in post-HSE patients using the test developed by Parkin et al. (1990b; see Chapter 2). Her data show, in comparison with WKS patients, poorer performance by the HSE group, with some patients exhibiting virtually no recall.

Warrington and McCarthy (1988) have presented a detailed study of RA in their patient R.F.R. The patient's RA was severe, he was unable to give a coherent account of any public or personal event from his past, could not identify old friends and he had considerable problems identifying photographs of his family. Assessment of R.F.R.'s autobiographical memory using the probe word technique indicated access to only a few specific personal experiences. When asked 20 questions about events occurring in the last 15 years, he only answered one correctly. Given the density of this amnesia, it was surprising to find that R.F.R. had no difficulty identifying new words and company names that had come into being in the last 20 years. On a famous faces test based on that of Sanders and Warrington (1971), R.F.R. could identify only one face out of 45. On a forced-choice version of the task, where the correct name was presented alongside two plausible distractors, R.F.R. performed at chance. In a subsequent test, R.F.R. was asked to name famous people and, if he failed, he was cued with the person's first name and initial letter of their surname. Under these conditions, R.F.R.'s performance was quite good and, when asked to guess the name of a person from the same type of cue in the absence of a photograph, his performance exceeded that of controls. A final experiment examined whether R.F.R. could recognise famous faces and names as familiar even though he had previously been unable to recall those names. He was presented with triads of faces or names in which one item was a famous person and the other two unknown people. R.F.R.'s performance on this task was well within normal limits.

R.F.R.'s retrograde impairment is of considerable interest for two reasons. First, he shows preservation of word information acquired during time periods from which he cannot recall personal events. Thus he can define the meaning of AIDS but is unable to recall that his mother died 6 years ago. This striking dissociation suggests that the system underlying our ability to define names acquired in the more recent pre-morbid period is in some way different to the system underlying retrieval of events, a finding that contrasts with that noted in cases P.Z. (Chapter 3) and M.R.L. (Chapter 5) in which pre-morbidly acquired terminology and event memory were equally affected. Secondly, R.F.R. shows remarkable facilitation from cueing and is able to pick out famous people in a test based on familiarity. This suggests that R.F.R's deficit is in conscious access to the verbal information associated with a face rather than in recognition *per se*. The type of problem was also encountered in the temporal lobe amnesic T.J. (Parkin & Hunkin, 1991; see Chapter 5) and has also been reported in some of Hunkin's HSE patients.

De Renzi, Liotti and Nichelli (1987) present another unusual pattern of RA in an HSE patient, L.P. This patient had a dense anterograde and retrograde amnesia as assessed by standard clinical procedures. She could not, for example, provide any information about the Second World War, recalled nothing about famous people such as Hitler, Mussolini and Kaddafyi, wrongly classified Mozart as a politician, Garibaldi as a professor, and performed at chance on a forced-choice test of public event memory. In contrast, she gave precise and correct answers on a 20-item questionnaire concerning personal events in her life. Even more remarkably, she retained information about new personal events despite performing extremely poorly on tests of free recall and recognition. Thus, despite poor test performance, she could remember the test encounter including details of conversations.

L.P.'s amnesia is certainly puzzling. Why should she perform so badly on laboratory memory tests yet show such good recollection of autobiographical material? One explanation is that L.P.'s amnesia reflects a fundamental deficit in verbal coding which is very sensitive to the formal test procedures used. L.P. is certainly anomic (see below), but this would not explain shy she performs so dismally on visual memory tasks such as remembering the Rey Figure which, as we argued in Chapter 2, does not lend itself well to verbal description. De Renzi et al. interpret L.P.'s memory performance as a selective preservation of autobiographical memory, i.e. memories related to one's own experience. This is exemplified by L.P.'s ability to remember a fatal car crash involving a relative in the complete absence of any recall of a major public event that had no personal connotations and that had occurred around the same time.

There are a number of problems with De Renzi and co-workers' (1987) interpretation of L.P. First, although they conducted a fairly structured interview, their claim that autobiographical memory is preserved selectively is based entirely on anecdotal report with no formal evaluation using cueing procedures (e.g. Robinson, 1976). Moreover, listening to a story (such as the logical memory component of WMS) or looking at the Rey Figure are, fundamentally, personal experiences, and so it is difficult to understand why L.P.'s amnesia should have been so selective. It would therefore have been interesting to see how L.P. performed on malingering tests. One possibility not considered by De Renzi et al. is that L.P.'s performance may have had an hysterical component in that, for some reason, she performed way below her capabilities on standard memory tests.

Hanley, Young and Pearson (1989) present patient B.D. who had particular problems in recognising people who had once been familiar. On any overt test of facial recognition, B.D. performed extremely poorly and he did no better when attempting to recognise someone from their voice. However, when his knowledge of famous people was tested by covert means, he showed considerable evidence of preserved knowledge. On one task, B.D. was asked to learn the occupation of famous people he had failed to recognise. Half the names were paired with their correct occupation (e.g. Mark Spitz—swimmer) and half with their incorrect occupation (Bjorn Borg—criminal). B.D. learnt the correct pairings more quickly than the incorrect pairings, indicating that he had some residual knowledge of people he could not identify consciously. Another task exploited B.D.'s previous interest in soccer. Using the same basic procedure, it was found that he had learnt to associate famous footballers with their correct club (e.g. Pat Crerand—Manchester United) more easily than incorrect pairings (e.g. Terry Paine—Arsenal), despite the fact that he did not recognise any of the footballers' names. Hanley et al. interpret B.D.'s performance as an instance of prosopagnosia rather than as a consequence of a more generalised amnesic syndrome. However, in the absence of sufficient general information about B.D.'s memory impairment, this claim is difficult to evaluate.

Semantic Memory

Gordon et al. (1990) reported significant language deficits in four HSE patients treated with acyclovir. More theoretically oriented studies have also revealed semantic memory deficits in this patient group. Warrington and Shallice (1984) investigated four HSE patients, two of whom had marked expressive speech difficulties and two who had normal fluent speech. However, all four were better at identifying inanimate objects compared with living things and foods. In two patients, it was possible to show that this anomia occurred in both the visual and verbal modalities. Within each modality there was consistency in these naming deficits but no consistency between modalities. One patient also showed better naming of abstract as opposed to concrete words, a finding that runs contrary to the normal superiority of concrete words. Warrington and Shallice interpret these findings as evidence for category specificity within semantic systems which are themselves modality-specific. In addition, they raise the possibility that the selective difficulty with food and food names might be related to the Kluver-Bucy Syndrome. L.P. (De Renzi et al., 1987) also had selective difficulty in identifying foods in addition to a more generalised anomia reflected in impaired category generation and confrontation naming.

Category-specific naming impairments in HSE patients are also reported by Pietrini et al. (1988), Sartori and Job (1988) and Silvera and Gainotti (1988). HSE patients B.D. (Hanley et al., 1989) and M.S. (Young, Newcombe, Hellawell & De Haan, 1989) both performed better when trying to identify non-living as opposed to living things from brief descriptions. M.S.'s impairment for nouns from living categories was most marked for low typicality exemplars, but despite this inability he exhibited reliable priming effects in pronouncing those nouns when preceded by their category name, indicating implicit access to semantic information that was not consciously available.

Recently, Stewart et al. (1992) have cast some doubt on the interpretation of apparent category-specific picture-naming deficits in HSE. Their patient, H.O., showed less accurate naming of living things with picture sets matched only for name frequency. But when additional controls for visual familiarity and complexity were applied to the selection of category exemplar sets, no evidence of category specificity was found. Because these controls were not present in other studies showing category-specific deficits, it is possible that these patients' impairments may have been misinterpreted. The view of Stewart et al. is reinforced by a recent study by Funnell and Sheridan (1992), who point out that the picture set devised by Snodgrass and Vanderwart (1980)—items from this picture set were used by Warrington and Shallice (1984, experiment 5) in their demonstration of category-specifc effects in their patient J.B.R.—differ systematically in the relationship between category membership and concept frequency. Categories of non-living things are more familiar than living things. As a result, item sets matched only on word frequency (the norm in this area of research) are likely to confound category with concept familiarity. To emphasise this, a re-analysis of J.B.R.'s naming performance is presented showing that naming performance is determined by concept familiarity, not the living/non-living distinction.

Implicit Memory

A number of studies have reported normal learning of pursuit rotor in HSE patients (Brooks & Baddeley, 1976; Cermak & O'Connor, 1983; Kapur, 1988b). This concurs with clinical observations that HSE has no adverse effects on motor skills (see example cases 10 and 11 described on pp. 100–101). Warrington and Weiskrantz (1982) showed that an HSE patient had good acquisition of a classically conditioned eyeblink response which was maintained over a period of 1 day. A notable feature of this study was the patient's complete inability to remember the previous conditioning procedure. Kapur (1988b) demonstrated substantial savings in perceptual learning in patient T.B., but he showed no priming in either a homonym spelling task or a category generation task which had been shown to be sensitive to priming effects in WKS patients (Gardner, Boller, Moreines & Butters, 1974). Finally, M.K. (Starr & Phillips, 1970) showed preserved implicit memory in that he was able to learn new tunes on the piano even though he could not remember having learned them.

On a perceptual priming task, S.S. showed significantly lower recognition thresholds for both repeated words and nonwords. S.S. also demonstrated bias effects in the spelling of homophones and showed higher stem completion rates for previously exposed items. More interestingly, he also exhibited a word enhancement effect. This finding, along with enhanced recognition of previously exposed nonwords, indicates that S.S. can retain novel information at an implicit level. This constrasts with Korsakoff patients who, as we have seen, perform poorly on the implicit learning of novel information.

Frontal Symptoms

Orbito-frontal pathology is a frequent feature of HSE, but systematic evaluation of frontal symptoms in HSE patients is uncommon. The cognitive estimation task (see Chapter 2) is known to be impaired in patients with frontal lobe damage (e.g. Milner, Petrides & Smith, 1985), and Leng and Parkin (1988a) found marked impairment on this test in seven HSE patients. The same survey also investigated the WCST, but the degree of impairment here was relatively mild compared with a WKS group. Hunkin (1991) noted a significant degree of frontal impairment in her HSE patients, including poor cognitive estimation, poor word fluency and some WCST difficulties. Other frontal symptoms noted were emotional disinhibition and palilalia. However, unlike certain other forms of amnesia (e.g. closed-head injury, ruptured aneurysms of the anterior communicating artery), gross changes of personality were not a prominent feature of this patient group.

Confabulation is a well-established feature of frontal lobe pathology, but its incidence in HSE appears to be rare. D.R.B. (Damasio & Van Hoesen, 1985, p. 253) "readily produced elaborate fabrications that may have involved the examiner and that, in spite of good intrinsic logic, had no basis in reality". Generally speaking, case reports of HSE patients do, from time to time, mention confabulation as a symptom, but it does not have the prominence found in other disorders, notably ruptured aneurysms of the anterior communicating artery (see Chapter 7).

HSE in Childhood

HSE is just as likely to strike children as it is adults (Olson, Buescher, Artenstein & Parkman, 1967). It is therefore surprising to find so little evidence of post-encephalitic amnesia in childhood. One possibility is that encephalitis due to type 2 herpes has a different clinical course to the acute necrotising effects of adult type 1 infections (Baringer, 1978). In addition, children who have recovered from encephalitis will almost certainly exhibit learning and other difficulties which may place them in other diagnostic categories that do not emphasise memory impairment *per se*. Lelord et al. (1971) report the presence of the controversial Gerstmann's Syndrome in a 9-year-old child recovering from HSE. DeLong, Bean and Brown (1981) describe an "autistic syndrome" in a 12-year-old girl following HSE. Computerised tomography revealed left medial temporal lobe pathology, and therefore it would seem likely that a verbal memory deficit would have been present. Similarly, Gillberg (1986) also reports "autistic" features in a 14-year-old survivor of HSE. Greer, Lyons-Crews, Maudlin and Brown (1989) describe a 14-year-old boy who developed severe psychological impairments following HSE. Eighteen months after developing the illness, he was described as "aggressive, hyperactive, non-compliant, and socially isolated except when aggressing towards others" (p. 322). Elements of the Kluver-Bucy Syndrome were also noted and disturbed language characterised by anomia and repetition of incomprehensible speech was also present. Only immediate memory ability was assessed, and on these tasks the patient ranged between mild and moderate impairment.

The only clear-cut amnesic syndrome following childhood HSE is described by Wood, Brown and Felton (1989). The patient, T.C., contracted HSE at the age of 9, and this resulted in a dense amnesia with relatively intact language function. Physical recovery continued over a 2-year period but there was no improvement in memory. She could recall nothing about a simple story 15 min later, although with extensive training some learning was possible. However, despite severe memory impairment, her Wechsler Intelligence Scale for Children (WISC) score has continued to improve and, 6 years post-onset, it is approaching the average for her age group. Preserved learning was also indicated by tests of scholastic achievement. As a senior, she managed to pass her state competence exam and graduated from high school. Yet, when reassessed at the age of 20, she could recall nothing of two complex figures she had copied accurately 30 min earlier, nor recall anything about a short story after a delay.

T.C. shows the striking dissociation that can occur between acquiring knowledge about personal events and certain other forms of knowledge. It would be wrong, however, to conclude that patients such as T.C. could exhibit normal learning across a whole range of subjects. Linguistic and mathematical skills may be relatively easy to acquire because they have a strong implicit component (see Chapter 1), in that both involve learning procedures and are less dependent on specific factual recollection than subjects such as geography or history.

Overview of Herpes Simplex Encephalitis

HSE results in a rapid necrotising process which first attacks temporal lobe structures followed by other cortical structures (notably the orbito-frontal cortex) and, less commonly, subcortical structures. The major neuropsychological sequelae of HSE are a severe anterograde amnesia and a retrograde amnesia that may vary considerably but tends to be quite extensive. Associated problems are also likely to be present, particularly anomia. Frontal pathology also contributes to the behavioural deficits of HSE patients and will be manifest primarily in cognitive disorders, although some alteration of personality will often be apparent. Implicit memory can be demonstrated in HSE patients.

Paraneoplastic Limbic Encephalitis

Paraneoplastic syndromes reflect the remote effects of cancer rather than direct effects such as nutritional and infectious complications. One form of this, paraneoplastic limbic encephalitis (PLE), was first emphasised by Brierley, Corsellis, Hierons and Nevin (1960) and has subsequently been described in over 40 case reports (Bakheit, Kennedy & Behan, 1990; Newman, Bell & McKee, 1990). Onset of the disorder usually occurs between 50 and 70 years and the primary features are severe memory problems along with an affective disorder.

At autopsy, the principal brain damage includes the hippocampus, amygdala and other medial temporal structures, and damage may also extend to the orbito-frontal cortex, other cortical structures and the hypothalamus. The associated malignancy of PLE is usually oat cell carcinoma of the lung but other primary malignancies can also be associated with the disorder (Newman et al. 1990).

Newman et al. (1990) provide a detailed case report of PLE in a 76-year-old man. The patient experienced sudden onset amnesia which was soon accompanied by affective changes and a gait disorder. Severe anterograde amnesia as evident from poor performance on recall tests and remote memory also seemed impaired. However, his language abilities were largely intact. Death occurred 4 months after the onset of memory problems. Autopsy revealed severe medial temporal lobe gliosis and the mamillary bodies were also affected. Other limbic structures were unaffected. General pathological examination revealed oat cell renal carcinoma. We also have observed a case of PLE.

Example Case History

Case 12, a 60-year-old plumber, developed an acute confusional state in which he showed considerable aggression, he became calmer but then exhibited a profound amnesic syndrome. On tests of new learning he performed very poorly, recalling virtually nothing of short stories immediately after hearing them and being completely incapable of learning unrelated paired associates. However, on digit span, his performance was close to the normal range as were his linguistic abilities.

In conversation, he was extremely confused. He gave the year as 1959 rather than 1989 and was unable to state how old he was. His premorbid memory was badly affected: out of a series of 30 famous people he could identify only Winston Churchill and Mrs Thatcher. Memory for his own past was also extremely hazy, particularly for events during the last 25 years. He could, for example, talk in some detail about the British motor cycles he rode in his youth but could not recognise names like Honda or Suzuki.

He had some insight into his poor memory but would nevertheless cover up his memory failures with repetitive excuses (e.g. "I've never been good at remembering names"). From time to time he would also confabulate, e.g. that he was working at the hospital. Despite his immense difficulties, he appeared quite cheerful although occasionally seeking reassurance. During his 4-month stay in hospital he learnt very little about his surroundings. Neuroradiological examination indicated extensive bilateral temporal lobe damage and, at autopsy, carcinoma of the lung was found.

PLE produces a particularly severe disorder with many similarities to HSE. However, because of poor prognosis, detailed neuropsychological accounts have not appeared.

7 Aneurysms of the Anterior Communicating Artery

An aneurysm is a localised dilation of the walls of a blood vessel, usually an artery, due to weakening through infection, injury, degenerative illness or congenital defect. In many instances of aneurysm, the blood vessel remains intact, but in a substantial proportion of cases it ruptures and causes a haemorrhage. Various types of aneurysms occur in the cerebral arterial system and they can often give rise to lasting impairments of memory (Larsson et al., 1989; Richardson, 1989; 1991; Vilkki et al., 1990), either directly because of rupture and subsequent haemorrhage or as a consequence of the operative procedure required to repair the aneurysm. With advances in operational procedures, particularly microsurgery, the outcome of operations for non-ruptured aneurysms has improved markedly.

One form of aneurysm—that involving the anterior communicating artery (ACoA)— is particularly associated with memory disorder as well as additional cognitive deficits. Aside from clinical interest, memory loss from ACoA aneurysms is of theoretical interest because it arises from damage centred on structures other than those limbic regions identified in Chapters 3, 4, 5 and 6. Furthermore, the behavioural characteristics of these patients suggest that their amnesia may take a qualitatively different form to that associated with diencephalic and temporal lobe damage.

Neuropathology

The anterior communicating artery (ACoA) is part of the Circle of Willis and it interconnects the two anterior cerebral arteries just rostral to the

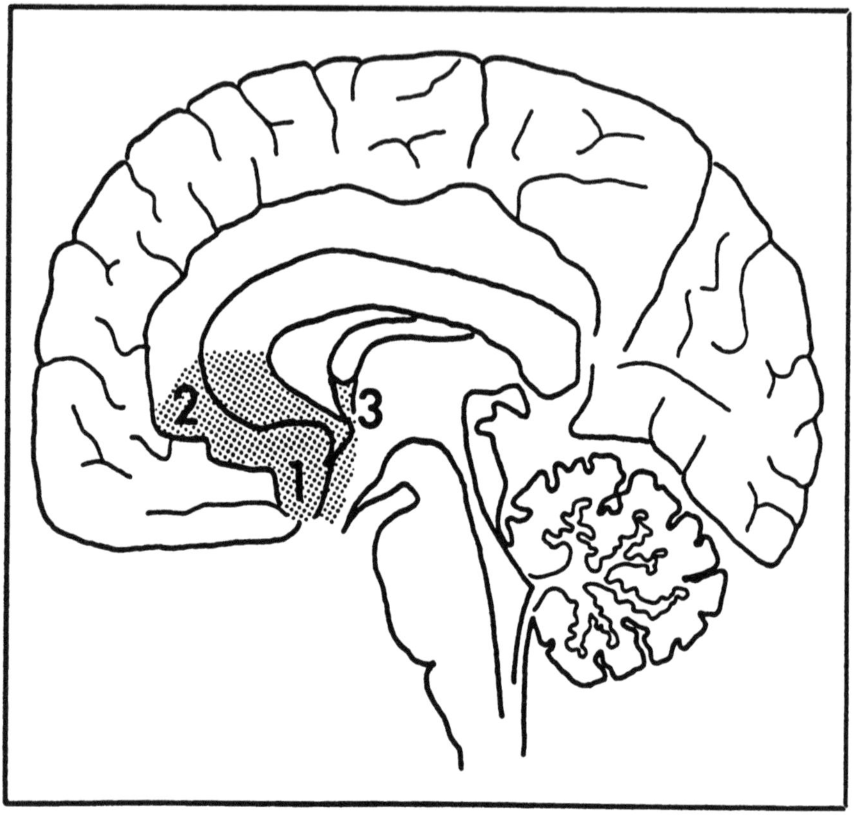

FIG. 7.1 Dotted area indicates the distribution of the ACoA and its perforators. 1, Basal forebrain; 2, anterior cingulate; 3, anterior hypothalamus. Reproduced with permission from Alexander and Freedman (1984).

optic chiasm. The ACoA is particularly prone to the development of saccular aneurysms and it is estimated that between 30 and 40% of all patients that have a ruptured aneurysm have it located in the ACoA (Gade, 1982; Steinman & Bigler, 1986). The structures supplied by the ACoA include the basal forebrain, the anterior cingulate, the anterior hypothalamus, the anterior columns of the fornix, the septal nuclei, the anterior commissure and the genu of the corpus callosum (Crowell & Morawetz, 1977; Dunker & Harris, 1976; see Fig. 7.1).

Rupture of an ACoA aneurysm can have a number of neuropathologic effects. First, those areas directly supplied by the ACoA are liable to infarction (tissue damage). Subarachnoid haemorrhage is common and may affect one or both of the frontal lobes. Rupture also affects the anterior circulation, resulting in infarction of the mesial aspects of the frontal lobes. Vasospasm, a spasmodic constriction of the artery causing reduced blood flow, is another major complication of ACoA aneurysm, sometimes causing infarction in structures quite distant from the site of the aneurysm (Maurice-Williams, 1987). The management of vasospasm, particularly post-operatively, appears crucial to the quality of survival in ACoA aneurysm patients (Stenhouse, Knight, Longmore & Bishara, 1991).

Gade (1982) noted a significant relationship between the outcome of ACoA aneurysms and the type of operative procedure used. A "trapping" approach, in which the aneurysm was isolated by placing a ligature on either side, was associated with amnesia in 9 out of the 11 cases in which it was used. However, a second approach in which the aneurysm was ligatured at the neck, was associated with amnesia in only 6 out of 37 patients. Gade dismissed the view that the association of amnesia with trapping was spurious and argued that trapping disrupted important branches of the ACoA. It should be noted, however, that many centres never used ligation, and it is more important to emphasise how the development of microsurgery and other techniques have improved outcome (e.g. Maurice-Williams, 1987; Teissier du Cros & Lhermitte, 1984). None the less, it is still the case that the operative procedure, as well as the effects of the haemorrhage, have important consequences for neuropsychological outcome.

The neuropathological sequelae of ruptured ACoA aneurysms are not as systematic as those found with other forms of brain insult partly, perhaps, because of anatomical variation (Gomes et al., 1986; Ogawa, Suzuki, Sakurai & Yoshimoto, 1990). Steinman and Bigler (1986) report that their seven patients all suffered bilateral medial frontal infarction with two patients showing more widespread cerebral infarction. Logue et al. (1968) reported frontal damage in four of their ACoA patients along with some evidence of parieto-temporal damage. Alexander and Freedman's (1984) patients are mainly characterised by the presence of either right, left or bilateral infarction in the territory of the anterior cerebral artery (ACA). The distribution of the ACA includes the internal frontal, fronto-polar and orbito-frontal cortex, paracentral, superior and inferior parietal cortex, pericallosal region and the basal ganglia (see Fig. 7.1). Eslinger and Damasio (1984) report CT findings in two ACoA patients, both of whom had bilateral infarction of the basal forebrain with one showing additional symmetrical lesions in the anterior cingulate cortex. In the series of five patients reported by Vilkki (1985), two were noted to have bilateral frontal low-density areas. Patient J.B. (Parkin et al., 1988b) was found to have a large left frontal horn with an adjacent low-density area indicating both basal forebrain and frontal lobe disturbance. The patient reported by Hanley, Davies and Downes (in press) appeared free of frontal damage but showed a large lesion in the left caudate nucleus.

Although there is marked variation in the above cases, there are certain consistencies. The most frequent lesion site involves one or more aspects of the frontal lobes with associated deficits in the basal forebrain. What is perhaps most striking is that there are no recorded instances of lesions in the brain regions normally associated with the amnesic syndrome, the medial aspects of the temporal lobe and midline structures of the diencephalon. This state of affairs suggests the nature of persisting memory deficits following ruptured ACoA aneurysm may well be different from those that we have so far considered.

Acute Phase

The immediate consequence of recovery following repair of a ruptured ACoA aneurysm can be compiled from a number of case reports (Alexander & Freedman, 1984; Eslinger & Damasio, 1984; Parkin et al., 1988b; Parkin & Barry, 1991; Vilkki, 1985; Volpe & Hirst, 1983b). There is a severe confusional state and attentional disturbance, and confabulation—sometimes fantastic—with lack of insight may also be found. There will often be a severe retrograde amnesia and the patient may orient to an earlier time period. In contrast, there is unlikely to be any impairment of language and general knowledge. It must be stressed, however, that the majority of ACoA aneurysms are operated on prior to rupture and recovery here is generally remarkably good (e.g. Maurice-Williams, Willison & Hatfield, 1991). Patients exhibiting severe memory loss, such as those in the following case histories, have usually suffered ruptured aneurysms and are comparatively rare. None the less, it is patients such as these that are emphasised in the memory pathology literature.

Example Case Histories

Case 13 (M.T.) suffered a sub-arachnoid haemorrhage followed a year later by a ruptured ACoA aneurysm. After an initial acute confusional state, her condition has remained relatively stable. Her performance on standard memory tests is very poor, except that there is not any great indication of retrograde amnesia. Her memory problems have a number of direct effects on her day-to-day life. If she attempts to shop she forgets that she has a list and simply grabs anything she fancies. She also tends to wash herself repeatedly if not supervised. She also feeds the dog over and over again and has difficulty in controlling her own eating.

M.T. also exhibits marked frontal impairments. She achieves only one category on the Wisconsin Card Sorting Test (WCST), has very poor word fluency and cannot attempt the cognitive estimates task. These deficits have implications for her everyday life. Housework is difficult because she has difficulty planning activities such as ironing and washing. Cooking is problematic because she selects the wrong ingredients and can no longer estimate quantities properly. She also has difficulty crossing the road because she cannot estimate the distance to the other side or assess the speed of oncoming traffic. She lives at home where her husband looks after her.

Case 14 (J.B.), aged 42, collapsed at work and on admission to hospital was found to have a ruptured ACoA aneurysm. A CT scan 9 months post-operation revealed a comparatively large left frontal horn and an adjacent low-density area. In the acute phase, he exhibited a severe amnesic syndrome with complete lack of insight and "fantastic" confabulation (Berlyne, 1972). His behaviour was based on intact memories from 20 years ago. He believed that he was studying at a college in which "brain stimulation" was a normal part of the curriculum. When asked to explain his inability to work, he gave numerous different accounts, all of them confabulatory. These included being hit by an exploding lawn mower and banging his head on a branch after being chased up a tree by a goblin. He would often announce spontaneously that a friend who he had lost contact with years ago had just rung up and that he was off to meet him in the pub. When it was explained to him that this could not possibly have happened, he greeted it with indifference.

After about 18 months, the deficit began to ameliorate. He began to remember events in his life, such as his divorce and the death of his father, which he had previously denied knowledge of. However, he remained temporally confused in that even though he could remember most events quite clearly, he could not, unless there were obvious logical constraints, remember the order in which these events occurred. Further improvements have occurred but recall and recognition memory is still severely impaired, particularly for verbal material. On tests of frontal lobe dysfunction, he performs well except for a mild impairment on cognitive estimation. However, he does have more subtle problems that can be attributed to frontal dysfunction, including an inability to apply strategies spontaneously. His memory difficulties do not preclude some lower forms of employment, but the personality disturbance he has undergone has presented a serious obstacle to obtaining any kind of employment. He is also incapable of managing his financial affairs and, unless closely supervised, he rapidly sinks into debt. He currently lives semi-independently.

Case 15 (C.B.), a businessman, was admitted to hospital with a 1-week history of frontal headache. A scan confirmed a sub-arachnoid haemorrhage and a ruptured aneurysm of the ACoA was clipped 4 days later. Initially, he exhibited a right-sided weakness and offered nothing in the way of spontaneous communication. After 2 months, there was a significant improvement in his psychological state. His memory abilities were clearly impaired but superior to those typical of patients with an amnesic syndrome—he could, for example, show learning of hard paired associates and exhibited good recognition memory. There were, however, other signs of cognitive impairment. Both his verbal and non-verbal IQ were down substantially from his estimated pre-morbid IQ. He also showed marked impairment on tests of frontal lobe dysfunction, particularly word fluency and cognitive estimation. His personality and motivation had also changed substantially following his operation. He has continued to improve, although he still experiences memory lapses and other cognitive deficits which have resulted in his early retirement.

Severity of Amnesia

Table 7.1 shows the FSIQ–WMSMQ difference scores from studies of ACoA aneurysm patients in which memory loss was considered a primary feature—data from larger samples in which many of the patients made excellent recoveries (e.g. Sengupta, James, Chiu & Brierley, 1975) are not included. The pattern bears some similarity with other patient groups but the average discrepancy score tends to be smaller and the MQ higher than that encountered in other patient groups.

TABLE 7.1
WAIS FSIQ–WMSMQ Discrepancies in ACoA Aneurysms

	FSIQ	*WMSMQ*	*Difference*
Alexander and Freedman (1984)	93	83	10
Corkin et al. (1985)	114	98	16
Delbecq-Derouesne et al. (1990)	95	94	1
Parkin et al. (1988b)	116	89	27
Steinman and Bigler (1986)	99	84	15
Volpe and Hirst (1983b)	101	102	−1

Immediate Memory

Delbecq-Derouesne, Beauvois and Shallice (1990), Logue et al. (1968) and Parkin et al. (1988b) considered digit span to be normal in their ACoA patients. However, Teissier du Cros and Lhermitte (1984) noted a mild impairment of memory span in 38% of their ACoA sample. Similarly, Laiacona et al. (1989) report memory span deficits in 23% of the 43 patients in their sample.

Short-term Memory

J.B. (Parkin et al., 1988b) performed poorly on a version of the Brown-Peterson (BP) task involving the retention of a single word over distractor intervals ranging from 5 to 30 sec. G.O. (Talland, Sweet & Ballantine,

1967) also showed impaired BP performance but a second ACoA patient, E.R., performed well on the task. Corkin et al. (1985) examined BP performance in seven ACoA patients and found evidence of impairment in three. Volpe and Hirst (1983b) examined immediate recall and recall after 30 sec of 10-word lists by two ACoA aneurysm patients. No differences were found with immediate recall, but the ACoA patients were significantly worse at 30 sec. Vilkki (1985) demonstrated short-term memory impairments in five ACoA patients using Luria's (1976) homogeneous interference task in which a subject is presented with two sequential word triples, recalls the first, and then the second until criterion is reached. The same patients also showed deficits on a version of the Benton visual retention test, particularly with delayed testing. Gade and Mortensen (1990) found that ACoA patients were worse than controls and no better than amnesic and demented patients on the SR task.

Parkin et al. (1988b) examined J.B.'s ability to learn five pairs of hard paired associates under different learning conditions. Under rote learning conditions, J.B. found the task very difficult with an error rate comparable to WKS and post-HSE amnesics. However, when given instructions to use imagery, his performance improved dramatically, averaging only three errors before reaching the criterion of three errorless trials. In contrast, the amnesic subjects continued to make large numbers of errors. This experiment indicates an important difference between J.B. and amnesic patients in that his performance can be radically improved by supplying strategic information. This suggests a more "executive" basis to J.B.'s deficit in comparison with the amnesic patients in whom a more fundamental deficit is present (see Chapter 8 for a fuller discussion of this point).

Anterograde Amnesia

Corkin et al. (1985) examined the performance of ACoA patients on seven measures of long-term memory and, on average, six patients exhibited significant impairments on each task. Vilkki (1985) reports impaired free recall and cued recall of verbal material in his ACoA group. Volpe and Hirst (1983b) found that free recall of verbal and visual material by their ACoA patients was extremely impaired after 5 min, but there was no difference between the patients and controls on recognition. Parkin et al. (1988b) report that JB had a level of free recall significantly below his controls, but on recognition he performed well within normal limits. In a follow-up study, Parkin and Binschaedler (in prep.) have investigated J.B.'s recall and recognition deficits more extensively and it is now evident that both recall and recognition under certain circumstances is markedly impaired. On yes–no recognition, J.B. performs extremely poorly and his deficit is characterised by large numbers of false positives, whereas on three alternative forced-choice problems he performs reasonably well. The authors conclude that J.B.'s poor recognition memory stems from an inability to adopt normal levels of bias.

Moscovitch (1989) reports that his ACoA patient, H.W. (see below), produced recognition scores within the normal range despite very poor recall performance. Hanley et al. (in press) found that their patient had exceptionally poor recall relative to recognition, even when using a test procedure in which normal recall and recognition memory were equated. These findings generally suggest that ACoA patients tend to show a much greater discrepancy between recall and recognition performance than that found in other groups of amnesic patients.

An exception to this pattern of recognition superiority is provided by Delbecq-Derouesne et al. (1990). Their patient, R.W., showed defective recognition on tests involving words, faces and paintings. In contrast, his performance on tests of recall fell within normal limits. Additional analyses showed that these discrepant findings could not be considered as an extreme but predictable position in the bivariate distribution of recognition and recall scores. One must, however, note that R.W. made a substantial number of intrusion errors in free recall. Thus if one were to score his recall as a proportion of correct items plus intrusions, his recall performance is far from normal.

Larsson et al. (1989) examined long-term memory for word lists and found evidence of impairment in 62% of their ACoA patients. These authors compared performance of the impaired ACoA group and a non-impaired group on a Swedish version of the Bennett-Levy and Powell (1980) subjective memory questionnaire, which asks various questions about memory impairment such as how good is your memory for faces, how often do you forget a word in mid-sentence, etc. No differences were found between the impaired and non memory-impaired groups, thus indicating substantial lack of insight in the ACoA group. This finding was not simply a question of poor memory, because patients with equally impaired memory arising from other forms of vascular disorder did show significant awareness of their memory problems on the same questionnaire.

Retrograde Amnesia

Cases 11, 12 and 13 (described above) were tested on the Parkin et al. (1990b) famous faces test. J.B. and C.B. performed at above normal levels, whereas M.T. showed a mild degree of impairment. Alexander and Freedman (1984) report an interview-based assessment of retrograde amnesia in their 11 ACoA patients and significant impairments were noted in 7. A much lower incidence of retrograde amnesia is recorded in the series of 53 ruptured ACoA aneurysm cases studied by Logue et al. (1968), where only 7 patients were considered to have a significant loss of remote memory. The studies of Talland et al. (1967) and Volpe and Hirst (1983b) indicate variable retrograde amnesia but none as severe as that encountered in other amnesic disorders such as WKS and HSE. Eslinger and Damasio (1984) note that both their ACoA patients assessed for retrograde amnesia showed impairments, but only one is classed as severely impaired.

Gade and Mortensen (1990) compared 20 ACoA patients with other amnesics, demented patients and controls on a remote memory events test in which recall was tested first, followed by forced-choice recognition. All three patient groups performed worse than the controls on recall, were indistinguishable from one another, and showed significant temporal gradients. However, on recognition performance it was notable that the ACoA group had a level of performance intermediate between that of the controls and the other patient groups, a finding which may again indicate a relative sparing of recognition relative to recall in this patient group.

Frontal Symptoms

Given the neuropathological aspects of ruptured ACoA aneurysm, one should expect to find evidence of frontal lobe impairment in this patient group. This was demonstrated quite clearly in our example case histories and is also borne out by other studies. Difficulties in concept formation are a well-established feature of frontal lobe pathology and, in line with this, Talland et al. (1967) found that one of their two ACoA patients could not detect the pattern in a card sequence, whereas the other patient, although unable to verbalise what this pattern was, learned it easily and retained it across testing sessions.

Ljungrenn, Saveland, Brandt and Zygmunt (1985) report that 66% of their patients were impaired on the WCST. Both Volpe and Hirst's (1983b) patients achieved six categories on the WCST but one made 45 errors in the process. Corkin et al.'s (1985) ACoA patients achieved a mean score of four categories with four of the eight patients judged as impaired. Alexander and Freedman (1984) found that their ACoA patients generally performed very poorly on the FAS word fluency test. Case J.B. (Parkin et al., 1988b) was unimpaired on the WCST and FAS but he did have problems with cognitive estimation. M.P. (Parkin & Barry, 1991) was grossly impaired on the WCST, showed reduced word fluency, but cognitive estimation was normal. R.W. (Delbecq-Derouesne et al., 1990) was impaired on only one of 13 frontal lobe tests administered. The recent study of Stenhouse et al. (1991) indicated significant deficits on the WCST, and the patient of Hanley et al. (in press) also had some frontal problems.

Behavioural disturbance, particularly associated with personality change, is a frequent feature of frontal lobe pathology and there is ample evidence of this kind of deficit in ACoA patients. Logue et al. (1968) observed a considerable range of personality changes, including instances of "autoleucotomy" in which the aneurysm resulted in the development of a more favourable personality. Okawa, Maeda, Nukui and Kawafuchi (1980) also found evidence of personality change of varying degrees in 34% of the 73 ACoA cases they followed up between 6 months and 9 years post-operation. All three of Eslinger and Damasio's (1984) patients exhibited personality changes in varying degrees, as did Alexander and Freedman's (1984) 11 patients.

Steinman and Bigler (1986) report the most detailed assessment of personality change in ACoA patients. They explored behavioural disturbance in seven patients in relation to the six categories of change. All of the patients showed significant changes (ranging from 54 to 100%) despite notable individual variation. However, consistencies were observed in the changes, such as loss of self-criticism, impatience and impulsivity, learned social behaviour, and apathy.

Confabulation

In the series of ACoA cases followed by Logue et al. (1968), 18 of the 56 patients showed evidence of confabulation which, on the basis of the examples given, appeared to be primarily of the fantastic type. Interestingly, the authors note the lack of relationship between this group's confabulatory tendencies and recall ability as measured by the logical memory component of the WMS. Two of Stuss et al.'s (1978) "extra-ordinary" confabulators were ruptured ACoA aneurysm cases and, in the subsequent series of ACoA cases reported by Alexander and Freedman (1984), 5 of their 11 patients showed evidence of marked and persistent confabulation. Kapur and Coughlan (1980) describe a single case in some detail. Following an initial period of bizarre behaviour, there was a long period in which fantastic confabulations were observed, such as the invention of fictitious business meetings. The patient was also impaired on cognitive estimation which, as we noted earlier, is symptomatic of frontal dysfunction. The link between frontal dysfunction and confabulation was further emphasised in that confabulatory behaviour receded significantly at the same time as improvements in the performance of frontal tests were noted.

A recent study by De Luca and Cicerone (1991) examined the relationship between probability and form of confabulation and the site of cerebral aneurysm. "Severe" (i.e. fantastic) confabulation was only found in ACoA cases and, furthermore, it was found to persist in three patients even when orientation to person, place and time was re-established. An intriguing feature of the confabulation observed in some ACoA cases is that it can often be maintained despite its self-evident implausibility. Our own patient, J.B., for example, was asked what month it was and immediately replied "February". It was in fact a beautiful summer afternoon and we were seated overlooking a garden in full flower. Rather than change his reply, J.B. said "It's a very mild February". This kind of persistence has been documented in Moscovitch's (1989) patient H.W.

Q. How old are you?
A. I'm 40, 42, pardon me, 62.
Q. Are you married or single?
A. Married.
Q. How long have you been married?
A. About four months.
Q. What's your wife's name?
A. Martha.
Q. How many children do you have?
A. Four. (He laughs.) Not bad for four months.
Q. How old are your children?
A. The eldest is 32, his name is Bob, and the youngest is 22, his name is Joe.
Q. How did you get these children in 4 months? (He laughs again.)
A. They're adopted.
Q. Who adopted them?
A. Martha and I.
Q. Immediately after you got married you wanted to adopt these older children?
A. Before we were married we adopted one of them, two of them. The eldest girl Brenda and Bob, and Joe and Dina since we were married.
Q. Does it all sound a little strange to you, what you are saying?
A. (He laughs.) I think it is a little strange.
Q. I think when I looked at your record it said that you've been married for over 30 years. Does that sound more reasonable to you if I told you that?
A. No.
Q. Do you really believe that you have been married for 4 months?
A. Yes.

This commitment, despite its implausibility, has many similarities with the degree of conviction seen in patients with delusions and it is therefore perhaps significant that the maintenance of delusions has recently been attributed to frontal lobe disturbance (Benson & Stuss, 1990).

ACoA Aneurysms and the "Split Brain" Syndrome

The ACoA distribution includes the genu of the corpus callosum. Ruptured ACoA aneurysms can therefore affect the corpus callosum directly and, in addition, can cause damage indirectly via induced vasospasm of the ACA. A survey of ACoA aneurysm cases, however, reveals that callosal damage and a resulting "split brain" or "disconnection" syndrome is rare. None the less, two cases have been reported, the most detailed being that of Parkin and Barry (1991).

Example Case History

Case 16 (M.P.) is a 46-year-old woman who suffered a ruptured ACoA aneurysm complicated by vasospasm. A CAT scan indicated left frontal lobe damage but, in addition, a substantial lesion in the genu of the corpus callosum. On initial recovery she was totally aphasic and lethargic. Recovery progressed and it became clear that she had marked memory loss, although this was not considered severe enough to be an amnesic syndrome. Her most notable deficit was "alien hand" behaviour in which the left hand would frequently act in a way opposite to the actions of the right hand (e.g. closing a drawer that had just been opened, undoing buttons just done up).

Formal neuropsychological testing indicated left-hand asterognosis (inability to identify items by touch) and left-hand agraphia and apraxia. Performance on the WMS-R indicated relatively intact immediate memory but some impairment on delayed recall (62 percentile), and comparison of the WAIS and NART indicated a substantial degree of intellectual deterioration. Performance on word fluency was poor and she could not understand WCST. However, cognitive estimation was normal.

A year later, she had shown a considerable improvement but the alien hand sign was still intermittently observed. She also had residual memory difficulties and experienced difficulties in planning and initiating movement.

Parkin and Barry interpreted M.P.'s additional impairments as evidence of callosal disconnection, although they cast doubt on whether the "alien hand" sign itself was of purely disconnection origin, suggesting instead that the deficit required a conjoint lesion of the corpus callosum plus extra-callosal damage which they suspected involved the supplementary motor area. The patient reported by Beukelman, Flowers and Swanson (1980), A.B., also exhibited an alien hand sign following ruptured ACoA aneurysm, but other tests revealed far less callosal disconnection than in patient M.P.

Callosal disconnection may simply be a rare phenomenon in ACoA cases. A more intriguing possibility, however, is that some less dramatic disconnection may be present in other cases but that appropriate testing to reveal it has not been carried out. Furthermore, such deficits in inter-hemispheric transfer might contribute to the memory impairment in this group. Future investigations of ACoA patients might take this into account.

Overview of Memory Loss Following Ruptured ACoA Aneurysm

Systematic detailed accounts of memory loss following ACoA aneurysm are far less frequent than those for other aetiologies of amnesia. None the less, the available evidence allows some interim conclusions about the nature of these patients' memory disorder. First, there seems to be considerable variation in the severity of the disorder, but patients who suffered a ruptured aneurysm are more severely affected. The recovery profile in these patients may also be variable (e.g. J.B. of Parkin et al., 1988b). Despite variation, there is a tendency for the amnesia exhibited by these patients to be less severe than in the other types of amnesia we have considered. In particular, there are indications that memory-impaired ACoA patients still show relatively good levels of recognition memory in relation to their recall ability. Frontal lobe dysfunction appears to be a relatively consistent feature of ACoA cases, manifest in poor performance on frontal tests, the frequency of fantastic confabulation and personality change. The possibility of callosal disconnection signs in ACoA patients should also not be overlooked.

8 Some Theoretical Issues

Aside from its clinical importance, the amnesic syndrome is of considerable scientific interest because the consistency of the dissociations observed must have some bearing on our understanding of human memory. Interest in the theoretical significance of amnesia is not new. Korsakoff (1889, p. 518), for example, noted the importance of residual learning phenomena observing:

> . . . that a whole series of traces which could in no way be restored to consciousness . . . continue to direct the course of ideas of the patients. . . . That seems to me to be one of the most interesting peculiarities of the disturbance about which we are speaking.

Residual learning phenomena continued to occupy the minds of various early theoreticians (e.g. Claparede, 1911; Gillespie, 1937; MacCurdy, 1928) whose writings may be seen as precursors of the implicit memory movement (Schacter, 1987).

Despite these early writers, theoretical interest in amnesia was aroused in the majority of psychologists by descriptions of the temporal lobe amnesic H.M. (see Chapter 5). During the 1960s, memory research was dominated by attempts to verify the modal model of memory (see Chapter 1) and anecdotal accounts of H.M.'s phenomenal inability to retain knowledge for even a few minutes (e.g. Milner, 1959) provided persuasive evidence for the STS/LTS dichotomy leading Atkinson and Shiffrin (1986, p. 97) to conclude that the pattern of memory loss in H.M. was "perhaps the single most convincing demonstration of a dichotomy in the memory system". From that point on, studies of amnesic patients have featured regularly in human memory research providing important insights into various theoretical issues, some of which we now consider.

Amnesia and the Modularity of Memory

As the above suggests, studies of amnesia have played an important role in supporting a primary distinction between STS and LTS. Amnesic patients provide numerous instances of preserved immediate memory as shown by normal performance on various span tasks. Indeed, 25 years on, much of the normal evidence concerning the distinction between STS and LTS is now questioned (e.g. Baddeley, 1986; Parkin, in press c), but the evidence from amnesia, although based essentially on a one-way dissociation, remains unchallenged.

Revived interest in amnesia led to the proposal that the amnesic syndrome provided strong evidence for dissociable episodic and semantic memory systems (e.g. Parkin, 1982). Most compelling, perhaps, was the consistent observation of grossly defective explicit memory performance in the presence of relatively normal language and intellect, a fact embodied by the regular observation of large FSIQ–MQ discrepancies. However, more refined analyses of amnesia have undermined this view.

If semantic memory is preserved in amnesia, the process of language acquisition ought to be normal. Some instances of amnesia, such as Wood et al.'s (1989) childhood amnesic and Hirst et al.'s (1988b) second language learner, support this contention but, equally, there are instances of a complete inability to acquire new vocabulary in the amnesic syndrome (Gabrieli et al., 1988; Grossman, 1987). Results as conflicting as these are difficult to accommodate but, minimally, they show that evidence for preserved language acquisition in amnesia is far from unequivocal.

A factor which may have some bearing on the above discrepancies is that acquisition of a new vocabulary item could depend, initially, on retention of the episode when it was encountered and that this must be retained until the item has been assimilated into semantic memory. However, even if correct, impairment of episodic memory should not have any influence on pre-existing semantic memories.

Another difficulty is that normal FSIQ cannot be considered as proof that semantic memory is entirely intact, because the attainment of normal performance on WAIS rests largely on the availability of knowledge acquired by early adulthood. At various points in this book, we have shown how retrograde impairments are most apparent for memories acquired towards the end of the pre-morbid period. Normal performance on WAIS might reflect nothing more than the lesser vulnerability of early memories as opposed to the selective preservation of the semantic system.

This conclusion is supported by studies which show, alongside poor premorbid event memory, marked retrograde loss for vocabulary and other aspects of knowledge acquired later in life (see Chapter 3, especially patient P.Z., and Chapter 5, patient M.R.L). None the less, we must note patient R.F.R. (Chapter 6), in whom knowledge of abbreviations and company names remained intact despite gross impairments of personal memories formed during the same time period.

The episodic/semantic distinction also falters in that many of the tests used to demonstrate retrograde amnesia (e.g. the BRMB) are more properly thought of as tests of general knowledge rather than the recollection of events. Knowing that the *Torrey Canyon* was an oil tanker that ran adrift off Cornwall and was finally bombed by the RAF does not imply memory for the episode itself (i.e. remembering the news bulletin), merely knowledge that that was what happened—knowledge that may be no different to that underlying historical knowledge for which we could not possibly have personal event memory available (e.g. that Wellington won the Battle of Waterloo). Even knowledge retrieved under autobiographical cueing conditions (see Chapter 2) must be treated with caution because of verification difficulties and because it can reflect semantic knowledge about oneself rather than the true recollection of events (Cermak & O'Connor, 1983). Moreover, even if an episodic deficit is established with this technique, there are difficulties inferring a selective episodic problem because a task of comparable difficulty in the semantic domain has not yet been devised (Moscovitch, 1989).

Although odd cases still suggest a functional distinction between episodic and semantic memory (e.g. patient R.F.R.), the weight of evidence argues against any distinction. Despite this, we believe that the dichotomy still has some clinical and descriptive value in that amnesic patients more readily demonstrate episodic rather than semantic memory impairments. However, this most likely reflects differences in the way a single system stores different kinds of knowledge rather than different underlying systems. Rejection of the episodic/semantic distinction leads us to accept "declarative memory" as an all-embracing term for the form of memory disrupted in the amnesic syndrome. But, apart from stressing the link between conscious inspection and certain aspects of memory, this term sheds little light on the nature and organisation of long-term storage.

The preceding chapters have recorded many instances of normal or near-normal performance by amnesics on various tests of implicit memory. This indicates the preservation of some distinct memory ability not linked to conscious awareness; but how should this be conceived of in terms of a modular memory system? A simplistic view might be to consider all learning demonstrated under implicit conditions as the function of a single procedural learning system. We consider this unlikely because of variations in the nature of preserved procedural learning. Motor skill memory, which might be considered the purest form of procedural learning, shows uniform preservation in all patients where it has been evaluated. However, data from other tasks that are considered procedural present a more confusing picture. Verbal priming measures, for example, do not consistently show evidence of learning.

We believe that most of the difficulties can be avoided by developing a proper taxonomy of procedural learning tasks and a parallel acceptance that the term "implicit memory" specifies a set of task conditions rather than reference to a putative single memory system. Differential performance of amnesics on different procedural tasks may be determined by a number of factors. First, the neural substrates will be different and this may directly influence the extent to which implicit learning abilities survive. Motor skills, for example, are likely to be mediated, in part at least, at sites somewhat distal from those usually damaged in amnesia. Non-motor measures of procedural memory, in contrast, may depend on the intactness of sites more adjacent to memory regions. It is likely, for example, that verbal priming is dependent on left temporal lobe language centres (Schacter, Rapscak, Rubens et al., 1990). Because of the imprecise nature of brain lesions, it is therefore likely that the extent of verbal priming found in temporal lobe amnesics might be unpredictable because of varying degrees of damage to the language system.

A second factor affecting variability is that measures of procedural memory may vary in their "purity", i.e. the extent to which they are unambiguous measures of procedural memory and nothing else. Motor skills, such as mirror drawing and pursuit rotor, are perhaps unique in that explicit recollection of the prior learning episode cannot facilitate performance, thus producing a truly implicit test of memory. In contrast, there is considerable evidence that both perceptual learning and verbal priming can be facilitated by explicit recollection (Parkin, in press c; Russo & Parkin, in press) and the presence of this may be part of what constitutes normal performance. Variations in the severity of the amnesia may therefore have uneven effects on the preservation of procedural learning abilities.

Our view is that the term "procedural" is being applied too broadly in that it currently embraces tasks with different neural substrates and performance characteristics. If applied to modular accounts of human memory, the term "procedural" seems most apt for motor skill learning because the modularity of this system is strongly indicated by the amnesia evidence. Specifying the modularity of systems underlying other forms of procedural learning must await a better understanding of the mechanisms involved and the variables determining performance.

The Neuroanatomy of Memory

Studies of the amnesic syndrome have begun to play an increasingly important role in attempts to identify the neural substrate of human memory. The first question one can ask is whether, despite its varying aetiologies, the amnesic syndrome is caused by a single critical lesion. Many amnesic patients do have large and diffuse lesions, but sufficient data exist to rule out a single lesion account. In Chapter 4, we considered several amnesic states caused by discrete thalamic lesions (see Fig 4.1), and patients such as R.B. (Chapter 5) provide convincing evidence of amnesia following localised medial temporal damage.

An alternative view of the pathology amnesia stems from the fact that all the key sites involved are part of the limbic system (see Fig. 1.4). This has led a number of workers to suggest that the commonality of symptoms shown by amnesic patients with varying lesions arises because the different structures form part of a "memory circuit" and that interruption at any point could therefore produce the same outcome. For a considerable time, the circuitry view was undermined by an inability to demonstrate the lesions of the fornix also give rise to amnesia. The fornix is the primary afferent pathway from the hippocampus to the mamillary bodies and its interruption should, if the circuitry theory is correct, produce an amnesia as extensive as that caused by damage to either the hippocampus or mamillary bodies.

The literature on fornix lesions in humans has, until recently, been somewhat inadequate (e.g. Parkin, 1984), but the general conclusion was that fornix damage did not produce an amnesic syndrome. Recent developments have changed this view to some extent. Gaffan and Gaffan (1991) have reassessed the earlier literature and concluded that the most reliable studies involving fornix lesions—studies of patients who underwent fornix sectioning for removal of colloid cysts—do show evidence of memory loss. In addition, Hodges and Carpenter (1991; see also Gaffan, Gaffan & Hodges, 1991) have reported psychometric memory evaluation on two fornix lesion patients and show that WMS performance of these patients is comparable with that seen in patients with the amnesic syndrome. However, it must be noted that, despite their poor levels of recall, these two patients did surprisingly well on the Recognition Memory Test (RMT)—this contrasts with the performance of most amnesic patients, in whom performance is usually at or near chance. There are grounds, therefore, for supposing that the memory loss in these patients is rather mild. These patients will be reconsidered shortly, but first we must consider a new and influential idea about the neuroanatomical basis of memory.

Using non-human primates, Mishkin and his colleagues (see Mishkin, 1982) have argued that the limbic system contains two neuroanatomically

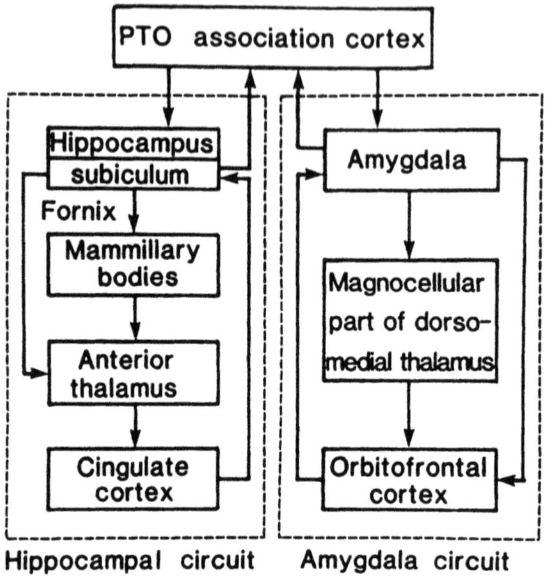

FIG. 8.1 Mishkin's dual circuit account of the neuroanatomy of memory. Reproduced from Mayes (1988) with the permission of Cambridge University Press.

distinct pathways (see Fig. 8.1). The "hippocampal" pathway projects from the hippocampus to the mamillary bodies via the fornix, from the mamillary bodies to the anterior thalamus via the mamillo-thalamic tract, on to the cingulate gyrus before returning to the hippocampus. The "amygdalar" pathway projects to the dorso-medial thalamic nucleus (DMTN), on to the orbito-frontal cortex, and then back to the amygdala. Mishkin found that lesions of either pathway alone were insufficient to produce severe memory defects in monkeys, although some disruption was noted. Severe impairments occurred only when both pathways were lesioned. If applied to humans, this theory would predict only mild memory loss rather than amnesia as a consequence of fornix lesions, a prediction possibly borne out by the patients studied by Hodges and Carpenter (1991).

H.M. (see Chapter 5), who underwent bilateral temporal lobe resection, lost both the hippocampus and amygdala bilaterally, and so his dense amnesia would be consistent with a dual circuit view. Victor et al.'s (1989) account of WKS concludes that memory loss is only reliably found when both the mamillary bodies and DMTN are damaged (see also the studies of Mair et al., 1979; Mayes et al., 1987b)—findings again consistent with a dual circuit lesion. The dual circuit theory may also account for some anomalous findings such as patients with no amnesia despite mamillary body lesions (Victor et al., 1989), isolated DMTN lesions (Kritchevsky,

Graff-Radford & Damasio, 1987), amydalectomy (Sarter & Markowitsch, 1985) and congenital absence of the fornix (Nathan & Smith, 1950).

The dual circuitry hypothesis gains further support from Graff-Radford et al.'s (1990) neuroradiological study of four thalamic infarction patients. Cases 1 and 2 were severely amnesic and had anterior lesions involving both the mamillo-thalamic tract and the pathway from the inferior thalamic peduncle to the DMTN. Cases 3 and 4 were not amnesic and had lesions affecting the DMTN but sparing the mamillo-thalamic tract. The presence/absence of amnesia was not a function of lesion size. The authors also determined the neuroanatomical relationship between the hippocampal and amygdalar pathways in the thalamic region of the monkey and found that these pathways were most adjacent in the anterior thalamus, a finding consistent with their human lesion data which had shown an association between anterior lesions and amnesia. Cramon et al. (1985) summarised CAT scan findings in 11 thalamic infarction cases and also concluded that amnesia was associated with more anterior lesions centred on the paramedian territory. Reviewing this and other studies, Graff-Radford et al. (1990) conclude that thalamic infarction is far more likely to produce amnesia if the lesion is anterior. Given that the hippocampal and amygdalar pathways are most adjacent in the anterior thalamus, the thalamic infarction data can be seen as supporting a dual circuitry view of amnesia.

The dual circuitry theory has wide applicability to other instances of the amnesic syndrome. Herpes simplex encephalitis (HSE) is most often associated with extensive necrosis which could easily affect both pathways. Similarly, midline tumours (e.g. case 5, Chapter 4) could exert pressure on both pathways and cause a temporary amnesic state. The theory may also have some bearing on Harper et al.'s (1986) observation that, of 131 patients exhibiting signs of Wernicke's disease at autopsy, only 20% had received a diagnosis of WKS during life. If development of amnesia depends on a dual circuit lesion, it is reasonable to suppose that these conditions would not be met in all cases. This point is strengthened by Harper and coworkers' additional finding that the modal lesion in their sample was the mamillary bodies, structures involved only in the hippocampal pathway.

A difficulty for the dual circuit hypothesis is case R.B. (Chapter 5), who suffered a highly discrete lesion affecting only the CA1 field of the hippocampus yet manifested severe anterograde amnesia but, interestingly, no significant retrograde impairment. The amygdala and other critical memory regions also appeared normal and only the somato-sensory cortex was damaged. R.B. would therefore seem to provide crucial evidence against the dual circuit hypothesis because, in these instances, amnesia is present when only one circuit is damaged—although, given the caveats raised about the two fornix patients (see above), it is unfortunate that R.B. was not given any test of recognition memory.

It may therefore be the case that damage to the hippocampal region alone may be sufficient to produce amnesia—this would certainly be consistent with recent neurophysiological work linking the hippocampus critically to the processes of consolidation (e.g. Rolls, 1988). However, if we accept this, we must explain why interruptions of the hippocampal circuit further on (e.g. mamillary bodies) are not reliably correlated with memory loss (e.g. Harper's findings). A compromise might be that for lesions in the midline diencephalon to produce amnesia, both pathways need to be disturbed (e.g. Graff-Radford's studies), whereas, within the medial temporal lobe, a lesion restricted to the hippocampus may be sufficient.

Memory and the Frontal Lobes

There is now incontrovertible evidence that the frontal lobes play a critical role in certain aspects of memory function. Chapters 3–7 have emphasised the presence of frontal lobe damage in perhaps the majority of amnesic syndrome patients, and therefore an understanding of how the frontal lobes influence memory is a prerequisite for any theoretical account of the functional deficit responsible for human amnesia.

Corsi (cited by Milner, 1971) asked subjects to read sequentially presented word pairs. At various intervals, a probe card appeared and the subjects had to state which of the two words had been presented most recently. On some trials, both words had been presented previously, whereas on others only one had. The latter task just involved *recognition*, whereas the former required *temporal discrimination*. Patients with discrete frontal removals performed normally on recognition but were markedly impaired on temporal discrimination. Other studies have also indicated frontal involvement in memory for temporal disorder. Shimamura et al. (1990) found frontal patients to be poor at reconstructing the sequence of a previously presented word list despite normal recognition memory. Frontal patients were also highly impaired at reconstructing the chronological sequence of public events they were able to describe accurately.

Vreizen and Moscovitch (1990) examined various aspects of memory performance in Parkinson's disease (PD) patients—in this group, the primary lesion lies within the basal ganglia but, because of the high degree of interconnectivity between this region and the frontal cortex, PD can be considered as compromising the frontal lobes. PD patients were found to be poor at reconstructing the temporal order of lists, both verbal and non-verbal, and the extent of this deficit was unrelated to the patients' recognition memory for the same stimuli.

Amnesic subjects have also been tested on various tasks measuring memory for temporal order. Squire et al. (1981) examined temporal discrimination in patients rendered temporarily amnesic as a result of ECT and the amnesic patient N.A. (see Chapter 4). Deficits on temporal discrimination were found but, importantly, these deficits disappeared when the patients' poor recognition memory was allowed for, i.e. poor temporal memory was a direct consequence of poor recognition. Other studies of amnesia, however, indicate that the impairment in temporal discrimination is *disproportionate* to the recognition deficit (e.g. Huppert & Piercy, 1978b; Squire, 1982) and it has further been proposed that this disproportionate impairment of temporal order memory is directly related to the extent of frontal lobe disturbance as measured by psychometric tests (Moscovitch, 1989; Squire, 1982).

Impaired memory for temporal order in amnesic patients could, on the basis of the above evidence, be attributed to the frontal damage present in these patients superimposing a "frontal" memory impairment on top of a core deficit arising from limbic pathology. However, there is a major difficulty with this argument, because several studies have shown gross impairments of temporal order memory in patients without any frontal pathology (see also Chapter 3 for further criticism of Squire, 1982).

Bowers et al. (1988) describe T.R., a patient who developed amnesia following a retrosplenial lesion which interrupted pathways between the hippocampus and the anterior thalamic nucleus. T.R. performed very poorly on anterograde tests of temporal order memory and his ability to make temporal discriminations was unrelated to his recognition ability. However, his ability to make temporal judgements about information in remote memory (e.g. deciding on the chronological sequence of various public events) was normal. We have recently described a similar situation in our two patients (R.K. and J.R.: see Chapter 4), neither of whom shows any evidence of frontal pathology. These two patients performed very poorly on an anterograde test of temporal discrimination, but normally on Kapur and co-workers' (1989) "Dead or Alive Test"—a test which requires the accurate dating of remote memory (see Chapter 2). The above cases indicate that disproportionate deficits in temporal discrimination can be found in patients without frontal involvement, although, importantly, all three cases appeared to have normal temporal memory when remote memory was assessed (see also the studies of Parkin & Hunkin, in press b; Kopelman, 1989; Shimamura et al., 1990; all of which found no relationship between memory for temporal order and frontal dysfunction).

At this point, it is necessary to consider in more detail what memory for temporal context might involve and how it could be related to the known functions of the frontal lobes. It is highly unlikely that the brain has evolved a direct "date stamping" function affixing a date tag to each new memory. More likely is that memory for temporal order involves some *problem-solving* exercise in which certain aspects of retrieved information are used to make some form of temporal decision. Two events might, for example, be correctly sequenced because key information is extracted which then logically determines that one must have preceded the other.

On the basis of the above framework, Bowers et al. (1988) have proposed two possible loci for impaired memory for temporal information:

1. Failure to encode information needed for temporal memory.
2. Failure to process retrieved information concerning temporal information effectively.

In patients T.R., J.R. and R.K., one can propose that the deficit lies at (1) because here the problem-solving aspects appear intact, as shown by normal temporal judgements about remote memory, but there are impairments on anterograde tests of temporal memory. In frontal patients, however, the deficit minimally lies at (2), because there is defective temporal memory on both anterograde and retrograde tests.

The above discussion indicates that structures of the midline diencephalon may be critically involved in the encoding of temporal information and that this, in turn, may provide a basis for explaining the functional deficit in amnesia. We return to this point in the next section, but for the moment we consider a second aspect of memory impairment that could be attributable to the disturbance of frontally based problem-solving abilities.

As we have seen, frontal lesions can often have no effect on recognition memory, but a number of studies indicate that frontally disturbed patients often show marked impairments on recall. Jetter, Poser, Freeman and Markowitsch (1987), for example, found that frontal patients showed marked impairments on tests of delayed recall but normal recognition memory. Moscovitch (1989) has argued that retrieval involves both strategic, problem-solving activities and less effortful local routines. Strategic activities include decisions about whereabouts in the memory database retrieval processes should be performed, whereas local routines reflect decisions made about a stimulus once retrieved. In terms of task, free recall makes the maximum demands on strategic activities and recognition the least, because presentation of a target can, depending on the circumstances (see below), reduce the search to a minimum.

In this book, we have encountered what might be termed the "frontal memory impairment" in our account of memory loss following ruptured ACoA aneurysms (Chapter 7). We noted a number of instances in this group of patients with grossly impaired recall but relatively good recognition—the most clear-cut case being that of Hanley et al. (in press), in which the sparing of recognition memory was observed using a recognition task that was matched for difficulty with a recall task showing substantial deficit.

An important point to note here, however, is that, like anterograde temporal memory deficits, the critical lesion may not be restricted to the frontal cortex. Ruptured ACoA aneurysms produce variable lesions with structures of the basal forebrain often principally involved and, in connection with this, it is important to note that Hanley et al.'s patient had a lesion restricted to the caudate nucleus. The critical lesion for disproportionately impaired recall may therefore be any interruption of critical pathways arising in the basal ganglia and terminating in the frontal cortex.

A second point is that not all ACoA patients exhibit a sparing of recognition memory and, in one case, R.W. (Delbecq-Derouesne et al., 1990), recall has been shown to be better than recognition, although it must be stressed that the large number of intrusions rule out normal recall in this case. Better recall than recognition can be accommodated by arguing that the "frontal" deficit in retrieval can itself be fractionated into a deficit affecting search and one influencing decisions about the output of the search process (Hanley et al., in press). Recognition is thus badly affected because inappropriate decisions are made about distractor stimuli, but recall is less affected because correct responses are produced among intrusions which are themselves a consequence of a faulty decision stage.

Parkin, Pitchford and Binschaedler (in prep.) provide a recent account of an ACoA patient in which executive deficits affected recognition *and* recall. Like Hanley and co-workers' patient, C.B. was found to show impaired recall relative to recognition on tasks matched for difficulty. However, the authors further demonstrated that C.B.'s recognition memory was not intact when conditions required more executive decisions to be made. On forced choice recognition, for example, C.B. performed well, but when single probe recognition was used, his performance was highly defective due to large numbers of false positives. This latter finding was interpreted as showing that C.B. had problems in performing recognition when some internal response criterion needed to be established.

In this section, we have described some of the features of frontal lobe memory deficits and examined how they relate to the memory deficits exhibited in the amnesic syndrome. It has been pointed out that frontal lesions can disrupt memory for temporal order, although, in the various instances of amnesic patients showing disproportionate impairment of temporal memory, frontal lobe dysfunction does not appear critically implicated. Frontal lobe impairments also disproportionately affect recall relative to recognition and we have indicated how this might have particular implications for interpreting memory impairment following ruptured ACoA aneurysms. Moreover, the recall deficits exhibited by other amnesic patients might also owe something to frontal involvement, a point to which we return later.

The Contextual Deficit Theory of Amnesia

There have been many attempts to explain the functional deficit experienced by amnesic syndrome patients but, in our opinion, only two theories are at present viable. The first, and the most straightforward, is the *consolidation theory*, which states that amnesics forget because they have lost the physiological ability to form permanent memory traces. A possible argument against this theory is that, under certain conditions, amnesic patients have been shown to have normal rates of forgetting on a recognition task if allowed sufficient acquisition trials. Kopelman (1985) found that, after equating learning, WKS patients forgot at the same rate as controls over a 1-week period and suggested that the amnesic deficit might be a fundamental learning deficit rather than one influencing storage processes.

An important point about the Kopelman study is that recognition was tested using a yes–no recognition paradigm in which the target stimuli had to be distinguished from distractor stimuli that had not been seen previously. To understand the significance of this, we must digress briefly to consider the nature of recognition memory in more detail.

Memory theorists now consider recognition to be a composite response based on information that can be derived from at least two independent sources (Gardiner & Parkin, 1990; Mandler, 1988). A target stimulus can be recognised simply on the grounds that it seems *familiar*, a response thought to arise from *perceptual fluency* with the stimulus (Jacoby, 1983). A response based on *familiarity* is one that is devoid of any *context*. The term "context" has a chequered history in cognitive psychology, but here it can be defined relatively unambiguously as the information in memory that allows a re-presented stimulus to be categorised in place or time. Returning to Kopelman's experiment, we can see that for WKS patients to perform the recognition task adequately, they need only have had access to familiarity information because, given that the distractors were novel, familiarity information would have been sufficient to discriminate targets from distractors.

In the preceding section, we saw data from patients T.R., J.R. and R.K. indicating that diencephalic lesions can result in a disproportionate impairment of memory for temporal order. Chapter 3 also described several studies (e.g. Huppert & Piercy, 1978b) in which WKS memory performance was adversely affected when the temporal order of stimuli was crucial for memory performance. The defective performance on these tasks can be attributed to an inability to remember the temporal context of the target stimuli (e.g. was the target on list one or two?, seen yesterday or today?) and reliance instead on just familiarity information which, because all of the items are familiar, provides no basis for a correct response.

Data such as the above have provided the basis for the *contextual deficit theory* of amnesia (Mayes, 1988; Mayes, Meudell & Pickering, 1985; Mayes, Meudell & MacDonald, 1991), which attributes amnesia to some inability to remember the contextual attributes essential for normal recognition memory. We have already noted how defective contextual memory can reduce the efficiency of recognition memory, and in free recall the effect is far more drastic—if no contextual memory is available, the general event specified by the experimenter (e.g. the word list I read to you 5 min ago) would not be accessible and the process of recall not even initiated.

The contextual deficit theory therefore provides a plausible account of some key findings in recent amnesia research. A problem, however, is that virtually all these studies have involved only patients with diencephalic lesions and, where this is not the case (e.g. Mayes et al., 1991), the number of non-WKS patients is too small for a valid comparison. To be generally acceptable, therefore, we must consider how it relates to other forms of amnesia. This leads us to consider whether all amnesics are alike with particular reference to whether the contextual deficit theory applies universally.

How Many Kinds of Amnesia?

Our preceding discussion has given us good reason to distinguish patients who have become amnesic following ruptured ACoA aneurysms from other amnesic patients on the grounds that the former exhibit a pattern of memory impairment more akin to that found in patients with frontal lesions. The question remains, however, as to whether the remaining patients constitute a single group or whether different functional deficits arise from different lesions. This question has typically been addressed by examining whether patients with amnesia following lesions focused on the medial temporal lobe region differ from those with diencephalic lesions (Parkin & Leng, 1988b). As we have already seen, the contextual deficit theory provides a plausible account of diencephalic amnesia, and therefore the question becomes, quite easily, whether medial temporal lobe amnesia can also be explained in this way. If so, the conditions for a unitary theory would be met and, if not, the case for functional heterogeneity would be supported. Before examining this, however, two other lines of evidence have to be considered.

In Chapters 3 and 5, evidence was presented showing that temporal lobe amnesics might forget more rapidly than diencephalic patients. It was noted that this evidence was itself equivocal and that significant methodological flaws exist. A particular problem is matching the groups of patients for severity. FSIQ−MQ provides a rule of thumb but could not be expected to rule out differences in severity sufficient to produce statistically different rates of forgetting. Moreover, given that the forgetting rate hypothesis is, in effect, a severity hypothesis, one might well expect poorer performance by temporal lobe patients on *a priori* grounds, particularly if delayed testing on WMS is used.

The above discussion suggests that the question of whether or not medial temporal lobe and diencephalic amnesia differ can only be answered using experimental tasks which demonstrate *qualitative* rather than *quantitative* differences between patient groups. This condition appeared to be met by the various studies comparing different amnesic patients on the Brown-Peterson (BP) task. Chapters 3 and 4 showed that the great majority of diencephalic amnesics showed impaired BP performance with recall declining exponentially as a function of distraction interval. In contrast, temporal lobe amnesics and post-HSE patients perform far better, often as well as controls, and are not particularly sensitive to distraction interval.

Differential BP performance might therefore be indicative of functional differences in the amnesia caused by medial temporal and diencephalic lesions. However, recent investigations have suggested that this may not be the case. Earlier, we noted that frontal lobe damage can "contaminate" memory impairments arising from limbic lesions and we highlighted two particular areas—memory for temporal order and the disproportionate impairment of recall relative to recognition. BP is, in effect, a recall task, and therefore it is possible, on *a priori* grounds, that differences in performance by the two patient groups could reflect differential frontal involvement. This possibility was explored directly by Leng and Parkin (1989), who found that the poorer performance of WKS patients on the BP was correlated with the extent of their frontal deficits as measured by the WCST. Further evidence has accrued to indicate their BP performance is significantly determined by the intactness of frontal lobe function (see Parkin & Walter, 1991) and this fact may also clear up a minor controversy concerning the anomalously good BP performance of the two WKS patients reported by Mair et al. (1979). Detailed autopsy evidence is available for these patients and this indicates that, uncharacteristically, these WKS patients were free of frontal damage.

We turn now to comparative studies of the context deficit hypothesis, which revolves around recent work in our own laboratory. In our first study (Parkin et al., 1990a), we examined whether a contextual manipulation had comparable effects on the short-term memory of medial temporal lobe and diencephalic amnesics. The patients were shown a 2 × 2 array of pictures and immediate recall was tested until perfect. After a 60-sec distractor period, the patients had to pick the targets from a 16-picture array. This procedure was then repeated on three more trials, except that items that had been distractors became targets and vice versa. On these subsequent trials, the subjects' task was to identify the items they were asked to remember most recently. The critical feature of this was that, after trial 1, some record of temporal context must be maintained for correct performance—familiarity information alone is insufficient. As Fig. 8.2 shows, WKS patients showed a marked drop in performance from trial 2 onwards, a deficit expected from the contextual deficit theory, but the temporal lobe group showed much better performance.

In a further experiment, Hunkin and Parkin (in press) examined whether group differences on the recency task arose because the WKS patients were more sensitive to proactive interference, i.e. doing four trials in quick succession. The task was therefore repeated, but this time completely different items were used on each trial. Under these conditions, there is no effect of trial for either group (see Fig. 8.2), thus indicating that poor WKS performance in the original condition stems directly from a failure to remember temporal context. The recency judgement data suggest that only WKS amnesia can be characterised as an impairment in memory for temporal context.

A second study (Hunkin, Parkin & Longmore, in press) supports this interpretation. Temporal lobe amnesics (all survivors of HSE) and diencephalic amnesics were compared on the list discrimination task (see Chapter 3). Levels of recognition memory were comparable in the two groups; what differed was the relation between discrimination and recognition. In WKS, there was no correlation between recognition performance and temporal discrimina- tion, but in the HSE group performance on recognition and temporal discrimination were highly correlated.

Data from the recency judgement and list discrimination tasks indicate that WKS patients are poor at remembering temporal context regardless of their recognition ability, whereas in HSE patients the two forms of memory are highly correlated (a finding comparable to the post-ECT data of Squire et al., 1981). However, in the previous section, we saw that discrete frontal lobe lesions can disrupt discrimination performance, and therefore it was possible that this apparent difference between the groups might constitute differential frontal pathology rather than a functional difference stemming from each group's pattern of limbic damage. However, analysis indicated that frontal pathology did not appear to be implicated in the WKS temporal order deficit. These data thus suggest that the observed differences between the patient groups stem directly from their different patterns of subcortical damage, a conclusion consistent with other data showing that subcortical deficits can impair memory for temporal order (see above).

This series of findings supports an intepretation of WKS in terms of a contextual encoding deficit, but this theory cannot accommodate the data from HSE patients who, to recap, have lesions centred on the medial

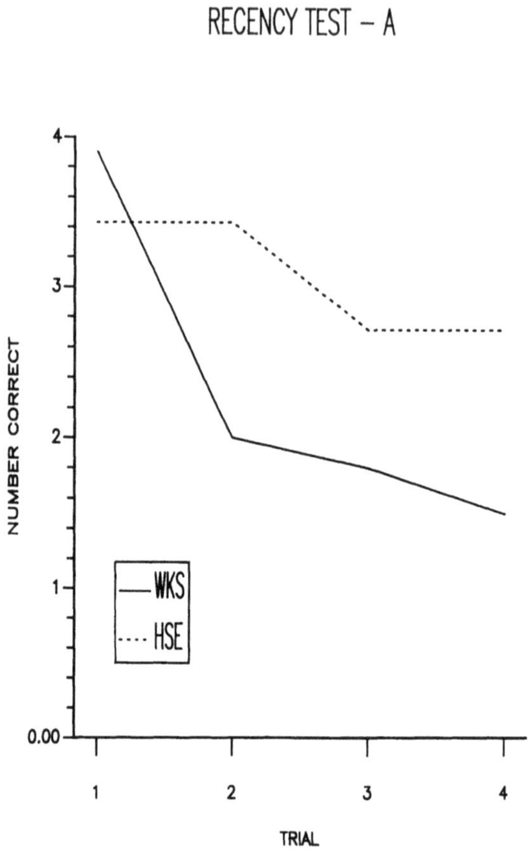

FIG. 8.2 A, Recency judgements with same materials on all trials; B, recency judgements with new materials on each trial. Reproduced from Hunkin and Parkin (in press) with the permission of Masson publishers.

temporal lobes and in whom one can reasonably assume hippocampal lesions. Parkin (in press a) has provided a possible framework for understanding the differing impairments of WKS and HSE patients on tests of temporal context. His argument, which will be described only briefly here, derives from recent views (e.g. Rolls, 1988) that the hippocampus is the neural substrate for forming the context within which a target stimulus is stored in memory. Parkin suggests that the WKS deficit can be conceived as defective input to the hippocampal systems, i.e. memory fails because the information input to the hippocampal system for storage is inadequate. As a result of this, memory for context will always be poor because the information needed to form it is not made available.

In post-HSE amnesia, the primary deficit lies in the efficiency of the hippocampal system to consolidate its input, which comprises information

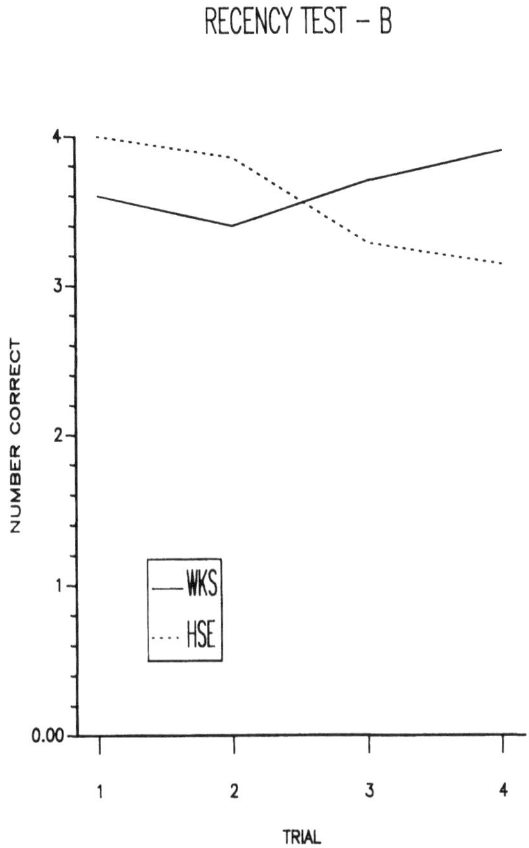

about both the target and context. Here, the critical factor determining memory performance is the probability that some degree of consolidation will occur, rather than an impoverishment of memory for context relative to target memory. The result of this, therefore, is a memory system that is defective but not biased to the loss of one kind of information, thus resulting in the correlation between target and context memory.

The Relationship Between Anterograde and Retrograde Amnesia

Given our conclusions about aetiological factors in the generation of anterograde deficits, this topic is best handled by treating diencephalic and temporal lobe groups separately. Chapter 3 showed that WKS patients exhibit both a severe anterograde amnesia, manifest by poor performance on memory tasks such as free recall and recognition, and retrograde amnesia, as shown by an inability to recall or recognise information relating to the pre-morbid period. Reviews indicate that this co-occurrence is a persistent feature of WKS, with no well-described instance of WKS in which this relationship has not been reported. This state of affairs leads directly to the possibility that the anterograde and retrograde deficits may have a common origin.

The widespread association of WKS with chronic alcoholism has been the basis of one attempt to explain the relationship between anterograde and retrograde deficits. The continuity hypothesis (e.g. Ryback, 1971) suggests that there is a continuum between the neurological impairments arising from chronic alcoholism and those sustained following an identifiable Wernicke's episode. Within this view, the acute anterograde impairment observed at diagnosis can be considered an exacerbation of a milder anterograde impairment present in the pre-morbid period. The apparent retrograde amnesia is therefore more properly considered the consequence of a milder anterograde impairment. This theory also explains the temporal gradient in retrograde amnesia on the grounds that chronic alcoholism exerts a cumulative effect on pre-morbid memory processes.

One prediction that has been held consistent with the continuity hypothesis is that the severity of the anterograde and retrograde deficits might be expected to correlate if they are both anterograde deficits. Shimamura and Squire (1986) correlated the performance of WKS patients on the BRMB, with their anterograde memory impairments being assessed using 12 learning measures. No overall correlation between remote memory impairments and anterograde amnesia was found, but sub-analyses indicated a significant positive relationship between the anterograde deficits and retrograde amnesia for the most recent decades of the pre-morbid period. Kopelman (1989) reports similar findings in his remote memory study with correlations only evident between anterograde measures and tests for the most recent period of pre-morbid memory.

Research on the Sussex WKS population reveals a similar picture. We correlated performance of our patients on a prototype famous faces test for U.K. populations (see Parkin et al., 1990b) with performance on a variety of anterograde learning tests. These data, summarised by Parkin (1991b), indicated no overall correlation between the anterograde and retrograde measures, but significant correlations when only the most recent pre-morbid period was considered. A further aspect of these data was that only anterograde tests measuring explicit, context-dependent memory (e.g. Parkin et al., 1990b) showed a significant correlation. Indirect, implicit measures did not correlate significantly with retrograde amnesia.

The general absence of correlations between anterograde and retrograde measures in WKS does not necessarily rule out a common explanation for both deficits. This is because of the *a priori* basis for assuming that the severity of a pre-morbid anterograde impairment should, of necessity, determine the additional impairment arising from the acute lesions associated with Wernicke's encephalopathy. Other lines of evidence do allow us to settle the issue (Parkin, 1991a).

Patient P.Z. (Chapter 3) is an academic scientist who, following a history of chronic alcoholism, developed WKS. Just prior to this episode, P.Z. produced his autobiography, thus providing an objective pre-morbid measure of his remote memory. Post-morbidly P.Z.'s memory for facts in his autobiography was extremely impaired and showed a temporal gradient similar to that shown by alcoholic WKS patients on standardised remote memory tests. It seems difficult to accommodate this finding within a continuity framework because this would predict preservation of remote memory at approximately the same level as it was pre-morbidly.

The three cases of non-alcoholic WKS described in Chapter 5 also bear directly on this issue. All three showed a pattern of anterograde impairment similar to alcoholic WKS and temporally graded retrograde amnesia. As chronic alcoholism was not a significant factor, one can only conclude that their retrograde deficit had an acute onset and, on the grounds of parsimony, the same deficit in alcoholic WKS should also be interpreted as an acute phenomenon unrelated to pre-morbid alcoholism.

The available evidence therefore argues against chronic pre-morbid alcoholism as the factor linking anterograde and retrograde amnesia in WKS. An alternative possibility is that the two deficits have a common acute cause. As we have seen, the context deficit theory is a plausible explanation of the WKS anterograde impairment, and therefore it is possible that it might also explain the retrograde deficit. Parkin et al. (1990b) speculated that a single contextual processing system is involved both in the encoding of new contextual information and the maintenance of existing contextual relationships in long-term storage. If correct, this theory predicts that remote memory performance should be enhanced by contextual cueing in the same way that anterograde deficits in WKS can be ameliorated by contextual cues (Mayes, 1988). To test this theory, WKS performance on a famous faces test was examined under two conditions—a "no context" condition in which no extraneous information concerning a person's identity was provided, and a "context" condition in which some clue concerning the person's identity was provided. Cueing was found to have progressively less effect in more recent periods of remote memory. A contextual deficit account would have predicted the opposite and the data instead supported a storage deficit. This interpretation is supported by Squire et al. (1989b), who demonstrated that alcoholic WKS patients show no improvement when tested repeatedly on the same remote memory tests. This is consistent with a storage deficit account but incompatible with a retrieval account because the latter would, on the assumption that the accessibility of memories would vary across time, predict a cumulative increase in overall performance.

The only finding favouring a link between anterograde and retrograde deficits in WKS are the three demonstrations of a correlation between anterograde impairment and the most recent portions of remote memory. However, even these data have important caveats. WKS can often have an insidious onset and it is quite possible that significant correlations between anterograde amnesia and the most recent pre-morbid memories reflect an evolving anterograde impairment more characteristic of WKS than any milder deficit that may have been present earlier. Furthermore, Cohen and Squire (1981) have argued that retrieval of remote memories may be partly determined by learning that occurs after the events themselves have occurred—the argument being that events continue to be discussed after their occurrence and that this contributes partly to their eventual memorability. If one assumes that recent remote memories are more likely to be strengthened by this process, then the correlation between anterograde amnesia and only recent remote memory can be attributed to a purely post-morbid memory impairment.

Finally, one must also consider evidence from diencephalic cases other than WKS. In Chapter 4, we saw that extensive retrograde amnesia is not a consistent adjunct of anterograde amnesia in patients with thalamic lesions. This variability supports our analysis of WKS impairments by suggesting that anterograde and retrograde impairments are independent of one another. However, two questions remain unanswered. First, why is it that severe anterograde and retrograde deficits are always present in WKS patients, whereas this is not the case in other diencephalic amnesias? One possible answer is that co-occurrence depends on the general extent of the lesions. In WKS patients, and other diencephalic patients showing severe retrograde loss, the underlying lesions are quite extensive, whereas in those thalamic amnesias showing little evidence of retrograde impairment, the lesions are much more circumscribed to key diencephalic loci.

Within temporal lobe amnesias, the extent of retrograde impairment is much more variable. At one end of the spectrum lie patients such as R.B. who present minimal impairments and, at the other end, many post-HSE patients in which the retrograde loss is almost total. There have been no studies of the relationship between anterograde and retrograde deficits primarily because few studies have incorporated sufficient subjects to justify the exercise. However, as we noted with diencephalic amnesia, there is a tendency for patients with smaller lesions to show less evidence of retrograde loss. Temporal lobe amnesics have shown some evidence of a temporal gradient, but there is not the systematic pattern found in WKS patients. However, the general rule applies that it is early remote memories that show greater preservation. Temporal lobe amnesics have also provided the few instances of retrograde amnesia without anterograde amnesia (Andrews, Poser & Kessler, 1982; Stuss & Guzman, 1988).

Explaining the Temporal Gradient

In this book, we have seen that retrograde amnesia is frequently characterised by temporal gradients and that this cannot be considered an artefact of alcoholism or any other pre-morbid factor. Instead, demonstrations of what is frequently termed *Ribot's Law* (Ribot, 1882) must be revealing something about the organisation of long-term memory that makes older memories less vulnerable to disruption. One view, once forwarded by Squire, Cohen and Nadel (1984), is that consolidation is a long-term process and that sudden brain injury can therefore still disrupt memories formed several years ago. Consolidation is certainly not an instant process but, on purely adaptive grounds, it seems unlikely that memories should remain labile for years.

More likely is the idea that the temporal gradient in retrograde amnesia reflects a *storage deficit*. One explanation of the gradient is to consider the possible effects of a brain lesion on a memory store built up as a *parallel distributed system* (see McClelland & Rumelhart, 1986). A feature of these systems is *redundancy*, in that every time a new memory is added it is represented again. If one makes the assumption that older memories will have a higher degree of redundancy—this arises because each use of an existing memory creates a new memory featuring the old one—then random damage to the system is more likely to spare older memories simply because they have a higher degree of multiple representation.

The above argument is, at present, largely speculative, and experimental evidence supporting it has yet to come forward. It will therefore be of interest to investigate this hypothesis and compare it with other theories. Conway (in press), for example, has drawn links between the temporal gradient of amnesic retrograde amnesia and the "reminiscence" hump found in autobiographical cueing experiments on older people. This "hump" represents the greater recall of personal events from early adulthood and this has also been found in amnesics (Mackinnon & Squire, 1989). The appearance of the hump has been attributed to the fact that early adulthood is the major period of self-definition and, for this reason, memories formed during that time are of particular salience to the self-initiated retrieval strategies underlying cued autobiographical memory. Investigations into this hypothesis and its relevance to amnesia are awaited with interest.

9 Remediation

The material covered in Chapters 1–8 indicates both the enormity of published research into amnesia and a preoccupation with the clinical description and scientific understanding of memory disorders that has been evident since the middle of the last century. In the last 10 years, there has been a remarkable growth in research concerning non-invasive methods of remediating memory disorders. The reasons for this late development are not altogether clear, but one likely explanation is the changing role of the clinical psychologist. Until relatively recently, the primary role of clinicians within the neurological arena was assessment on tests considered to have good lesion-localising value. However, the development of new neuroradiological techniques such as CAT scans has reduced this role and allowed clinicians greater scope to explore remediation strategies.

One of the first and most important publications in this area was Wilson and Moffat's *Clinical management of memory problems* (1984). Since then, there have been a large number of other publications concerned with this issue (e.g. O'Connor & Cermak, 1987; Salmon & Butters, 1987; Seron & Deloche, 1989; Sohlberg & Mateer, 1989a; Wilson, 1987). In this chapter, we outline some current approaches to rehabilitation and evaluate their effectiveness. The research on drug approaches to remediation is extensive, but our concern here is with an understanding of the psychological approaches to remediation.

Restitution or Functional Adaptation?

A fundamental issue in memory remediation is whether therapy should aim at restitution of the damaged function or devise some alternative functional adaptation which will circumvent memory difficulties. Belief in the restitution of memory function has its origins in the idea that weak memory is analogous to a weak muscle and that an impaired memory can therefore be improved through repeated use. In a survey of occupational therapists (Harris & Sunderland, 1981), many of the respondents thought that memory could be improved by simple repetitive practice and this view undoubtedly influenced these therapists' approach to memory therapy. Furthermore, the increasing availability of inexpensive personal computers has seen the development of software packages that allow patients to engage in repetitive and lengthy memory drills, freeing the therapist from tedious supervision, and allowing the patient greater autonomy in the therapeutic process.

Given the above advantages, it is a pity that there is such little evidence to show that repetitive practice leads to any significant improvement in memory. Only the study of Ethier et al. (1989) reports *on-task* improvements and the issue of generalisation is not examined. Prigatano et al. (1984) put a group of head-injured amnesics through a 6-month remediation programme that included repeated practice on several memory tasks. The programme did produce modest improvements with the WMS subtest scores being about 1 point higher than at the outset of training. As Schacter and Glisky (1986) point out, this represents an improvement rate of 1/625th of an item per hour of practice—not a cost-effective proposition in any health organisation with low staff–patient ratios. From their review of memory training packages, Bradley, Welch and Skilbeck (1993) conclude "that there is little evidence of effectiveness in enhancing scores on untrained memory tasks or of improved functional memory". However, one should not overlook the possibility that improvements may occur that are not detected by psychometric measures. Bradley et al. (1991) got quite convincing reports from patients and relatives of improved everyday memory despite no evidence of memory impairment on test scores.

Although the possible benefits of repetitive practice may not have been fully researched (e.g. use of repetitive practice during intitial recovery stage), the study of Prigatano et al. (1984), along with others providing similar results (e.g. Godfrey & Knight, 1985), indicate that memory does not improve through simple repetitive practice. Repetition will only improve matters if it leads the patient to devise better ways of remembering information. This point is illustrated by Ericsson and Chase (1980), who report that a student, through repetitive practice, was able to increase his digit span to 80! However, when given digit span using letters, his performance dropped to within normal limits (i.e. 7 ± 2). The student's memory had not improved generally but he had, through practice, incorporated a specific strategy for remembering numbers. For this reason, the preferred approach to memory remediation must be one in which functional adaptation is the primary aim (Miller, 1984).

External Memory Aids

Memory prostheses, or external memory aids, fall into two categories: environmental and personal. Environmental memory aids include sign-posts, noticeboards, arrows, calendars, colour-coded areas and Twenty-Four Hour Reality Orientation Therapy. Personal memory aids are suitable for the more moderately impaired patient who has insight into their memory loss (although, see Sohlberg & Mateer, 1989b, for a successful application of external memory aids in a case of severe memory disorder using a behavioural training procedure). Personal memory aids must achieve two things to be effective. First, information must be stored in a suitable and convenient form and, secondly, they must cue the person to retrieve information at the right place and time. Suitable storage aids include timetables, diaries, notebooks and lists. A diary or filofax is a more comprehensive, and arguably more normal, storage aid than a timetable, but it does not cue the patient and the patient may forget to use it. A cueing device, such as a buzzer, may therefore be required as well. However, in our experience, several memory-disordered patients have successfully learnt to use diaries without the need for a cueing device, because they carry them around constantly and therefore the diary itself also acts as the cue. Modern technology has produced electronic memory aids which are, in effect, small hand-held microcomputers capable of storing and retrieving information and incorporating an alarm to remind the person that an appointment is due. A typical device will store names, telephone numbers, etc., as well as acting as a diary and automatically cueing the person to do a particular task. Generally, these devices are only suitable for more mildly impaired patients. A variant of this is a device for reminding patients to take pills. Many amnesic patients have epileptic complications and this kind of device can be useful in helping them to remember to take their anticonvulsive medication.

In sum, external memory aids do have the potential for storing information, for helping patients get to the right place at the right time, and they therefore have an important role to play in the management of many patients. The second way of approaching functional adaptation is to utilise the patient's residual or preserved capabilities. The first of these we can call *elaborative encoding strategies*.

Elaborative Encoding Strategies

One example of this approach is called the PQRST technique (Robinson, 1970). Each of the letters stands for a stage in the learning process: P =

preview, Q = question, R = read, S = state and T = test. The subject briefly previews the material to be learned in order to grasp the main theme. He or she then asks key questions about the text. The script is then read thoroughly with the aim of answering the questions. The information derived from this is then rehearsed. Finally, the subject has to test him or herself on the questions. The PQRST technique also significantly increases study time, which presumably affords more elaborate encoding of the information. Following an earlier study by Glasgow, Zeiss, Barrera and Lewinsohn (1977), Wilson (1982) reports that a patient of hers became quite efficient at using the PQRST technique, although retention of what had been learned was not very good a day later. Similarly, Davidoff, Butters, Gerstmann et al. (1984) found that short-term retention of a passage could be improved in Korsakoff patients by ensuring more elaborate encoding, but longer-term performance was not improved.

Imagery

The facilitatory effects of mental imagery upon memory have been known since at least the time of the ancient Greeks, but the first attempt to examine the ability of amnesic patients to benefit from the use of mental imagery did not appear in the literature until Patten (1972) anecdotally reported his work with a small number of memory-impaired cases. He taught patients to use the "peg" method, which involved first teaching them a list of peg words, each of which could then be attached to the to-be-remembered word by forming a mental image connecting the two words. Thus, if the peg word was "bun" and the to-be-remembered word was "bacon", the subject was taught to form the mental image of a bun with a slice of bacon in it. When he wanted to recall the word, he first had to recall the peg word, and this would bring to mind the image and hence the word to be remembered. Patten reported that several patients were able to acquire and use this method, but noted that severity and lack of insight limited its effectiveness.

Nevertheless, several subsequent reports have clearly demonstrated that amnesic patients can at least form mental images, even though not all studies report a facilitatory effect. Thus, Kapur (1978) argued that while Korsakoff patients seemed capable of "reading off" images, they were poor at utilising them, and Baddeley and Warrington (1973) reported that their patients were able to form mental images but, despite this, their memory performance did not improve. Complexity of the memory task may have caused this result because Cermak (1975) did find improved recall and recognition performance in Korsakoff patients on a simpler mental imagery task, although performance did not reach the level of the control group. However, a subsequent study showed that imagery improved the memory of S.S. (post-HSE) to a level similar to controls.

Howes (1983) also found that Korsakoff patients show enhanced performance with imagery, the effect being stronger with supplied rather than self-generated images, and Gianutsos (1981) reported that a post-HSE patient showed modest improvements with imagery.

Other researchers have noted complete failure in using imagery to promote amnesic memory performance. Cutting (1978), for example, failed to find any facilitatory effect of imagery upon memory performance in his WKS group, although the opportunity for learning, which is known to proceed slowly in these patients, may not have been sufficient enough for the effect to become apparent. Similarly, Jones (1974) failed to find an effect in H.M., but again only a few learning trials were given. Our own patients, who comprise both diencephalic and bilateral medial temporal lobe amnesics, do show improved recall with both supplied and self-generated imagery, but we have shown that a large number of trials is required to produce this effect (Leng & Parkin, 1988b). However, instructions to use imagery can produce far more dramatic improvements in some memory-impaired patients (e.g. case J.B. and case L.E.).

Heinrichs (1989) reports a fairly spectacular failure to observe preserved learning in a WKS patient. The study was based on previous work by Kovner and his associates (Kovner, Mattis & Goldmeier, 1983; Kovner, Mattis & Pass, 1985), in which some amnesics were shown to be capable of recalling large amounts of verbal information when learning involved an elaborate, imagery-laden narrative. Heinrichs (1989) followed a similar procedure and, across 30 learning sessions, showed a modest increase in his subject's recall by the end of each session. However, there was no evidence of transfer across sessions with initial recall of the items being zero at the commencement of every training session. Discussing his failure, Heinrichs suggests that previous successes with the technique may have arisen because the patients used were only mildly amnesic. Kovner et al., for example, used patients with MQs of 100 and 83, whereas Heinrich's patient had an MQ of 63. This study may therefore highlight the pitfalls of research that does not adhere to a rigorous definition of amnesia (Squire & Shimamura, 1986).

There can be no doubt that, when instructed to do so, many amnesic patients show a marked improvement on memory tasks when instructed to use various elaborative encoding strategies when attempting text recall or paired-associate learning. But these apparent advantages are undermined by two serious problems. First, there are few recorded instances of patients using elaborative strategies spontaneously. This problem arises because, in order to make use of an elaborative strategy, a patient must remember that they have a strategy available. A second problem is that elaborative strategies, particularly those involving imagery, have little practical value. The *method of loci* is a visuo-spatial mnemonic which, when used by amnesics, can promote good levels of recall. Often, the technique is used to learn items such as a short shopping list. However, one is bound to ask why not just write it down? Thus the use of imagery may show the memory-impaired patient that they can, under certain circumstances, remember more effectively, but the practical value of these techniques may be rather restricted.

Spaced Retrieval

An alternative approach is to try and optimise the conditions under which a patient utilises their own spontaneous learning strategies. One technique is *spaced retrieval*, in which learning is shown to improve as the interval between learning and retrieving an item of information is gradually increased. This is illustrated by a study reported by Landauer and Bjork (1978). Normal subjects were given a continuous paired-associate learning test, which involved being presented with a forename followed by a surname during the learning phase, and then having to produce the surname in response to the forename in the recall phase. For each of the names, there was an initial study trial and this was followed by three tests, but the timing of the tests was varied. Under the uniform condition, an equal number of study trials of other names separated each of the three tests, whereas under the expanding condition an increasingly larger number of study trials intervened. Maximum benefits occurred under the expanding conditon.

In a pilot study, Schacter, Rich and Stampp (1985) examined the performance of two mild amnesic patients on a spaced retrieval task. Both showed the expanding condition effect, in common with Landauer and Bjork's (1978) normal subjects, but only when they were explicitly instructed to use the spaced retrieval technique. Their performance returned to baseline level on subsequent sessions in which no explicit instructions were given to use the spaced retrieval technique. In a second experiment, four patients—two with mild memory problems and two with severe deficits—underwent four study phases each involving memory for faces. Phase one (baseline) involved the subject remembering a characteristic of a face with a cue being given if recall failed. Phase two consisted of an expanding spaced retrieval condition, using memory for characteristics of faces as before. In phase three, the subject was given self-cued training, and prompts to initiate spaced retrieval were gradually faded. The final phase was essentially the same as the baseline phase. A comparison of the baseline and final assessment showed that spaced retrieval had improved the patients' performance. However, because the study employed only the expanding spaced retrieval condition, it is possible, as the authors concede, that the patients were benefiting just from repetition of items. Two of the patients showed evidence of spontaneously using the spaced retrieval technique after training, whereas the other two continued to require some prompts. However, this did not seem to depend upon severity of amnesia, because one of the severe amnesics showed the spontaneous use of the technique and one mild case did not.

Memory Manuals

Recently, a number of psychologists have produced "memory manuals". Kapur's (1989) *Wessex memory manual*, now known as *Managing your memory*, is aimed at patients suffering from memory problems, rather than those caring for them, and therefore it is likely to be of use to people with milder memory problems. The manual addresses various typical day-to-day difficulties likely to be encountered, such as remembering people's names, where you have to put things, when to do something, what people tell you, how to get somewhere, and what you are reading. General strategies advocated by Kapur include ensuring that better attention is paid at the time of input of information, rehearsing information, using memory aids and trying to recall information logically (e.g. carrying out an alphabetical search if you cannot remember a person's name). Patients with milder memory problems who have insight will find many ideas which they can try out. Beaulieu, Knipe, Selley and Sunderland (1990) have produced the *Burden memory group manual*. This is primarily for patients attending their memory group but its contents are also of general use to the mild amnesic sufferer. Finally, Wilson has produced a helpful leaflet on various strategies for overcoming memory problems.

Memory Groups

One popular approach to memory remediation is the *memory group*. This involves a regular meeting between a therapist and a group of memory-disordered patients. The aim of these groups is to illustrate various ways of improving memory and get the patients to try and use them. Wilson and Moffat (1984) describe the kinds of tasks they used in memory groups. At the Rivermead Rehabilitation Centre, a group comprising 4–6 patients met on a daily basis for 3 weeks. The aim was to complete at least one memory exercise in each session from each of three main areas: general memory exercises (e.g. memory games and tests), external memory aids and internal memory strategies. A wide range of exercises was used including reality orientation therapy, everyday exercises (e.g. remembering the location of a belonging), visual imagery training, initial letter cues, alphabetic cues and the PQRST method.

Wilson and Moffat also describe the running of a less intensive memory group in Birmingham. In contrast, this group comprised six head-injured patients, with a further six acting as a control group. The group met once per week for 15 weeks, each session lasting approximately 90 min. The main activities were similar to the Rivermead groups, with the emphasis being placed upon external aids, first-letter mnemonics and visual imagery methods. Wilson and Moffat provide a discussion of the problems in evaluating memory groups, and they give some guidelines as to how this might be done. But they note the lack of published research in this area, with most studies having been carried out with individual patients or using specific methods (e.g. Wilson, 1987), and they do not apparently provide any data on their own memory groups.

Memory groups are clearly limited by the value of the various strategies that get taught during each session. As we have seen, the practical value of many of these strategies is rather limited, and therefore this may question the value of running memory groups. However, simply showing patients that they can improve their memories, even under artificial conditions, has its benefits. Evans and Wilson (1992), for example, have recently shown reduced depression and anxiety in amnesic patients who regularly attend a memory group. Moreover, these groups provide an important regular contact between patient, carer and therapist, which would be unlikely to occur in other circumstances.

Exploiting Residual Learning Ability

At many points in this book, we have emphasised that amnesic patients often show a range of residual learning abilities. So far in this chapter, the various approaches to functional adaptation have aimed at devising ways in which patients can use damaged function more effectively. A radical alternative is to concentrate on residual learning abilities as the basis of remediation, the idea being that these preserved memory processes could be harnessed in some way to substitute for impaired memory processes. This approach is very new and, to date, has only been explored in one remedial technique—vanishing cues.

Vanishing Cues

The "vanishing cues" (VC) method was developed by Glisky, Schacter and Tulving (1986a; 1986b). The method works by first presenting the patient with a definition of a computer term. If the patient fails to give the correct answer, he or she is given the first letter of it, followed by subsequent letters as necessary until he or she responds correctly. On subsequent learning trials, the patient is again presented with the definition, but with one less letter cue than was required for correct responding on the previous trial. The learning procedure continues until the patient is able to respond correctly without any cues. VC has been found by Glisky et al. to produce faster learning and better retention than learning by anticipation (i.e. no cues given). Glisky and co-workers also showed that densely amnesic patients were able to learn computer-based vocabulary and to carry out elementary computer operations such as loading and storing programs. They focused upon computer-related information because of its practical value. One patient returned to work as a computer operator, but even in less ambitious cases one could argue in favour of training a patient to use word processing or to use micro-computers as prosthetic aids or for recreational purposes.

We have designed our own computer-based VC program to teach patients computer-related vocabulary. The program consists of a pre-test, followed by training sessions and then a post-test. The pre- and post-tests measure the ability of the patient to recall and then recognise the answers to 30 definitions of computer terms. The training sessions consist either of anticipation learning or 15 items of information to be learnt in both conditions. Leng, Copello and Sayegh (1991) found that an amnesic patient learned successfully with VC and anticipation learning, but that the former was quicker. After 1 month, the patient had retained 87% of the information learned by each method, indicating that the main advantage in VC is faster learning rather than superior retention. Glisky et al. report that their patients showed little evidence of generalisation but our patient showed good retention when definitions were presented in a different surface form and reworded slightly. One should also note that, after an initial lack of optimism, our patient became highly motivated using the VC technique. Partly, this is because the patient never fails. He is simply given as much help as he needs to produce the response. In this way, the method is actually highly rewarding for the patient who is able not only to experience repeated success but also improvement over trials. He was also able to make use of the acquired knowledge outside of the laboratory in that he produced a series of articles about the history of motorcycles.

Glisky and her colleagues have argued that VC depends on intact priming mechanisms (see Chapter 3), but Wilson and Patterson (1990) query this. They argue that VC is just another instance of "backward chaining". Chaining is a behaviour modification procedure used a lot with mentally handicapped people and has been used successfully by Giles and Morgan (1989) to improve personal hygiene in a post-HSE patient. Chaining a sequence of steps (e.g. the procedure for putting on a hearing aid) is taught gradually, either by presenting new steps once earlier steps have been learned (forward chaining) or demonstrating the entire sequence and then gradually reducing the number of steps demonstrated beginning with the last (backward chaining).

VC does bear a similarity to backward chaining but this comparison may well be superficial. First of all, the inflexible nature of VC learning does not appear to have a parallel in chaining, in that learning achieved by the latter does not appear to be hyper-specific, in that more generalisation seems to occur. Secondly, VC is essentially a perceptual learning phenomenon with close links to current theoretical and experimental evidence concerning priming. Chaining, in contrast, is an atheoretical learning principle which applies to the learning of motor sequences.

Long-term Prospects

Despite the flurry of interest in non-interventive memory remediation, progress has not been great. Much initial enthusiasm for the use of elaborative strategies has waned with the realisation that patients will rarely implement these strategies spontaneously. The availability of inexpensive personal computers has resulted in the increasing use of software packages in memory rehabilitation. However, much of this software consists of memory "games" as opposed to proper rehabilitation packages. Part of the problem is the lack of an appropriate theory-driven approach to memory rehabilitation which, when available, will enable clinicians to choose training tasks that are most likely to be effective.

On the positive side, interest in memory rehabilitation has drawn attention to the long-term plight of amnesic patients and doubtless encouraged a more sensible attitude to the long-term management of patients. On the research side, we are most enthusiastic about remediation procedures such as vanishing cues, because these build on intact functions rather than on attempts to boost impaired functions. Vanishing cues is one instance of success in this area, but it has the disadvantage of being domain-specific.[1] It remains possible, however, that more generalised benefits might accrue from patients becoming more reliant on residual memory abilities. In a recent study, Gardiner and Parkin (1990) have shown that effective recognition can, under certain circumstances, be achieved on the basis of memory processes resembling those preserved in amnesic subjects. It may therefore be possible that training strategies involving implicit memory tasks might have some benefits for patients by making them more reliant on residual learning abilities.

One final point is that remediation procedures using computer packages might become more "intelligent". In a recent study, Aldrich (1990) has pointed out that computer-based memory remediation packages take no account of the user's initial status, as measured by psychometric measures, and the patient's rate of progress. She advocates an "intelligent tutoring system approach" to memory remediation in which psychometric factors and on-line measures of performance mediate the characteristics of the training programme.

[1] Since this book was written, we have carried a more extensive investigation of the VC technique and we have been unable to show that this technique confers any general advantage in learning relative to a standard rote learning procedure (Aldrich, submitted; Hunkin & Parkin, submitted). It may be the case, therefore, that the kind of success reported by Glisky et al. can only be expected in certain cases, although, at present, it is not clear from our research what the relevant factors might be.

References

Akiguchi, I., Tadashi, I., Hidehiko, N., Udaka, F., Matsubayashi, K., Fukuyama, H. & Kameyama, M. (1987). Acute-onset amnesic syndrome with localized infarct on the dominant side: Comparison between anteromedial thalamic lesion and posterior cerebral artery territory lesion. *Japanese Journal of Medicine, 26*, 15–20.

Albert, M. A., Butters, N. & Levin, J. A. (1979). Temporal gradients in the retrograde amnesia of patients with alcoholic Korsakoff's disease. *Archives of Neurology, 36*, 211–216.

Aldrich, F. K. (1990). *A tutoring system for people with amnesia*. Unpublished MSc thesis, University of Sussex.

Aldrich, F.K. (submitted). Vanishing cues versus serial anticipation learning following head injury: A case study.

Aldrich, F. K. & Wilson, B. A. (1991). Rivermead Behavioural Memory Tests for Children (RBMT-C): A preliminary evaluation. *British Journal of Clinical Psychology, 30*, 161–168.

Alexander, M. P. & Freedman, M. (1984). Amnesia after anterior communicating artery aneurysm rupture. *Neurology, 34*, 752–759.

Andrews, E., Poser, C. M. & Kessler, M. (1982). Retrograde amnesia for forty years. *Cortex, 18*, 441–458.

Assal, P. G., Probst, A., Zander, E. & Rabinowicz, T. (1976). Syndrome amnesique par infiltration tumorale. *Archives Suisses de Neurologie, Neurochirurgie et de Psychiatrie, 119*, 317–324.

Atkinson, R. C. & Shiffrin, R. M. (1968). Human memory: A proposed system and its control processes. In K. W. Spence & J. T. Spence (Eds), *The psychology of learning and motivation*, Vol. 2. New York: Academic Press.

Auer, R. N., Jensen, M. L. & Whishaw, I. Q. (1989). Neurobehavioural deficit due to ischemic brain damage limited to half of the CA1 sector of the hippocampus. *Journal of Neuroscience, 9*, 1641–1647.

Baddeley, A. D. (1986). *Working memory*. Oxford: Oxford University Press.

Baddeley, A. D. & Hitch, G. J. (1974). Working memory. In G. A. Bower (Ed.), *The psychology of learning and motivation*, Vol. 8, pp. 47–90. New York: Academic Press.

Baddeley, A. D. & Warrington, E. K. (1970). Amnesia and the distinction between long- and short-term memory. *Journal of Verbal Learning and Verbal Behavior, 9*, 178–189.

Baddeley, A. D. & Warrington, E. K. (1973). Memory coding and amnesia. *Neuropsychologia, 11*, 159–165.

Baddeley, A. D. & Wilson, B. A. (1986). Amnesia, autobiographical memory and confabulation. In D. Rubin (Ed.), *Autobiographical memory*. New York: Cambridge University Press.

Bakheit, A. M. O., Kennedy, P. G. E. & Behan, P. O. (1990). Paraneoplastic limbic encephalitis: Clinico-pathological correlations. *Journal of Neurology, Neurosurgery and Psychiatry, 53*, 1084–1088.

Barbizet, J. (1970). *Human memory and its pathology*. San Francisco: W. H. Freeman.

Barbizet, J., Degos, J. D., Louarn, F., Nguyen, J. P. & Mas, J. L. (1981). Amnesie par lesion ischemique bi-thalamique. *Revue Neurologique, 137*, 415–424.

Baringer, J. R. (1978). Herpes simplex virus infections of the nervous system. In P. J. Vinken & G. W. Bruyn (Eds), *Handbook of clinical neurology*, Vol. 34. Amsterdam: North-Holland.

Beardsall, L. & Huppert, F. A. (1989). A comparison of clinical psychometric and behavioural memory tests: Findings from a community study of dementia. *International Journal of Geriatric Psychiatry, 6*, 295–306.

Beatty, W. W., Bailly, R. C. & Fisher, L. (1988). Korsakoff-like amnesic syndrome in a patient with anorexia and vomiting. *International Journal of Clinical Neuropsychology, 11*, 55–65.

Beatty, W. W., Salmon, D. P., Bernstein, N. & Butters, N. (1987a). Remote memory in a patient with amnesia due to hypoxia. *Psychological Medicine, 17*, 657–665.

Beatty, W. W., Salmon, D. P., Bernstein, N., Martone, M., Lyon, L. & Butters, N. (1987b). Procedural learning in a patient with amnesia due to hypoxia. *Brain and Cognition, 6*, 386–402.

Beaufils, B., Ramirez, D. & Feline, A. (1988). Malnutrition psychogene ayant entraine une encephalopathie de Gayet-Wernicke avec nevrite optique retrobulbaire chez une schizophrene deficitaire. *Annales Medicopsychologiques, 146*, 471–475.

Beaulieu, K., Knipe, C., Selley, S. & Sunderland, A. (1990). *Burden memory group manual*.

Becker, J. T., Furman, J. M. R., Panisset, M. & Smith, C. (1990). Characteristics of the memory loss of a patient with Wernicke-Korsakoff's syndrome without alcoholism. *Neuropsychologia, 23*, 171–179.

Bennett-Levy, J. & Powell, G. E. (1980). The subjective memory questionnaire (SMQ): An investigation into the self-reporting of real-life memory skills. *British Journal of Social and Clinical Psychology, 19*, 177–183.

Benson, D. F. & Geschwind, N. (1968). Shrinking retrograde amnesia. *Journal of Neurology, Neurosurgery and Psychiatry, 30*, 539–544.

Benson, D. F., Marsden, C. D. & Meadows, J. C. (1974). The amnesic syndrome of posterior cerebral artery occlusion. *Acta Neurologica Scandinavica, 50*, 133–145.

Benson, D. F. & Stuss, D. T. (1990). Frontal lobe influences on delusions. *Schizophrenia Bulletin, 16*, 403–411.

Berlyne, N. (1972). Confabulation. *British Journal of Psychiatry, 120*, 31–39.

Berlyne, N. & Strachan, M. (1968). Neuropsychiatric sequelae of attempted hanging. *British Journal of Psychiatry, 114*, 411–422.

Berman, K. F., Zec, R. F. & Weinberger, D. R. (1986). Physiological dysfunction of dorsolateral prefrontal cortex in schizophrenia. II. Role of neuroleptic treatment, attention, and mental effort. *Archives of General Psychiatry, 43*, 126–135.

Bernard, L. C. (1990). Prospects of faking believable memory deficits on neuropsychological tests and the use of incentives in simulation research. *Journal of Clinical and Experimental Neuropsychology, 12*, 715–728.

Bernard, L. C. & Fowler, W. (1990). Assessing the validity of memory complaints: Performance of brain-damaged and normal individuals on Rey's task to detect malingering. *Journal of Clinical Psychology, 46*, 432–436.

Beukelman, D. R., Flowers, C. R. & Swanson, P. D. (1980). Cerebral disconnection associated with anterior communicating artery aneurysm: Implications for evaluation of symptoms. *Archives of Physical Medicine and Rehabilitation, 61*, 18–23.

Bigler, E. D. (1988). Frontal lobe damage and neuropsychological assessment. *Archives of Clinical Neuropsychology, 3*, 279–297.

Bigler, E. D. & Alfano, M. (1988). Anoxic encephalopathy: Neuroradiological and neuropsychological findings. *Archives of Clinical Neuropsychology, 3*, 383–396.

Binder, L. M. & Pankratz, L. (1987). Neuropsychological evidence of a facticious memory complaint. *Journal of Clincal and Experimental Neuropsychology, 9*, 167–171.

Blass, J. P. & Gibson, G. E. (1979). Genetic factors in Wernicke-Korsakoff syndrome. *Alcohol Clinical Experimental Research, 3*, 126–134.

Bogousslavsky, J., Regli, F. & Uske, A. (1988). Thalamic infarcts: Clinical syndromes, etiology, and prognosis. *Neurology, 38*, 837–848.

Borrini, G., Dall'Ora, P., Della Sala, S., Marinelli, L. & Spinnler, H. (1989). Autobiographical memory: Sensitivity to age and education of a standardized enquiry. *Psychological Medicine, 19*, 215–224.

Bowers, D., Verafaellie, M., Valenstein, E. & Heilman, K. M. (1988). Impaired acquisition of temporal information in retrosplenial amnesia. *Brain and Cognition, 8*, 47–66.

Bradley, V. A., Welch, J. L. & Skilbeck, C. E. (1993). *Cognitive retraining using microcomputers*. Hove: Lawrence Erlbaum Associates Ltd.

Brierley, J. B., Corsellis, J. A. N., Hierons, R. & Nevin, S. (1960). Subacute encephalitis of later adult life mainly affecting the limbic areas. *Brain, 83*, 357–368.

Broadbent, D. E., Cooper, P. E., Fitzgerald, P. & Parkes, K. R. (1982). Cognitive Failures Questionnaire (CFQ). *British Journal of Clinical Psychology, 21*, 1–16.

Brooks, D. N. & Baddeley, A. D. (1976). What can amnesic patients learn? *Neuropsychologia, 14*, 111–112.

Brown, G. G., Kieran, S. & Patel, S. (1989). Memory functioning following a left medial thalamic hematoma. *Journal of Clinical and Experimental Neuropsychology, 11*, 206–218.

Brown, J. (1958). Some tests of the decay theory of immediate memory. *Quarterly Journal of Experimental Psychology, 10*, 12–21.

Bryer, J. B., Heck, E. T. & Reams, S. H. (1988). Neuropsychological sequelae of carbon monoxide toxicity at eleven-year follow-up. *Clinical Neuropsychologist, 2*, 221–227.

Buschke, H. (1973). Selective reminding for analysis of memory and learning. *Journal of Verbal Learning and Verbal Behavior, 12*, 543–550.

Butters, N. (1984). Alcoholic Korsakoff's syndrome: An update. *Seminars in Neurology, 4*, 226–244.

Butters, N. (1985). Alcoholic Korsakoff's syndrome: Some unresolved issues concerning aetiology, neuropathology, and cognitive deficits. *Journal of Experimental and Cinical Neuropsychology, 7*, 181–210.

Butters, N. & Cermak, L. S. (1980). *Alcoholic Korsakoff's syndrome: An information processing approach*. New York: Academic Press.

Butters, N., Granholm, E., Salmon, D. P., Grant, I. & Wolfe, J. (1987). Episodic and semantic memory: A comparison of amnesic and demented patients. *Journal of Clinical and Experimental Neuropsychology, 9*, 479–497.

Butters, N., Grant, I., Haxby, J., Judd, L. L., Martin, A., McClelland, J., Pequegnat, W., Schacter, D. & Stover, E. (1990). Assessment of AIDS-related cognitive changes: Recommendations of the NIMH Workshop on neuropsychological assessment approaches. *Journal of Clinical and Experimental Neuropsychology, 12*, 963–978.

Butters, N., Miliotis, P., Albert, M. S. & Sax, D. S. (1984). Memory assessment: Evidence of the heterogeneity of amnesic symptoms. *Advances in Clinical Neuropsychology, 1*, 127–159.

Butters, N., Wolfe, J., Granholm, E. & Martone, M. (1986). An assessment of verbal recall, recognition, and fluency abilities in patients with Huntington's disease. *Cortex, 22, 11–32.*

Carr, A. C. (1982). Memory deficit after fornix transection. *Neuropsychologia, 20*, 95–98.

Caramazza, A. & Badecker, W. (1991). Clinical syndromes are not God's gift to cognitive neuropsychology: A reply to a rebuttal to an answer to a response to the case against syndrome-based research. *Brain and Cognition, 16*, 211–227.

Cermak, L. S. (1975). Imagery as an aid to retrieval for Korsakoff patients. *Cortex, 11*, 163–169.

Cermak, L. S. (1976). The encoding capacity of a patient with amnesia due to encephalitis. *Neuropsychologia, 14*, 311–326.

Cermak, L. S., Beale, L. & Baker, E. (1978). Alcoholic Korsakoff patients' retrieval from semantic memory. *Brain and Language, 5*, 215–226.

Cermak, L. S., Bleich, R. P. & Blackford, S. P. (1988). Deficits in the implicit retention of new associations by alcoholic Korsakoff patients. *Brain and Cognition, 7*, 312–323.

Cermak, L. S., Lewis, R., Butters, N. & Goodglass, H. (1973). Role of verbal mediation in the performance of motor skills by Korsakoff patients. *Perception and Motor Skills, 37*, 259–262.

Cermak, L. S. & O'Connor, M. (1983). The anterograde and retrograde retrieval ability of a patient with amnesia due to encephalitis. *Neuropsychologia, 21*, 213–234.

Cermak, L. S., O'Connor, M. & Talbot, N. (1986). The semantic biasing of alcoholic Korsakoff patients. *Journal of Clinical and Experimental Neuropsychology, 8*, 543–555.

Cermak, L. S., Talbot, N., Chandler, K. & Wolbarst, L. R. (1985). The perceptual priming phenomenon in amnesia. *Neuropsychologia, 23*, 615–622.

Cermak, L. S., Verfaellie, M., Milberg, W., Letourneau, L. & Blackford, S. (1991). A further analysis of perceptual identification priming in alcoholic Korsakoff patients. *Neuropsychologia, 29*, 725–736.

Choi, D., Sudarsky, L., Schacter, S., Biber, M. & Burke, P. (1983). Medial thalamic hemorrhage with amnesia. *Archives of Neurology, 40*, 611–613.

Claparede, E. (1911). Recognition et moiite. *Archives de Psychologie Genève, 11*, 79–90.

Cohen, N. J. (1984). Preserved learning capacity in amnesia: Evidence for multiple memory systems. In L. R. Squire & N. Butters (Eds), *The neuropsychology of memory*. New York: Guilford Press.

Cohen, N. J. & Squire, L. R. (1980). Preserved learning and retention of pattern-analyzing skill in amnesia: Dissociation of knowing how and knowing that. *Science, 210*, 207–210.

Cohen, N. J. & Squire, L. R. (1981). Retrograde amnesia and remote memory impairment. *Neuropsychologia, 19*, 337–356.

Conrad, K. (1953). Iber einen fall von "Minuten-Gedachtnis". Beitrag zum problem des amnestischen symptomenkomplexes. *Archiv für Psychiatrie und Zeitschrift Neurologie, 190*, 471–502.

Conway, M. (1990). *Autobiographical memory*. Milton Keynes: Open University Press.

Coons, P. M., Milstein, V. & Marley, C. (1982). EEG studies of two multiple personalities. *Archives of General Psychiatry, 39*, 823–825.

Corkin, S. (1968). Acquisition of motor skill after bilateral medial temporal lobe excision. *Neuropsychologia, 6*, 255–265.

Corkin, S. (1982). Some relations between global amnesias and the memory impairments in Alzheimer's disease. In S. Corkin, K. L. Davis, J. H. Growden, E. Usdin & R. J. Wurtman (Eds), *Alzheimer's disease: A report of progress in research into aging*, Vol. 19, pp. 149–164. New York: Raven Press.

Corkin, S. (1984). Lasting consequences of bilateral medial temporal lobectomy: Clinical course and experimental findings in H. M. *Seminars in Neurology, 4*, 249–259.

Corkin, S., Cohen, N. J., Sullivan, E. V., Clegg, R. A. & Rosen, T. J. (1985). Analyses of global memory impairments of different etiologies. *Annals of the New York Academy of Sciences, 444*, 10–40.

Corsi, P. S. (1972). *Human memory and the medial temporal lobe of the brain*. Unpublished doctoral dissertation, McGill University.

Coughlan, A. & Hollows, S. E. (1985). *Adult Memory and Information Processing Battery*. Available from the first author, St James Hospital, Leeds, U.K.

Craik, F. I. M. & Lockhart, R. S. (1972). Levels of processing: A framework for memory research. *Journal of Verbal Learning and Verbal Behavior, 11*, 671–684.

Cramon, D. Y. V., Hebel, N. & Schuri, U. (1985). A contribution to the anatomical basis of thalamic amnesia. *Brain, 108*, 993–1008.

Crawford, J. R., Allan, K. M., Cochrane, R. H. B. & Parker, D. M. (1990). Assessing the validity of NART-estimated premorbid IQ's in the individual case. *British Journal of Clinical Psychology, 29*, 435–436.

Crawford, J. R., Stewart, L. E. & Moore, J. W. (1989). Demonstration of savings on the AVLT and development of a parallel form. *Journal of Clinical and Experimental Neuropsychology, 11*, 975–981.

Croen, K. D., Ostrove, J. M., Dragovic, L. J., Smialek, J. E. & Straus, S. E. (1987). Latent herpes simplex virus in human trigeminal ganglia. *New England Journal of Medicine, 317*, 23.

Crook, T. H., Youngjohn, J. R. & Larrabee, G. J. (1990). The misplaced objects test: A measure of everyday visual memory. *Journal of Clinical and Experimental Neuropsychology, 12*, 819–833.

Crovitz, H. F., Harvey, M. T. & McClanahan, S. (1981). Hidden memory: A rapid method for the study of amnesia using perceptual learning. *Cortex, 17*, 273–278.

Crovitz, H. F. & Schiffman, H. (1974). Frequency of episodic memories as a function of their age. *Bulletin of the Psychonomic Society, 4*, 517–518.

Crowell, R. M. & Morawetz, R. (1977). The anterior communicating artery has significant branches. *Stroke, 8*, 272–273.

Cummings, J. L., Tomiyasu, K., Read, S. & Benson, F. (1984). Amnesia with hippocampal lesions after cardiopulmonary arrest. *Neurology, 34*, 679–681.

Cutting, J. (1978). The relationship between Korsakoff's Syndrome and alcoholic dementia. *British Journal of Psychiatry, 132*, 240–251.

Czechmanek, K. (1954). Ein Korsahowsyndrom bei traumatisch er Schadigung des Hypothalamus durch Granatasplitter. *Nervenarzt, 25*, 158–161.

Dall'Ora, P., Della Sala, S. & Spinnler, H. (1989). Autobiographical memory: Its impairment in amnesic syndromes. *Cortex, 25*, 197–217.

Damasio, A. R., Eslinger, P. J., Damasio, H., Van Hoesen, G. W. & Cornell, S. (1985). Multi-modal amnesic syndrome following bilateral temporal and basal forebrain lesions. *Archives of Neurology, 42*, 252–259.

Damasio, A. R. & Van Hoesen, G. W. (1985). The limbic system and the localisation of herpes simplex encephalitis. *Journal of Neurology, Neurosurgery and Psychiatry, 48*, 297–301.

Davidoff, D. A., Butters, N., Gerstman, L. J., Zurif, E., Paul, I. H. & Mattis, S. (1984). Affective/motivational factors in the recall of prose passages by alcoholic Korsakoff patients. *Alcohol, 1*, 63–69.

Davis, L. E. & Johnson, R. T. (1979). An explanation for the localization of herpes simplex encephalitis? *Annals of Neurology, 5*, 2–5.

De Jong, R. N., Itabashi, H. H. & Olson, J. R. (1969). Memory loss due to hippocampal lesions. *Archives of Neurology, 20*, 339–348.

Delbecq-Derouesne, J., Beauvois, M. F. & Shallice, T. (1990). Preserved recall versus impaired recognition. *Brain, 113*, 1045–1074.

D'Elia, L., Satz, P. & Schretlen, D. (1989). Wechsler Memory Scale: A critical appraisal of the normative studies. *Journal of Clinical and Experimental Neuropsychology, 11*, 551–568.

Della Sala, S. & Spinnler, H. (1986). "Indifference amnesique" in a case of global amnesia following acute brain hypoxia. *European Neurology, 25*, 98–109.

DeLong, G. R., Bean, S. C. & Brown, F. R. (1981). Acquired reversible autistic syndrome in acute encephalopathic illness in children. *Archives of Neurology, 38*, 191–194.

De Luca, J. & Cicerone, K. D. (1991). Confabulation following aneurysm of the anterior communicating artery. *Cortex, 17*, 417–424.

De Renzi, E., Liotti, M. & Nichelli, P. (1987). Semantic amnesia with preservation of autobiographic memory: A case report. *Cortex, 23*, 575–597.

De Wardener, H. E. & Lennox, B. (1947). Cerebral beri-beri. *Lancet, 1*, 11.

Dricker, J., Butters, N., Berman, G., Samuels, I. & Carey, S. (1978). The recognition of and encoding of faces by alcoholic Korsakoff and right hemisphere patients. *Neuropsychologia, 16*, 683–695.

Dunker, R. O. & Harris, A. B. (1976). Surgical anatomy of the proximal anterior cerebral artery. *Journal of Neurosurgery, 44*, 359–367.

Dusoir, H., Kapur, N., Byrnes, D. P., McKinstry, S. & Hoare, R. D. (1990). The role of diencephalic pathology in human memory disorder: Evidence from a penetrating paranasal brain injury. *Brain, 13*, 1695–1706.

Duyckaerts, C., Derouesne, C., Signoret, J. L., Gray, F., Escourolle, R. & Castaigne, P. (1985). Bilateral and limited amygdalohippocampal lesions causing a pure amnesic syndrome. *Annals of Neurology, 18*, 314–319.

Eichenbaum, H., Morton, T. H., Potter, H. & Corkin, S. (1983). Selective olfactory deficits in case H.M. *Brain, 106*, 459–472.

Ellis, A. & Young, A. W. (1989). *Human cognitive neuropsychology*. Hove: Lawrence Erlbaum Associates Ltd.

Erickson, R. C. & Scott, M. L. (1977). Clinical memory testing. *Psychological Bulletin, 84*, 1130–1149.

Ericsson, K. A. & Chase, W. G. (1980). Acquisition of a memory skill. *Science, 208*, 1181–1182.

Eslinger, P. & Damasio, A. R. (1984). Behavioral disturbances associated with rupture of anterior communicating artery aneurysms. *Seminars in Neurology, 4*, 385–389.

Ethier, M., Baribeau, J. M. C. & Braun, C. M. J. (1989). Computer-dispensed cognitive-perceptual training of closed head patients after spontaneous recovery, Study 2: Non-speeded tasks. *Canadian Journal of Rehabilitation, 3*, 7–16.

Evans, J. J. & Wilson, B. A. (1992). A memory group for individuals with brain injury. *Clinical Rehabilitation, 6*, 75–81.

Faris, A. (1972). Wernicke's encephalopathy in uremia. *Neurology, 22*, 1293–1297.

Fensore, C., Lazzarino, L. G., Nappo, A. & Nicolai, A. (1988). Language and memory disturbances from mesencephalothalamic infarcts. *European Neurology, 28*, 51–56.

Ferla, S., Giometto, B., Meneghetti, G. & Schergna, E. (1981). Wernicke-Korsakoff Syndrome after sub-total gastrectomy. *Italian Journal of Neurological Science, 2*, 225–227.

Fisher, C. M. & Adams, R. D. (1958). Transient global amnesia. *Transactions of the American Neurological Association, 83*, 143–146.

Fodor, J. (1983). *The modularity of mind*. Cambridge, Mass.: MIT Press.

Foletti, G., Regli, F. & Assal, G. (1980). Syndrome amnesique d'origine encephalitique. *Revue Médicale de la Suisse Romande, 100*, 1979–1985.

Freed, D. M. & Corkin, S. (1988). Rate of forgetting in HM: 6 month recognition. *Behavioral Neuroscience, 102*, 823–827.

Freed, D. M., Corkin, S. & Cohen, N. J. (1987). Forgetting in HM: A second look. *Neuropsychologia, 25*, 461–471.

Freedman, M. & Cermak, L. S. (1986). Semantic encoding deficits in frontal lobe disease and amnesia. *Brain and Cognition, 5*, 108–114.

Funnell, E. & Sheridan, J. (1992). Categories of knowledge? Unfamiliar aspects of living and non-living things. *Cognitive Neuropsychology, 9*, 135–153.

Gabrieli, J. D. E., Cohen, N. J. & Corkin, S. (1988). The impaired learning of semantic knowledge following bilateral medial temporal-lobe resection. *Brain, 7*, 157–177.

Gabrieli, J. D. E., Milberg, W., Keane, M. M. & Corkin, S. (1990). Intact priming of patterns despite impaired memory. *Neuropsychologia, 28*, 417–427.

Gade, A. (1982). Amnesia after operations on aneurysms of the anterior communicating artery. *Surgical Neurology, 1*, 46–49.

Gade, A. & Mortensen, E. L. (1990). Temporal gradient in the remote memory impairment of amnesic patients with lesions in the basal forebrain. *Neuropsychologia, 28*, 985–1001.

Gaffan, D. & Gaffan, E. A. (1991). Amnesia in man following transection of the fornix. *Brain, 114*, 2611–2618.

Gaffan, E. A., Gaffan, D. & Hodges, J. R. (1991). Amnesia following damage to the left fornix and to other sites. *Brain, 114*, 1297–1313.

Gamper, E. (1928). Zur Frage der Polyencephalitis haemorrhagica der chronisichen Alkoholiker. *Deutsche Zeitschrift für Nervenheilkunde, 102*, 122–129.

Gantt, W. H. & Muncie, W. (1942). Analysis of mental defect in chronic Korsakoff's psychosis by means of the conditioned reflex method. *John Hopkins Hospital Bulletin, 70*, 467–487.

Gardiner, J. & Parkin, A. J. (1990). Attention and recollective experience. *Memory and Cognition, 18*, 579–583.

Gardner, H. (1977). *The shattered mind*. London: Routledge.

Gardner, H., Boller, F., Moreines, J. & Butters, N. (1974). Retrieval information from Korsakoff patients: Effects of categorical cues and reference to task. *Cortex, 12*, 163–175.

Gentilini, M., De Renzi, E. & Crisi, G. (1987). Bilateral paramedian thalamic artery infarcts: Report of eight cases. *Journal of Neurology, Neurosurgery and Psychiatry, 50*, 900–909.

Ghidoni, E., Pattacini, F., Galimberti, D. & Aguzzoli, L. (1989). Lacunar thalamic infarcts and amnesia. *European Neurology, 29*, 13–15 (suppl. 2).

Gianutsos, R. (1981). Training the short and long term verbal recall of a post-encephalitic amnesic. *Journal of Clinical Neuropsychology, 3*, 143–153.

Giles, G. M. & Morgan, J. H. (1989). Training functional skills following herpes simplex encephalitis: A single case study. *Journal of Clinical and Experimental Neuropsychology, 11*, 311–318.

Gillberg, C. (1986). Brief report: Onset at age 14 of a typical autistic syndrome. A case report of a girl with herpes simplex encephalitis. *Journal of Autism and Developmental Disorders, 16*, 369–375.

Gillespie, R. D. (1937). Amnesia. *Archives of Neurology and Psychiatry, 37*, 748–764.

Glasgow, R. E., Zeiss, R. A., Barrera, M. & Lewinsohn, P. M. (1977). Case studies in remediating memory in brain-damaged individuals. *Journal of Clinical Psychology, 33*, 1049–1054.

Glisky, E. L. & Schacter, D. L. (1988). Long-term memory retention of computer learning by patients with memory disorders. *Neuropsychologia, 26*, 173–178.

Glisky, E. L. & Schacter, D. L. (1989). Extending the limits of complex learning in organic amnesia: Computer training in a vocational domain. *Neuropsychologia, 27*, 107–120.

Glisky, E. L., Schacter, D. L. & Tulving, E. (1986a). Learning and retention of computer-related vocabulary in memory-impaired patients: Method of vanishing cues. *Journal of Clinical and Experimental Neuropsychology, 3*, 292–312.

Glisky, E. L., Schacter, D. L. & Tulving, E. (1986b). Computer learning by memory-impaired patients: Acquisition and retention of complex knowledge. *Neuropsychologia, 24*, 313–328.

Glosser, G., Butters, N. & Samuels, I. (1976). Failures in information processing in patients with Korsakoff's Syndrome. *Neuropsychologia, 14*, 327–334.

Godfrey, H. P. D. & Knight, R. G. (1985). Cognitive rehabilitation of memory functioning in amnesic alcoholics. *Journal of Consulting and Clinical Psychology, 53*, 555–557.

Goldberg, T. E., Weinberger, D. R., Pliskin, N. H., Berman, K. F. & Podd, M. H. (1989). Recall memory deficit in schizophrenia. *Schizophrenia Research, 2*, 251–257.

Gollin, E. S. (1960). Developmental studies of visual recognition of incomplete objects. *Perceptual and Motor Skills, 11*, 289–298.

Gomes, F. B., Dujovny, M., Umansky, F., Berman, S. K., Diaz, F. G., Ausman, J. I., Mirchandani, H. G. & Ray, W. J. (1986). Microanatomy of the anterior cerebral artery. *Surgical Neurology, 26*, 129–141.

Gordon, B., Selnes, O. A., Hart, J., Hanley, D. F. & Whiteley, R. J. (1990). Long-term cognitive sequelae of acyclovir-treated herpes simplex encephalitis. *Archives of Neurology, 47*, 646–647.

Graf, P. & Schacter, D. L. (1985). Implicit and explicit memory for new associations in normal and amnesic subjects. *Journal of Experimental Psychology: Learning, Memory and Cognition, 11*, 501–518.

Graf, P., Shimamura, A. P. & Squire, L. R. (1985). Priming across modalities and priming across category levels: Extending the domain of preserved function in amnesia. *Journal of Experimental Psychology: Learning, Memory and Cognition, 11*, 386–396.

Graf, P., Squire, L. R. & Mandler, G. (1984). The information that amnesic patients do not forget. *Journal of Experimental Psychology: Learning, Memory and Cognition, 10*, 164–178.

Graff-Radford, N. R., Eslinger, P. J., Damasio, A. R. & Yamada, T. (1984). Nonhemorrhagic infarction of the thalamus: Behavioral, anatomic and physiological correlates. *Neurology, 34*, 14–23.

Graff-Radford, N. R., Tranel, D., Van Hoesen, G. W. & Brandt, J. P. (1990). Diencephalic amnesia. *Brain, 113*, 1–25.

Greenwood, R., Bhalla, A., Gordon, A. & Roberts, J. (1983). Behaviour disturbances during recovery from herpes simplex encephalitis. *Journal of Neurology, Neurosurgery and Psychiatry, 46*, 809–817.

Greer, M. K., Lyons-Crews, M., Mauldin, L. B. & Brown, F. R. (1989). A case study of the cognitive and behavioral deficits of temporal lobe damage in herpes simplex encephalitis. *Journal of Autism and Developmental Disorders, 19*, 317–326.

Grossman, M. (1987). Lexical acquisition in alcoholic Korsakoff psychosis. *Cortex, 23*, 631–644.

Guberman, A. & Stuss, D. T. (1983). The syndrome of bilateral paramedian thalamic infarction. *Neurology, 33*, 540–546.

Handler, C. E. & Perkins, G. D. (1982). Anorexia nervosa and Wernicke's Encephalopathy: An underdiagnosed association. *Lancet, 2*, 771–772.

Hanley, J. R., Davies, A. D. M. & Downes, J. (in press). Impaired recall of verbal material following an anterior communicating artery aneurysm.

Hanley, J. R., Young, A. & Pearson, N. (1989). Defective recognition of familiar people. *Cognitive Neuropsychology, 6*, 179–210.

Hannay, H. J. & Levin, H. S. (1985). Selective reminding test: An examination of the equivalence of four forms. *Journal of Clinical and Experimental Neuropsychology, 7*, 251–263.

Hannay, H. J. & Levin, H. S. (1988). Visual continuous recognition memory in normal and closed-head-injured adolescents. *Journal of Clinical and Experimental Neuropsychology, 11*, 444–460.

Harper, C., Giles, M. & Finlay-Jones, R. (1986). Clinical signs in the Wernicke-Korsakoff complex: A retrospective analysis of 131 cases diagnosed at necropsy. *Journal of Neurology, Neurosurgery and Psychiatry, 49*, 341–345.

Harris, J. E. & Sunderland, A. (1981). A brief survey of the management of memory disorders in rehabilitation units in Britain. *International Rehabilitation Medicine, 3*, 206–209.

Hata, T., Meyer, J. S., Tanahashi, N., Ishikawa, Y., Imai, A., Shinohara, T., Velez, M., Fann, W. E., Kandula, P. & Sakai, F. (1987). Three-dimensional mapping of local cerebral perfusion in alcoholic encephalopathy with and without Wernicke-Korsakoff Sydrome. *Journal of Cerebral Blood Flow Metabolism, 7*, 35–44.

Heinrichs, R. W. (1989). Attempted clinical application of a technique for promoting robust free recall to a case of alcoholic Korsakoff's sydrome. *Brain and Cognition, 9*, 151–157.

Henry, G. K., Adams, R. L., Buck, P., Buchanan, W. L. & Altepeter, T. A. (1990). The American liner New York and Anna Thompson: An investigation of interference effects on the Wechsler Memory Scale. *Journal of Clinical and Experimental Neuropsychology, 12*, 502–506.

Herrmann, D. J. & Neisser, U. (1978). An inventory of everyday memory experiences. In M. M. Gruneberg, P. E. Morris & R. Sykes (Eds), *Practical aspects of memory*. New York: Academic Press.

Hirst, W., Phelps, E. A., Johnson, M. K. & Volpe, B. T. (1988). Amnesia and second language learning. *Brain and Cognition, 8*, 105–116.

Hirst, W. & Volpe, B. T. (1988). Memory strategies with brain damage. *Brain and Cognition, 8*, 1–33.

Hiscock, M. & Hiscock, C. K. (1989). Refining the forced-choice method for the detection of malingering. *Journal of Clinical and Experimental Neuropsychology, 11*, 967–974.

Hodges, J. R. & Carpenter, K. (1991). Anterograde amnesia with fornix damage following removal of IIIrd ventricle colloid cyst. *Journal of Neurology, Neurosurgery and Psychiatry, 54*, 633–638.

Hodges, J. R. & Ward, C. D. (1989). Observations during transient global amnesia: A behavioural and neuropsychological study of five cases. *Brain, 112*, 595–620.

Hodges, J. R. & Warlow, C. P. (1990a). The aetiology of transient global amnesia: A case-control study of 114 cases with prospective follow-up. *Brain, 113*, 639–657.

Hodges, J. R. & Warlow, C. P. (1990b). Syndromes of transient amnesia: Towards a classification. A study of 153 cases. *Journal of Neurology, Neurosurgery and Psychiatry, 53*, 834–843.

Howes, J. (1983). Effects of experimenter and self-generated imagery on the Korsakoff patient's memory performance. *Neuropsychologia, 21*, 341–349.

Hoyumpa, A. M. Jr, Nichols, S., Henderson, G. & Schenker, S. (1978). Intestinal thiamine transport: Effect of chronic ethanol administration in rats. *American Journal of Clinical Nutrition, 31*, 938–945.

Hunkin, N. M. (1991). *Comparative aspects of Korsakoff and post-encephalitic amnesia*. DPhil thesis, University of Sussex.

Hunkin, N. M. & Parkin, A. J. (in press). Recency judgements in Wernicke-Korsakoff and post-encephalitic amnesia: Influences of proactive interference and retention interval. *Cortex*.

Hunkin, N. M. & Parkin, A. J. (submitted). A critical evaluation of memory remediation using the 'vanishing cues' method.

Hunkin, N. M., Parkin, A. J. & Longmore, B. E. (in press). Aetiological variation in the amnesic syndrome: Comparisons using the list discrimination task. *Neuropsychologia*.

Huppert, F. A. & Piercy, M. (1978a). Recognition memory in amnesic patients: A defect of acquisition? *Neuropsychologia, 15*, 643–652.

Huppert, F. A. & Piercy, M. (1987b). The role of trace strength in recency and frequency judgments by amnesic and control subjects. *Quarterly Journal of Experimental Psychology, 30*, 346–354.

Huppert, F. A. & Piercy, M. (1979). Normal and abnormal forgetting in organic amnesia: Effect of locus of lesion. *Cortex, 15*, 385–390.

Ignelzi, R. J. & Squire, L. R. (1976). Recovery from anterograde and retrograde amnesia after percutaneous drainage of a cystic craniopharyngioma. *Journal of Neurology, Neurosurgery and Psychiatry, 39*, 1231–1235.

Illis, L. S. & Gostling, J. V. T. (1972). *Herpes simplex encephalitis*. Bristol: Scientechnica.

Jacobson, R. R. (1989). Alcoholism, Korsakoff's syndrome and the frontal lobes. *Behavioural Neurology, 2*, 25–38.

Jacobson, R. R. & Lishman, W. A. (1987). Selective memory loss and global intellectual deficits in alcoholic Korsakoff's syndrome. *Psychological Medicine, 17*, 649–655.

Jacobson, R. R. & Lishman, W. A. (1990). Cortical and diencephalic lesions in Korsakoff's syndrome: A clinical and CT scan study. *Psychological Medicine, 20*, 63–75.

Jacoby, L. L. (1983). Remembering the data: Analyzing interactive processing in reading. *Journal of Verbal Learning and Behavior, 22*, 485–508.

Jaeckle, R. S. & Nasrallah, H. A. (1985). Major depression and carbon monoxide-induced Parkinsonism: Diagnosis, computerized axial tomography, and response to L-dopa. *Journal of Nervous and Mental Disease, 173*, 503–508.

Jagadha, V., Deck, J. H. N., Halliday, W. C. & Smyth, H. S. (1987). Wernicke's encephalopathy in patients on peritoneal dialysis or hemodialysis. *Annals of Neurology, 21*, 87–94.

Jernigan, T. L., Schafer, K., Butters, N. & Cermak, L. S. (1991). Magnetic resonance imaging of alcoholic Korsakoff patients. *Neuropsychopharmacology, 4*, 175–186.

Jetter, W., Poser, U., Freeman, R. B. & Markowitsch, H. J. (1987). A verbal long-term memory deficit in frontal lobe damaged patients. *Cortex, 22*, 229–242.

Johnson, M. K., Kim, J. K. & Risse, G. (1985). Do alcoholic Korsakoff's Syndrome patients acquire affective reactions? *Journal of Experimental Psychology: Learning, Memory and Cognition, 11*, 22–36.

Jones, M. K. (1974). Imagery as a mnemonic aid after left temporal lobectomy: Contrast between material-specific and generalised memory disorders. *Neuropsychologia, 12*, 21–40.

Jones-Gotman, M. & Milner, B. (1977). Design fluency: The invention of nonsense drawings after focal cortical lesions. *Neuropsychologia, 15*, 653–674.

Kahn, E. A. & Crosby, E. C. (1972). Korsakoff's syndrome associated with surgical lesions involving the mamillary bodies. *Neurology, 22*, 117–124.

Kapur, N. (1978). Visual imagery capacity of alcoholic Korsakoff patients. *Neuropsychologia, 16*, 517–519.

Kapur, N. (1987). Some comments on the technical acceptability of Warrington's Recognition Memory Test. *British Journal of Psychology, 26*, 144–146.

Kapur, N. (1988a). *Memory disorders in clinical practice*. London: Butterworths.

Kapur, N. (1988b). Selective sparing of memory functioning in a patient with amnesia following herpes encephalitis. *Brain and Cognition, 7*, 184–200.

Kapur, N. (1989). *The Wessex memory manual*. Available from the author, Wessex Neurological Centre, Southampton, U.K.

Kapur, N. (1990). Transient epileptic amnesia: A clinically distinct form of neurological memory disorder. In H. J. Markowitsch (Ed.), *Transient global amnesia and related disorders*. Toronto: Hogrefe and Huber.

Kapur, N. & Coughlan, A. C. (1980). Confabulation and frontal lobe dysfunction. *Journal of Neurology, Neurosurgery and Psychiatry, 43*, 461–463.

Kapur, N., Young, A., Bateman, D. & Kennedy, P. (1989). A long-term clinical and neuropsychological follow-up of focal retrograde amnesia. *Cortex, 25*, 387–402.

Kessler, J., Irle, E. & Markowitsch, H. J. (1986). Korsakoff and alcoholic subjects are severely impaired in animal tasks of associative memory. *Neuropsychologia, 24*, 671–680.

Kimura, D. (1963). Right temporal-lobe damage. *Archives of Neurology, 8*, 264–271.

Klapper, P. E., Cleator, G. M. & Longson, M. (1984). Mild forms of herpes encephalitis. *Journal of Neurology, Neurosurgery and Psychiatry, 47*, 1247–1250.

Knight, R. G. & Godfrey, H. P. D. (1985). The assessment of memory impairment: The relationship between different methods of evaluating dysmnesic deficits. *British Journal of Clinical Psychology, 24*, 25–31.

Knight, R. G. & Longmore, B. (1990). What is an amnesic? In W. C. Abraham, M. C. Corballis & K. G. White (Eds), *Memory mechanisms: A tribute to G. V. Goddard*. Hillsdale, N.J.: Lawrence Erlbaum Associates Inc.

Kohnstamm, O. (1917). Uber das Krankheitsbild der retro-graden Amnesie und die Unterscheidung des spontanen und des lernenden Merkens. *Mschr. Psychiat. Neurol., 41*, 373–382.

Kolb, B. & Whishaw, I. Q. (1990). *Fundamentals of human neuropsychology*, 3rd edn. New York: W. H. Freeman.

Kopelman, M. D. (1985). Rates of forgetting in Alzheimer-type dementias and Korsakoff's Syndrome. *Neuropsychologia, 23*, 623–638.

Kopelman, M. D. (1987a). Crime and amnesia: A review. *Behavioural Sciences and the Law, 5*, 323–342.

Kopelman, M. D. (1987b). Two types of confabulation. *Journal of Neurology, Neurosurgery and Psychiatry, 50*, 1482–1487.

Kopelman, M. D. (1989). Remote and autobiographical memory, temporal context memory and frontal atrophy in Korsakoff and Alzheimer patients. *Neuropsychologia, 27*, 437–460.

Kopelman, M. D. (1990). *Autobiographical Memory Interview*. Reading: Thames Valley Test Company.

Kopelman, M. D. (1991). Frontal dysfunction and memory deficits in alcoholic Korsakoff Syndrome and Alzheimer-type dementia. *Brain, 114*, 117–137.

Kopelman, M. D., Wilson, B. A. & Baddeley, A. D. (1989). The Autobiographical Memory Interview: A new assessment of autobiographical and personal semantic memory in amnesic patients. *Journal of Clinical and Experimental Neuropsychology, 11*, 724–744.

Korsakoff, S. S. (1889). Etude medico-psychologique sur une forme des maladies de la memoire. *Revue Philosophique, 28*, 501–530.

Kovner, R., Mattis, S. & Goldmeier, E. (1983). A technique for promoting robust free recall in chronic organic amnesia. *Journal of Clinical Neuropsychology, 5*, 65–71.

Kovner, R., Mattis, S. & Pass, R. (1985). Some amnesic patients can freely recall large amounts of information in new contexts. *Journal of Clinical and Experimental Neuropsychology, 7*, 395–411.

Kritchevsky, M., Graff-Radford, N. R. & Damasio, A. R. (1987). Normal memory after damage to medial thalamus. *Archives of Neurology, 44*, 959–962.

Laiacona, M., De Santis, A., Barbarotto, R., Basso, A., Spagnoli, D. & Capitani, E. (1989). Neuropsychological follow-up of patients operated for aneurysms of the anterior communicating artery. *Cortex, 25*, 261–273.

Landauer, T. K. & Bjork, R. A. (1978). Optimum rehearsal patterns and name learning. In M. M. Gruneberg, P. E. Morris & R. N. Sykes (Eds), *Practical aspects of memory*. New York: Academic Press.

Larrabee, G. J. (1987). Further cautions in interpretation of comparisons between the WAIS-R and Wechsler Memory Scale. *Journal of Clinical and Experimental Neuropsychology, 9*, 456–460.

Larrabee, G. J., Kane, R. L. & Schuck, J. R. (1983). Factor analysis of the WAIS and Wechsler Memory Scale: An analysis of the construct validity of the Wechsler Memory Scale. *Journal of Clinical Neuropsychology, 5*, 159–168.

Larsson, C., Ronneberg, J., Forssell, A., Nilsson, L.-G., Lindberg, M. & Angquist, K.-A. (1989). Verbal memory function after subarachnoid haemorrhage determined by the localisation of the ruptured aneurysm. *British Journal of Neurosurgery, 3*, 549–560.

Lee, A. W., Ng, S. H., Ho, J. H., Tse, V. K., Poon, Y. F., Tse, C. C., Au, G. K., O, S. K., Lau, W. H. & Foo, W. W. (1987). Clinical diagnosis of late temporal lobe necrosis following radiation therapy for nasopharyngeal carcinoma. *Cancer, 61*, 1535–1542.

Lee, P. W. H., Hung, B. K. M., Woo, E. K. W., Tai, P. T. H. & Choi, D. T. K. (1989). Effects of radiation therapy on neuropsychological functioning in patients with nasopharyngeal carcinoma. *Journal of Neurology, Neurosurgery and Psychiatry, 52*, 488–492.

Leininger, B. E., Gramling, S. E., Farrell, A. D., Kreutzer, J. S. & Peck, E. A. (1990). Neuropsychological deficits in symptomatic minor head injury patients after concussion and mild concussion. *Journal of Neurology, Neurosurgery and Psychiatry, 53*, 293–296.

Lelord, G., Fauchier, C. I., Regy, J. M., Ciosi, C. I. & Combe, P. (1971). Etapes evolutives de l'amelioration d'un syndrome de Gerstmann postencephalitique. *Encephale, 60*, 58–73.

Leng, N. R. C. (1987). *A comparative study of diencephalic and bi-temporal lobe amnesias.* Unpublished DPhil thesis, University of Sussex.

Leng, N. R. C., Copello, A. G. & Sayegh, A. (1991). Learning after brain injury by the method of vanishing cues: A case study. *Behavioural Psychotherapy, 19*, 173–181.

Leng, N. R. C. & Parkin, A. J. (1988a). Double dissociation of frontal dysfunction in organic amnesia. *British Journal of Clinical Psychology, 27*, 359–362.

Leng, N. R. C. & Parkin, A. J. (1988b). Amnesic patients can benefit from instructions to use imagery: Evidence against the cognitive mediation hypothesis. *Cortex, 24*, 33–39.

Leng, N. R. C. & Parkin, A. J. (1989). Aetiological variation in the amnesic syndrome: Comparisons using the Brown-Peterson task. *Cortex, 25*, 251–259.

Lezak, M. D. (1983). *Neuropsychological assessment.* Oxford: Oxford University Press.

Lhermitte, F. & Signoret, J. L. (1972). Analyse neuropsychologique et differenciation des syndromes amnesiques. *Revue Neurologique, 126*, 161–178.

Lilly, R., Cummings, J. L., Benson, D. F. & Frankel, M. (1983). The human Kluver-Bucy syndrome. *Neurology, 33*, 1141–1145.

Lindboe, C. F. & Lobert, E. M. (1989). Wernicke's encephalopathy in non-alcohlics: An autopsy study. *Journal of the Neurological Sciences, 90*, 125–129.

Lishman, W. A. (1990). Alcohol and the brain. *British Journal of Psychiatry, 156*, 635–644.

Ljungrenn, B., Saveland, H., Brandt, L. & Zygmunt, S. (1985). Early operation and overall outcome in aneurysmal subarachnoid hemorrhage. *Journal of Neurosurgery, 62*, 547–551.

Logue, V., Durward, M., Pratt, R. T. C., Piercy, M. & Nixon, W. L. B. (1968). The quality of survival after rupture of anterior cerebral aneurysm. *British Journal of Psychiatry, 114*, 137–160.

Longmore, B. E. & Knight, R. G. (1988). The effect of intellectual deterioration on retention deficits in amnesic alcoholics. *Journal of Abnormal Psychology, 97*, 448–454.

Loring, D. W. & Papanicolaou, A. C. (1987). Memory assessment in neuropsychology: Theoretical considerations and practical utility. *Journal of Clinical and Experimental Neuropsychology, 9*, 340–358.

Luria, A. R. (1976). *Neuropsychology of memory.* Chichester: John Wiley.

MacCurdy, T. J. (1928). *Common principles in psychology and physiology.* Cambridge: Cambridge University Library.

MacKinnon, D. F. & Squire, L. R. (1989). Autobiographical memory and amnesia. *Psychobiology, 17*, 247–256.

Mair, R., Capra, C., McEntee, W. J. & Engen, T. (1980). Odor discrimination and memory in Korsakoff's psychosis. *Journal of Experimental Psychology: Human Perception and Performance, 6*, 445–458.

Mair, W. G. P., Warrington, E. K. & Weiskrantz, L. (1979). Memory disorder in Korsakoff's psychosis. *Brain, 102*, 749–783.

Malamud, N. & Skillicorn, S. A. (1956). Relationship between the Wernicke and the Korsakoff Syndrome. *Annals of Neurology and Psychiatry, 76*, 585–596.

Mandler, G. (1988). Memory: Conscious and unconscious. In P. R. Solomon (Ed.), *Memory: Interdisciplinary approaches.* New York: Springer-Verlag.

Markowitsch, H. J. (1983). Thalamic mediodorsal nucleus and memory: A critical evaluation of studies in animals and man. *Neuroscience and Biobehavioral Reviews, 6,* 351–380.

Markowitsch, H. J. (Ed.) (1990). *Transient global amnesia and related disorders.* Toronto: Hogrefe and Huber.

Marr, D. (1982). *Vision.* San Francisco: W. H. Freeman.

Marshall, R. C. (1982). Language and speech recovery in a case of viral encephalitis. *Brain and Language, 17,* 316–326.

Marslen-Wilson, W. D. & Teuber, H. L. (1975). Memory for remote events in anterograde amnesia: Recognition of public figures from newsphotos. *Neuropsychologia, 13,* 353–364.

Masur, D. M., Fuld, P.A., Blow, A. D., Crystal, H. & Aronson, M. K. (1990). Predicting development of dementia in the elderly with the Selective Reminding Test. *Journal of Clinical and Experimental Neuropsychology, 12,* 529–538.

Mattis, S. E., Kovner, R. & Goldmeier, E. (1978). Different patterns of mnemonic deficits in two organic amnesic syndromes. *Brain and Language, 6,* 179–191.

Mattis, S., Kovner, R., Gartner, J. & Goldmeier, E. (1981). Deficits in retrieval of category exemplars in alcoholic Korsakoff patients. *Neuropsychologia, 19,* 357–363.

Maurice-Williams, R. S. (1987). *Sub-arachnoid haemorrhage.* Bristol: Wright.

Maurice-Williams, R. S., Willison, J. R. & Hatfield, R. (1991). The cognitive and psychological sequelae of uncomplicated aneurysm surgery. *Journal of Neurology, Neurosurgery and Psychiatry, 54,* 335–340.

Mayes, A. R. (1988). *Human organic memory disorders.* Cambridge: Cambridge University Press.

Mayes, A. R., Baddeley, A. D., Cockburn, J., Meudell, P. R., Pickering, A. & Wilson, B. (1988). Why are amnesic judgements of recency and frequency made in a qualitatively different way from those of normal people? *Cortex, 25,* 479–488.

Mayes, A. R. & Gooding, P. (1989). Enhancement of word completion priming in amnesics by cueing with previously novel associates. *Neuropsychologia, 27,* 1057–1072.

Mayes, A. R., Meudell, P. R. & Fairbairn, A. (1987a). Amnesic sensitivity to proactive interference: Its relationship to priming and the causes of amnesia. *Neuropsychologia, 25,* 211–220.

Mayes, A. R., Meudell, P. R. & MacDonald, C. (1991). Disproportionate intentional spatial-memory impairments in amnesia. *Neuropsychologia, 29,* 771–784.

Mayes, A. R., Meudell, R., Mann, D. & Pickering, A. (1987b). Location of lesions in Korsakoff's Syndrome: Neuropsychological and neuropathological data on two patients. *Cortex, 24,* 367–388.

Mayes, A. R., Meudell, R. & Pickering, A. (1985). Is organic amnesia caused by a selective deficit in remembering contextual information? *Cortex, 21,* 167–202.

McClelland, J. L. & Rumelhart, D. E. (1986). *Parallel distributed processing: Explorations in the microstructure of cognition,* Vol. 2. Cambridge, Mass.: MIT Press.

McEntee, W. J., Biber, M. P., Perl, D. P. & Benson, F. D. (1976). Diencephalic amnesia: A reappraisal. *Journal of Neurology, Neurosurgery and Psychiatry, 39,* 436–441.

McEntee, W. J. & Mair, R. G. (1979). Memory enhancement in Korsakoff's psychosis by clonidine: Further evidence for a noradrenergic deficit. *Annals of Neurology, 16,* 466–470.

McKenna, P. & Warrington, E. K. (1983). *The Graded Naming Test.* Windsor: NFER Nelson.

McMillan, T. M. & Glucksman, E. E. (1987). The neuropsychology of moderate head injury. *Journal of Neurology, Neurosurgery and Psychiatry, 50,* 393–397.

Medalia, A. A., Merriam, A. E. & Ehrenreich, J. H. (1991). The neuropsychological sequelae of attempted hanging. *Journal of Neurology, Neurosurgery and Psychiatry, 54*, 546–548.

Meissner, I., Sapir, S., Kokmen, E. & Stein, S. D., (1987). The paramedian diencephalic syndrome: A dynamic phenomenon. *Stroke, 18*, 380–385.

Meissner, W. W. (1967). Memory function in the Korsakoff Syndrome. *Journal of Nervous and Mental Disorders, 145*, 106–122.

Meudell, P. & Mayes, A. (1981). The Claparede phenomenon: A further example in amnesics, a demonstration of a similar effect in normal people with attenuated memory and a reinterpretation. *Current Psychological Research, 1*, 75–88.

Meudell, P. R., Mayes, A. R., Ostergaard, A. & Pickering, A. (1985). Recency and frequency judgements in alcoholic amnesics and normal people with poor memory. *Cortex, 21*, 487–511.

Milberg, W. P., Hebben, N. & Kaplan, E. (1986). The Boston process approach to neuropsychological assessment. In I. Grant & K. M. Adams (Eds), Neuropsychological assessment of neuropsychiatric disorders. New York: Oxford University Press.

Miller, E. (1984). *Recovery and management of neuropsychological impairments.* Chichester: John Wiley.

Mills, R. P. & Swanson, P. D. (1978). Vertical oculomotor apraxic and memory loss. *Annals of Neurology, 4*, 149–153.

Milner, B. (1959). The memory defect in bilateral hippocampal lesions. *Psychiatric Association: Psychiatric Research Reports, 11*, 43–58.

Milner, B. (1966). Amnesia following operation on the temporal lobes. In C. W. M. Whitty & O. L. Zangwill (Eds), *Amnesia*, 1st edn. London: Butterworths.

Milner, B. (1971). Interhemispheric differences in the location of psychological processes in man. *British Medical Bulletin, 27*, 272–277.

Milner, B., Corkin, S. & Teuber, H.-L. (1968). Further analyses of the hippocampal amnesic syndrome: 14-year follow up study of H.M. *Neuropsychologia, 6*, 215–234.

Milner, B., Corsi, P. & Leonard, G. (1991). Frontal contribution to recency judgments. *Neuropsychologia, 29*, 601–618.

Milner, B., Petrides, M. & Smith, M. L. (1985). Frontal lobes and the temporal organisation of memory. *Human Neurobiology, 4*, 137–142.

Min, S. K. (1986). A brain syndrome associated with delayed neuropsychiatric sequelae following acute carbon monoxide intoxication. *Acta Psychiatrica Scandinavica, 73*, 80–86.

Mishkin, M. (1982). A memory system in the monkey. *Philosophical Transactions of the Royal Society, B298*, 85–95.

Mohr, J. P., Leicester, J., Stoddard, L. T. & Sidman, M. (1971). Right hemianopia with memory and colour deficits in circumscribed left posterior cerebral artery territory infarction. *Neurology, 21*, 1104–1113.

Mori, E., Yamadori, A. & Mitani, Y. (1986). Left thalamic infarction and disturbance of verbal memory: A clinicoanatomical study with a new method of computed tomographic stereotaxic localization. *Annals of Neurology, 20*, 671–676.

Morris, R. G. (1991). The nature of memory impairment in dementia. In J. Weinmann & J. Hunter (Eds), *Clinical and biochemical contributions to the understanding of human memory function*. London: Harwood.

Moscovitch, M. (1989). Confabulation and the frontal systems: Strategic versus associative retrieval in neuropsychological theories of memory. In H. L. Roediger III & F. I. M. Craik (Eds), *Varieties of memory and consciousness: Essays in honor of Endel Tulving.* Hillsdale, N.J.: Lawrence Erlbaum Associates Inc.

Mumenthaler, M., Kaeser, H. E., Meyer, A. & Hess, T. (1979). Transient global amnesia after clioquinol. *Journal of Neurology, Neurosurgery and Psychiatry, 42*, 1084–1090.

Muramoto, O., Kuru, Y., Sugishita, M. & Toyokura, Y. (1979). Pure memory loss with hippocampal lesions. *Archives of Neurology, 36*, 54–56.

Nadel, A. M. & Burger, P. C. (1976). Wernicke encephalopathy following prolonged intravenous therapy. *Journal of the American Medical Association, 235*, 2403–2405.

Nathan, P. W. & Smith, M. C. (1950). Normal mentality associated with a maldeveloped "Rhinencephalon". *Journal of Neurology, Neurosurgery and Psychiatry, 13*, 191–197.

Nelson, H. E. (1976). A modified card sorting test sensitive to frontal lobe deficits. *Cortex, 12*, 313–324.

Nelson, H. E. (1985). *National Adult Reading Test (NART): Test Manual.* Windsor: NFER-Nelson.

Nelson, H. E. (1991). *National Adult Reading Test (NART): Test Manual (Revised).* Windsor: NFER-Nelson.

Nelson, H. E. & O'Connell, A. (1978). Dementia: The estimation of premorbid intelligence levels using the New Adult Reading Test. *Cortex, 14*, 234–244.

Neuberger, K. (1937). Wernickersche-krankheit bei chronischer gastritis. Ein beitrag zu den bezeihungen zwischen magen und gehirn. *Zeitschrift die Gesamte Neurologie und Psychiatrie, 160*, 208–225.

Newman, N. J., Bell, I. R. & McKee, A. C. (1990). Paraneoplastic limbic encephalitis: Neuropsychiatric presentation. *Biological Psychiatry, 27*, 529–542.

Newman, S., Pugsley, W., Klinger, L., Harrison, M., Aveling, W. & Treasure, T. (1989). Neuropsychological consequences of circulatory arrest with hypothermia—A case report. *Journal of Clinical and Experimental Neuropsychology, 11*, 529–538.

Nichelli, P., Bahmanian-Behbahani, G., Gentilini, M. & Vecchi, A. (1988). Preserved memory abilities in thalamic amnesia. *Brain, 111*, 1337–1353.

Nissen, M. J. & Bullemer, P. (1987). Attentional requirements of learning: Evidence from performance measures. *Cognitive Psychology, 19*, 1–32.

Nissen, M. J., Ross, J. L., Willingham, D. B., Mackenzie, T. B. & Schacter, D. L. (1988). Memory and awareness in a patient with multiple personality disorder. *Brain and Cognition, 8*, 21–38.

Nissen, M. J., Willingham, D. & Hartman, M. (1989). Explicit and implicit remembering: When is learning preserved in amnesia? *Neuropsychologia, 27*, 341–352.

Nyssen, R. (1956). Des capacités de definition et d'évocation des mots dan la psychose de Korsakov alcoolique. *Evolution Psychiatrique, 1*, 303–314.

O'Connor, M. & Cermak, L. S. (1987). Rehabilitation of organic memory disorders. In M. J. Meier, A. L. Benton & L. Diller (Eds), *Neuropsychological rehabilitation.* New York: Guilford Press.

Ogawa, A., Suzuki, M., Sakurai, Y. & Yoshimoto, T. (1990). Vascular anomalies associated with aneurysms of the anterior communicating artery. *Journal of Neurosurgery, 72*, 607–709.

Ogden, J. A. & Corkin, S. (1991). Memories of H. M. In W. C. Abrahams, M. C. Corballis & K. G. White (Eds), *Memory mechanisms: A tribute to G. V. Goddard.* Hillsdale, N.J.: Lawrence Erlbaum Associates Inc.

Ogden, J. A., Growden, J. H. & Corkin, S. (1990). Deficits on visuospatial tests involving forward planning in high functioning parkinsonians. *Neuropsychiatry, Neuropsychology and Behavioural Neurology, 3*, 125–129.

Okawa, M., Maeda, S., Nukui, H. & Kawafuchi, J. (1980). Psychiatric symptoms in ruptured anterior communicating aneurysms: Social prognosis. *Acta Psychiatrica Scandinavica, 61*, 306–312.

Olson, L. C., Buescher, E. L., Artenstein, M. S. & Parkman, P. D. (1967). Herpes virus infections of the human nervous system. *New England Journal of Medicine, 277*, 1271–1277.

Orchinik, C. W. (1960). Some psychological aspects of circumscribed lesions of the diencephalon. *Confin. Neurol., 20*, 292–310.

Oscar-Berman, M. (1971). Hypothesis testing and focusing behaviour during concept formation by amnesic Korsakoff patients. *Neuropsychologia, 11*, 191–198.

Oscar-Berman, M., Sahakian, B. J. & Wikmark, G. (1976). Spatial probability learning by alcoholic Korsakoff patients. *Journal of Experimental Psychology: Human Learning and Memory, 2*, 215–222.

Palmai, G., Taylor, D. G. & Falconer, M. A. (1967). A case of craniopharyngioma presenting as Korsakoff's Syndrome. *British Journal of Psychiatry, 113*, 619–623.

Parkin, A. J. (1982). Residual learning capability in organic amnesia. *Cortex, 18*, 417–440.

Parkin, A. J. (1984). Amnesic syndrome: A lesion-specific disorder? *Cortex, 20*, 479–508.

Parkin, A. J. (1987). *Memory and amnesia: An introduction*. Oxford: Basil Blackwell.

Parkin, A. J. (1991a). The relation between anterograde and retrograde amnesia in alcoholic Korsakoff Syndrome. *Psychological Medicine, 21*, 11–14.

Parkin, A. J. (1991b). Recent advances in the neuropsychology of memory. In J. Weinmann & J. Hunter (Eds), *Clinical and biochemical contributions to the understanding of human memory disorders*. London: Harwood.

Parkin, A. J. (in press a). Functional significance of aetiological factors in human amnesia. In N. Butters & L. R. Squire (Eds), *Neuropsychology of memory*, 2nd edn. New York: Guilford Press.

Parkin, A. J. (in press b). Implicit memory across the life span. In P. Graf & M. Masson (Eds), *Implicit memory: New directions in cognition, development, and neuropsychology*. Hillsdale, N.J.: Lawrence Erlbaum Associates Inc.

Parkin, A. J. (in press c). *Memory: Phenomena, Experiment and Theory*. Oxford: Basil Blackwell.

Parkin, A. J. & Barry, C. (1991). Alien hand and other cognitive deficits following ruptured anterior communicating artery aneurysm. *Behavioural Neurology, 4*, 167–179.

Parkin, A. J., Bell, W. P. & Leng, N. R. C. (1988a). Metamemory in amnesic and normal subjects. *Cortex, 24*, 141–147.

Parkin, A. J. & Binschaedler, C. (in prep.). Defective memory following anterior communicating artery aneurysm with particular reference to the impairment of recognition.

Parkin, A. J., Blunden, J., Rees, J. E. & Hunkin, N. M. (1991). Wernicke-Korsakoff Syndrome of non-alcoholic origin. *Brain and Cognition, 15*, 69–82.

Parkin, A. J., Dunn, J. C., Lee, C. W., O'Hara, P. F. & Nussbaum, L. (in press a). Neuropsychological sequelae of Wernicke's encephalopathy in a 20-year-old woman: Selective impairment of a "frontal memory system". *Brain and Cognition*.

Parkin, A. J. & Hunkin, N. M. (1991). Memory loss following radiotherapy for naso-pharyngeal cancer: An unusual presentation of amnesia. *British Journal of Clinical Psychology, 30*, 349–357.

Parkin, A. J. & Hunkin, N. M. (in press). Impaired temporal context memory on anterograde but not retrograde tests in the absence of frontal pathology. *Cortex*.

Parkin, A. J. & Leng, N. R. (1988). Comparative studies of the amnesic syndrome. In H. Markowitsch (Ed.), *Information processing by the brain: Views and hypotheses from a physiological-cognitive perspective*. Toronto: Hans Huber.

Parkin, A. J., Leng, N. R. C. & Hunkin, N. (1990a). Differential sensitivity to contextual information in diencephalic and temporal lobe amnesia. *Cortex, 26*, 373–380.

Parkin, A. J., Leng, N. R., Stanhope, N. & Smith, A. P. (1988b). Memory impairment following ruptured aneurysm of the anterior communicating artery. *Brain and Cognition, 7*, 231–243.

Parkin, A. J., Miller, J. W. & Vincent, R. (1987). Multiple neuropsychological deficits due to anoxic encephalopathy—A case study. *Cortex, 23*, 655-665.

Parkin, A. J., Montaldi, D., Leng, N. R. C. & Hunkin, N. M. (1990b). Contextual cueing effects in the remote memory of alcoholic Korsakoff patients and normal subjects. *Quarterly Journal of Experimental Psychology, 42A*, 585–596.

Parkin, A. J., Pitchford, J. & Binschaedler, C. (in prep.). Analysis of an executive memory impairment.

Parkin, A. J., Rees, J. E., Hunkin, N. M. & Rose, P. (in press b). Impaired memory following discrete thalamic infarcation compromising both hippocampal and amygdalar pathways.

Parkin, A. J. & Stampfer, H. (in press). Memory following atypical psychosis. In R. Campbell & M. Conway (Eds), *Broken lives*. Oxford: Basil Blackwell.

Parkin, A. J. & Streete, S. (1988). Implicit and explicit memory in young children and adults. *British Journal of Psychology, 79*, 361–369.

Parkin, A. J. & Walter, B. (1991). Short-term memory, ageing, and frontal lobe dysfunction. *Psychobiology, 19*, 175–179.

Parkinson, S. R. (1979). The amnesic Korsakoff syndrome: A study of selective and divided attention. *Neuropsychologia, 17*, 67–75.

Patten, B. M. (1972). The ancient art of memory. *Archives of Neurology, 26*, 25–31.

Penfield, W. & Mathieson, G. (1974). Memory: Autopsy findings and comments on the role of hippocampus in experiential recall. *Archives of Neurology, 31*, 145–154.

Penfield, W. & Milner, B. (1958). Memory deficit produced by bilateral lesion in the hippocampal zone. *Archives of Neurology and Psychiatry, 79*, 475–497.

Pentland, B. & Maudsley, C. (1982). Wernicke's encephalopathy following hunger strike. *Postgraduate Medical Journal, 58*, 427–428.

Peterson, L. R. & Peterson, M. J. (1959). Short-term retention of individual verbal items. *Journal of Experimental Psychology, 58*, 193–198.

Pietrini, V., Nertempi, P., Vaglia, A., Revello, M. G., Pinna, V. & Ferro-Milone, F. (1988). Recovery from herpes simplex encephalitis: Selective impairment of specific semantic categories with neuroradiological correlation. *Journal of Neurology, Neurosurgery and Psychiatry, 51*, 1284–1293.

Press, G. A., Amaral, D. G. & Squire, L. R. (1989). Hippocampal abnormalities in amnesic patients revealed by high-resolution magnetic resonance imaging. *Nature, 341*, 54–57.

Prigatano, G. P. (1978). Wechsler Memory Scale: A selective review of the literature. *Journal of Clinical Psychology, 34*, 816–832.

Prigatano, G. P., Fordyce, D. J., Zeiner, H. K., Roueche, J. R., Pepping, M. & Wood, B. C. (1984). Neuropsychological rehabilitation after closed-head injury in young adults. *Journal of Neurology, Neurosurgery and Psychiatry, 47*, 505–513.

Putnam, F. W. (1989). *Diagnosis and treatment of multiple personality disorder*. New York: Guilford Press.

Randt, C. T., Brown, E. R. & Osbourne, D. P. (1980). A memory test for longitudinal measurement of mild to moderate memory deficits. *Clinical Neuropsychology, 11*, 184–194.

Redington, K., Bruce, T. & Gazzaniga, M. S. (1984). Failure of preference formation in amnesia. *Neurology, 34*, 536–538.

Reuler, J. B., Girard, D. E. & Cooney, T. G. (1985). Medical Intelligence Current Concepts: Wernicke's encephalopathy. *New England Journal of Medicine, 312*, 1035–1039.

Rey, A. (1964). *L'examen clinique en psychologie*. Paris: Presses Universitaires de France.

Ribot, T. (1882). *Diseases of memory*. New York: Appleton.

Richardson, J. T. E. (1989). Performance in free recall following rupture and repair of intracranial aneurysm. *Brain and Cognition, 9*, 210–226.

Richardson, J. T. E. (1990). *Clinical and neuropsychological aspects of closed head injury*. London: Taylor and Francis.

Richardson, J. T. E. (1991). Cognitive performance following rupture and repair of intracranial aneurysm. *Acta Neurologica Scandinavica, 83*, 110–112.

Rizzo, E. M. (1955). Sulla sindrome di Korsakoff. *Rassegna di studi psichiatrici, 44*, 801–816.

Robinson, F. P. (1970). *Effective study*. New York: Harper.

Robinson, J. A. (1976). Sampling autobiographical memory. *Cognitive Psychology, 8*, 578–595.

Rolls, E. G. (1988). Parallel distributed processing in the brain: Implications of the functional architecture of neural networks in the hippocampus. In R. G. M. Morris (Ed.), *Parallel distributed processing: Implications for psychology and neurobiology*. Oxford: Clarendon Press.

Rose, F. C. & Symonds, C. P. (1960). Persistent memory defect following encephalitis. *Brain, 83*, 195–212.

Roth, D. L., Conboy, T. J., Reeder, K. P. & Boll, T. J. (1990). Confirmatory factor analysis of the Wechsler Memory Scale—Revised in a sample of head-injured patients. *Journal of Clinical and Experimental Neuropsychology, 12*, 834–842.

Rousseaux, M., Cabaret, M., Lesoin, F., Dubois, F. & Petit, H. (1986). L'amnesie des infarctus thalamiques. *L'Encephale, XII*, 19–26.

Ruff, R. M., Light, R. H. & Evans, R. W. (1987). The Ruff figural fluency test: A normative study with adults. *Developmental Neuropsychology, 3*, 37–51.

Rumbach, L., Tranchant, C., Kiesmann, M., Marescaux, C., Chambron, J. & Kurtz, D. (1988). Imagerie par resonance magnetique et encephalite herpetique. *Revue Neurologique (Paris), 144*, 125–126.

Russell, E. W. (1975). A multiple scoring method for the assessment of complex memory functions. *Journal of Consulting and Clinical Psychology, 43*, 800–809.

Russell, E. W. (1988). Renorming Russell's version of the Wechsler Memory Scale. *Journal of Clinical and Experimental Neuropsychology, 10*, 235–249.

Russo, R. & Parkin, A. J. (in press). Age differences in implicit memory: More apparent than real.

Ryback, R. (1971). The continuum and specificity of the effects of alcohol on memory. *Quarterly Journal of Studies in Alcoholism, 32*, 995–1016.

Sagar, H. J., Gabrieli, J. D. E., Sullivan, E. V. & Corkin, S. (1990). Recency and frequency discrimination in the amnesic patient HM. *Brain, 113*, 581–602.

Salmon, D. P. & Butters, N. (1987). Recent developments in learning and memory: Implications for the rehabilitation of the amnesic patient. In M. J. Meyer, A. R. Benton & L. Diller (Eds), *Neuropsychological Rehabilitation*. Edinburgh: Churchill Livingstone.

Sanders, H. I. & Warrington, E. K. (1971). Memory for remote events in amnesic patients. *Brain, 94*, 661–668.

Sarter, M. & Markowitsch, H. J. (1985). The amygdala's role in human mnemonic processing. *Cortex, 21*, 7–24.

Sartori, G. & Job, R. (1988). The oyster with four legs: A neuropsychological study on the interaction of visual and semantic information. *Cognitive Neuropsychology, 5*, 105–132.

Savoy, R. L. & Gabrieli, J. D. E. (1991). Normal McCollough effect in Alzheimer's disease and global amnesia. *Perception and Psychophysics, 49*, 448–455.

Schacter, D. L. (1987). Implicit memory: History and current status. *Journal of Experimental Psychology: Learning, Memory and Cognition, 13*, 501–518.

Schacter, D. L. & Glisky, E. L. (1986). Memory remediation: Restoration, alleviation and the acquisition of domain-specific knowledge. In B. Uzzell & Y. Gross (Eds), *Clinical neuropsychology of intervention*. Boston: Martinus Nijhoff.

Schacter, D. L., Kihlstrom, J. F. & Kihlstrom, L. C. (1989). Autobiographical memory in a case of multiple personality disorder. *Journal of Abnormal Psychology, 98*, 508–514.

Schacter, D. L., Rapscak, S. Z., Rubens, A. B., Tharan, M. & Languna, J. (1990). Priming effects in a letter-by-letter reader depend on access to the word form system. *Neuropsychologia, 28*, 1079–1094.

Schacter, D. L., Rich, S. A. & Stampp, M. S. (1985). Remediation of memory disorders: Experimental evaluation of the spaced-retrieval technique. *Journal of Clinical and Experimental Neuropsychology, 7*, 79–96.

Schacter, D. L., Wang, P. L., Tulving, E. & Freedman, M. (1982). Functional retrograde amnesia: A quantitative case study. *Neuropsychologia, 20*, 523–532.

Schlitt, M. J., Morawertz, R. B., Bonnin, J. M., Zeiger, H. E. & Whitley, R. J. (1986). Brain biopsy for encephalitis. *Clinical Neurosurgery, 33*, 591–602.

Schneider, K. (1912). Uber einige klinisch-pathologische Unter-suchungsmethoden und ihre Ergebnisse. Zugleich ein Beitrag zur Psychopathologie der Korsakowschen Psychose. *Zeitschrift für Neurologie und Psychiatrie, 8*, 553–616.

Schonell, F. (1942). *Backwardness in the basic subjects*. London: Oliver and Boyd.

Schwartz, A. F. & McMillan, T. M. (1989). Assessment of everyday memory after severe head injury. *Cortex, 25*, 665–671.

Scoville, W. B. & Milner, B. (1957). Loss of recent memory after bilateral hippocampal lesions. *Journal of Neurology, Neurosurgery and Psychiatry, 20*, 11–12.

Seltzer, B. & Benson, D. F. (1974). The temporal pattern of retrograde amnesia in Korsakoff's disease. *Neurology, 24*, 527–530.

Sengupta, P., James, E., Chiu, S. P. & Brierley, H. (1975). Quality of survival following direct surgery for anterior communicating artery aneurysms. *Journal of Neurosurgery, 43*, 58–64.

Seron, X. & Deloche, G. (1989). *Cognitive approaches in neuropsychological rehabilitation*. Hillsdale, N.J.: Lawrence Erlbaum Associates Inc.

Shallice, M. T. & Evans, M. E. (1978). The involvement of the frontal lobes in cognitive estimation. *Cortex, 14*, 293–303.

Shallice, T. & Warrington, E. K. (1970). Independent functioning of verbal memory stores: A neuropsychological case study. *Quarterly Journal of Experimental Psychology, 22*, 261–273.

Shimamura, A. P., Janowsky, J. & Squire, L. R. (1990). Memory for temporal order of events in patients with frontal lobe lesions and amnesic patients. *Neuropsychologia, 28*, 803–813.

Shimamura, A. P., Jernigan, T. L. & Squire, L. R. (1988). Korsakoff's syndrome: Radiological (CT) findings and neuropsychological correlates. *Journal of Neuroscience, 8*, 4400–4410.

Shimamura, A. P. & Squire, L. R. (1986). Korsakoff's syndrome: A study of the relations between anterograde amnesia and remote memory impairment. *Behavioural Neuroscience, 100*, 165–170.

Shimauchi, M., Wakisaka, S. & Kinoshita, K. (1989). Amnesia due to bilateral hippocampal glioblastoma: MRI finding. *Neuroradiology, 31*, 430–432.

Shoqeirat, M. A., Mayes, A., MacDonald, C., Meudell, P. & Pickering, A. (1990). Performance on tests sensitive to frontal lobe lesions by patients with organic amnesia: Leng & Parkin revisited. *British Journal of Clinical Psychology, 29*, 401–408.

Signoret, J. L. (1972). Memory and Korsakoff's Syndrome: Persistence or extinction and memory traces. *International Journal of Mental Health, 1*, 103–108.

Signoret, J. L. & Goldenberg, G. (1986). Troubles de memoire lors des lesions du thalamus chez l'homme. *Revue Neurologique, 142*, 445–448.

Silvera, M. C. & Gainotti, G. (1988). Interaction between vision and language in category-specific semantic impairment. *Cognitive Neuropsychology, 5*, 677–709.

Singer, H. S. & Walkup, J. T. (1991). Tourette syndrome and other tic disorders: Diagnosis, pathophysiology, and treatment. *Medicine, 70*, 15–32.

Smith, M. L. (1988). Recall of spatial location by the amnesic patient H.M. *Brain and Cognition, 7*, 178–183.

Smith, M. L. & Milner, B. (1981). The role of the right hippocampus in the recall of spatial location. *Neuropsychologia, 19*, 781–793.

Snodgrass, J. G., Bradford, S., Feenan, K. & Corvin, J. (1987). Fragmenting pictures on the Apple Macintosh computer for experimental and clinical applications. *Behavior Research: Methods, Applications, and Computers, 19*, 270–274.

Snodgrass, J. G. & Vanderwart, M. (1980). A standardised set of 260 pictures: Norms for name agreement, image agreement, familiarity and visual complexity. *Journal of Experimental Psychology: Human Learning and Memory, 6*, 174–215.

Sohlberg, M. & Mateer, C. A. (1989a). *Introduction to cognitive rehabilitation*. Hillsdale, N.J.: Lawrence Erlbaum Associates Inc.

Sohlberg, M. M. & Mateer, C. A. (1989b). Training use of compensatory memory books: A three stage behavioural approach. *Journal of Clinical and Experimental Neuropsychology, 11*, 871–891.

Sommer, W. (1880). Eckrankung des Ammonshorns als aetiologisches Moment der Epilepsie. *Archiv Psychiatrie 10*, 631–675.

Speedie, L. J. & Heilman, K. M. (1982). Amnesic disturbance following infarction of the left dorsomedial nucleus of the thalamus. *Neuropsychologia, 20*, 597–604.

Spiegel, A., Wycis, H. T., Orchinik, W. & Freed, H. (1955). The thalamus and temporal orientation. *Science, 121*, 771–772.

Spinnler, H., Sterzi, R. & Vallar, G. (1980). Amnesic syndrome after carbon monoxide poisoning: A case report. *Archives Suisses de Neurologie, Neurochirurgie et de Psychiatrie, 1*, 79–88.

Squire, L. R. (1981). Two forms of human amnesia: An analysis of forgetting. *Journal of Neuroscience, 1*, 635–640.

Squire, L. R. (1982). Comparisons between forms of amnesia: Some deficits are unique to Korsakoff's Syndrome. *Journal of Experimental Psychology: Learning, Memory and Cognition, 8*, 560–571.

Squire, L. R., Amaral, D. G., Zola-Morgan, S., Kritchevsky, M. & Press, G. (1989a). Description of brain injury in the amnesic patient N.A. based on magnetic resonance imaging. *Experimental Neurology, 105*, 23–35.

Squire, L. R., Cohen, N. J. & Nadel, L. (1984). The medial temporal region and memory consolidation: A new hypothesis. In H. Weingartner & E. S. Parker (Eds), *Memory consolidation: Psychobiology of cognition*. Hillsdale, N.J.: Lawrence Earlbaum Associates Inc.

Squire, L. R., Haist, F. & Shimamura, A. P. (1989b). The neurology of memory: Quantitative assessment of retrograde amnesia in two groups of amnesic patients. *Journal of Neuroscience, 9*, 828–839.

Squire, L. R. & Moore, R. Y. (1979). Dorsal thalamic lesions in a noted case of human memory dysfunction. *Annals of Neurology, 6*, 603–606.

Squire, L. R., Nadel, L. & Slater, P. C. (1981). Anterograde amnesia and memory for temporal order. *Neuropsychologia, 19*, 141–145.

Squire, L. R. & Shimamura, A. P. (1986). Characterizing amnesic patients for neurobehavioral study. *Behavioral Neuroscience, 100*, 866–877.

Squire, L. R. & Slater, P. C. (1978). Anterograde and retrograde impairment in chronic amnesia. *Neuropsychologia, 16*, 313–322.

Squire, L. R. & Zola-Morgan, S. (1985). Neuropsychology of memory: New links between humans and experimental animals. In D. Olton, S. Corkin & E. Gamzu (Eds), *Memory dysfunctions: An integration of animal and human research from clinical and preclinical perspectives*, pp. 137–149. New York: New York Academy of Sciences.

Squire, L. R. & Zouzounis, J. A. (1988). Self-ratings of memory dysfunction: Different findings in depression and amnesia. *Journal of Clinical and Experimental Neuropsychology, 10*, 727–738.

Starr, A. & Phillips, L. (1970). Verbal and motor memory in the amnesic syndrome. *Neuropsychologia, 8*, 75–88.

Steinman, D. R. & Bigler, E. D. (1986). Neuropsychological sequelae of ruptured anterior communicating artery aneurysm. *International Journal of Clinical Neuropsychology, 8*, 135–140.

Stenhouse, L. M., Knight, R. G., Longmore, B. E. & Bishara, S. N. (1991). Long-term cognitive deficits in patients after surgery on aneurysms of the anterior communicating artery. *Journal of Neurology, Neurosurgery and Psychiatry, 54*, 909–914.

Stevens, M. (1979). Famous personality test: A test for measuring remote memory. *Bulletin of the British Psychological Society, 32*, 211.

Stewart, F., Parkin, A. J. & Hunkin, N. M. (1992). Naming impairments following recovery from herpes simplex encephalitis: Category specific? *Quarterly Journal of Experimental Psychology, 44A*, 261–284.

Strauss, E. & Spreen, O. (1990). A comparison of the Rey and Taylor figures. *Archives of Clinical Neuropsychology, 5*, 417–420.

Stroop, W. G. (1986). Herpes simplex virus encephalitis of the human adult: Reactivation of latent brain infection. *Pathology and Immunopathology Research, 5*, 156–169.

Stuss, D. T., Alexander, M. P., Lieberman, A. & Levine, H. (1978). An extraordinary form of confabulation. *Neurology, 28*, 1166–1172.

Stuss, D. T., Ely, P., Hugenholtz, H., Richard, M. T., La Rochelle, S., Poirier, C. A. & Bell, I. (1985). Subtle neuropsychological deficits in patients with good recovery after closed head injury. *Neurosurgery, 17*, 41–47.

Stuss, D. T., Guberman, A., Nelson, R. & La Rochelle, S. (1988). The neuropsychology of paramedian thalamic infarction. *Brain and Cognition, 7*, 1–31.

Stuss, D. T. & Guzman, D. A. (1988). Severe remote memory loss with minimal anterograde amnesia: A clinical note. *Brain and Cognition, 8*, 2–30.

Sunderland, A., Harris, J. & Baddeley, A. D. (1983). Do laboratory tests predict everyday memory? *Journal of Verbal Learning and Verbal Behavior, 122*, 341–357.

Swanson, R. A. & Schmidley, J. W. (1985). Amnesic syndrome and vertical gaze palsy: Early detection of bilateral thalamic infarction by CT and NMR. *Stroke, 16*, 823–827.

Symonds, C. P. (1962). Concussion and its sequelae. *Lancet, i*, 1–5.

Talland, G. A. (1965). *Deranged memory*. New York: Academic Press.

Talland, G. A., Sweet, W. H. & Ballantine, H. T. (1967). Amnesic syndrome with anterior communicating artery aneurysm. *Journal of Nervous and Mental Disease, 145*, 179–192.

Taylor, L. B. (1979). Psychological assessment of neurosurgical patients. In T. Rasmussen & R. Marino (Eds), *Functional neurosurgery*. New York: Raven Press.

Teissier du Cros, J. & Lhermitte, F. (1984). Neuropsychological analysis of ruptured saccular aneurysms of the anterior communicating artery after radical therapy (32 cases). *Surgical Neurology, 22*, 353–359.

Teitelbaum, J. S., Zatorre, R. J., Carpenter, S., Gendron, D., Evans, A. C., Gjedde, A. & Cashman, N. R. (1990). Neurologic sequelae of domoic acid intoxication due to the ingestion of contaminated mussels. *New England Journal of Medicine, 322*, 1781–1787.

Teuber, H.-L., Milner, B. & Vaughan, H. G. (1968). Persistent anterograde amnesia after stab wound to the basal brain. *Neuropsychologia, 6*, 267–282.

Torvik, A. (1987). Topographic distribution and severity of brain lesions in Wernicke's encephalopathy. *Clinical Neuropsychologia, 6*, 25–29.

Trennery, M. R., Crosson, B., DeBoe, J. & Leber, W. R. (1989). *Stroop Neuropsychological Screening Test*. London: NFER-Nelson.

Trillet, M., Fischer, C., Serclerat, D. & Schott, B. (1980). Le syndrome amnesique des ischemies cerebrales posterieures. *Cortex, 16*, 421–434.

Tsoi, M. M., Huang, C. Y., Lee, A. D. M. & Yu, Y. L. (1987). Amnesia following right thalamic haemorrhage. *Clinical and Experimental Neurology, 23*, 201–207.

Tulving, E. (1985). How many memory systems are there? *American Psychologist, 40*, 385–398.

Tulving, E. (1989). Remembering and knowing the past. *American Psychologist, 77*, 361–367.
Tulving, E., Hayman, C. A. G. & Macdonald, C. A. (1991). Long-lasting perceptual priming and semantic learning in amnesia: A case experiment. *Journal of Experimental Psychology, Learning, Memory and Cognition, 17*, 595–617.
Tulving, E., Schacter, D. L. & Stark, H. (1982). Priming effects in word-fragment completion are independent of recognition memory. *Journal of Experimental Psychology: Human Learning and Memory, 8*, 336–342.
Turner, S., Daniels, L. & Greer, S. (1989). Wernicke's encephalopathy in an 18 year-old woman. *British Journal of Psychiatry, 154*, 261–262.
Uchimura, J. (1928). Zur Pathogenese der ortlich elektiv en Ammonshornerkrankung. *Zeitschrift für Neurologie und Psychiatrie, 114*, 567–601.
Vallar, G. & Shallice, T. (1990). *Neuropsychological impairments of short-term memory*. Cambridge: Cambridge University Press.
Verfaellie, M., Cermak, L. S., Blackford, S. P. & Weiss, S. (1990). Strategic and automatic priming of semantic memory in alcoholic Korsakoff patients. *Brain and Cognition, 13*, 178–192.
Verfaellie, M., Cermak, L. S., Letourneau, L. & Zuffante, P. (1991). Repetition effects in a lexical decision task: The role of episodic memory in the performance of alcoholic Korsakoff patients. *Neuropsychologia, 29*, 641–657.
Victor, M., Adams, R. D. & Collins, G. H. (1989). *The Wernicke-Korsakoff Syndrome and related neurologic disorders due to alcoholism and malnutrition*, 2nd edn. Philadephia: Davis.
Victor, M., Angevine, J., Mancall, E. & Fisher, C. M. (1971). Memory loss with lesions of hippocampal formation. *Archives of Neurology, 5*, 244–263.
Victor, M., Hermann, K. & White, E. E. (1959). A psychological study of the Wernicke-Korsakoff syndrome. *Quarterly Journal of Studies in Alcoholism, 20*, 467–479.
Victor, M. & Yakolev, P. I. (1955). S. S. Korsakoff's psychic disorder in conjunction with peripheral neuritis: A translation of Korsakoff's original article with brief comments on the author and his contribution to clinical medicine. *Neurology, 5*, 394–406.
Vilkki, J. (1985). Amnesic syndromes after surgery of anterior communicating artery aneurysms. *Cortex, 21*, 431–444.
Vilkki, J., Holst, P., Ohman, J., Servo, A. & Heiskanen, O. (1990). Social outcome related to cognitive performance and computed tomographic findings after surgery for a ruptured intracranial aneurysm. *Neurosurgery, 26*, 579–585.
Villar, H. V. & Ranne, R. D. (1984). Neurological deficit following gastric partitioning: Possible role of thiamine. *Journal of Parenteral and Enteral Nutrition, 8*, 575–578.
Volpe, B. T., Herscovitch, P. & Raichle, M. E. (1984). Positron emission tomography defines metabolic abnormality in medial temporal lobes of two patients with amnesia after rupture and repair of anterior communicating artery aneurysm. *Neurology, 34*, 188.
Volpe, B. T. & Hirst, W. (1983a). The characterization of an amnesic syndrome following hypoxic ischemic injury. *Archives of Neurology, 40*, 436–440.
Volpe, B. T. & Hirst, W. (1983b). Amnesia following the rupture and repair of an anterior communicating artery aneurysm. *Journal of Neurology, Neurosurgery and Psychiatry, 46*, 704–709.
Volpe, B. T., Holtzman, J. D. & Hirst, W. (1986). Further characterization of patients with amnesia after cardiac arrest: Preserved recognition memory. *Neurology, 36*, 408–411.
Vreizen, E. R. & Moscovitch, M. (1990). Memory for temporal order and conditional associative-learning in patients with Parkinson's disease. *Neuropsychologia, 28*, 1283–1293.
Warrington, E. K. (1984). *Recognition Memory Test*. London: NFER-Nelson.
Warrington, E. K. & James, M. (1991). A new test of object decision: 2D silhouettes featuring a minimal view. *Cortex, 27*, 377–383.

Warrington, E. K. & McCarthy, R. A. (1988). The fractionation of retrograde amnesia. *Brain and Cognition, 7*, 184–200.

Warrington, E. K. & Shallice, T. (1984). Category specific semantic impairments. *Brain, 107*, 829–854.

Warrington, E. K. & Taylor, A. M. (1978). Two categorical stages of object recognition. *Perception, 7*, 695–705.

Warrington, E. K. & Weiskrantz, L. (1970). Amnesic syndrome: Consolidation or retrieval? *Nature, 228*, 628–630.

Warrington, E. K. & Weiskrantz, L. (1979). Conditioning in amnesic patients. *Neuropsychologia, 17*, 187–194.

Warrington, E. K. & Weiskrantz, L. (1982). Amnesia: A disconnection syndrome? *Neuropsychologia, 20*, 233–243.

Waugh, N. C. & Norman, D. A. (1965). Primary memory. *Psychological Review, 72*, 89–104.

Wechsler, D. (1945). A standardized memory scale for clinical use. *Journal of Psychology, 19*, 87–95.

Wechsler, D. (1955). *Adult Intelligence Scale*. New York: Psychological Corporation.

Wechsler, D. (1981). *Wechsler Adult Intelligence Scale—Revised*. New York: Psychological Corporation.

Wechsler, F. (1987). *Wechsler Memory Scale—Revised*. New York: Psychological Corporation.

Weiner, R. D. (1984). Does electroconvulsive therapy cause brain damage? *Behavioral and Brain Sciences, 7*, 1–53.

Weiskrantz, L. (1985). Issues and theories in the study of the amnesic syndrome. In N. M. Weinberger, K. F. Berham & G. Lynch (Eds), *Memory systems of the brain*. New York: Guilford Press.

Wernicke, C. (1881). *Lehrbuch der Gehirnkrankheiten für Aerzte und Studirende*, Vol. 2, pp. 229–242. Kassel: Theodor Fischer.

Whiting, S., Lincoln, N., Bhavnani, G. & Cockburn, J. (1985). *Rivermead Perceptual Assessment Battery*. London: NFER-Nelson.

Wickelgren, W. A. (1968). Sparing of short-term memory in an amnesic patient: Implications for a strength theory of memory. *Neuropsychologia, 6*, 235–244.

Wickens, D. D. (1970). Encoding categories of words: An empirical approach to meaning. *Psychological Review, 77*, 1–15.

Williams, J. M., Medwedeff, C. H. & Haban G. (1989). Memory disorder and subjective time estimation. *Journal of Clinical and Experimental Neuropsychology, 11*, 713–723.

Williams, M. & Pennybacker, J. (1954). Memory disturbances in third ventricle tumours. *Journal of Neurology, Neurosurgery and Psychiatry, 17*, 115–123.

Wilson, B. (1982). Success and failure in memory training following a cerebral vascular accident. *Cortex, 18*, 581–594.

Wilson, B. A. (1987). *Rehabilitation of memory*. London: Guilford Press.

Wilson, B., Cockburn, J., Baddeley, A. & Hiorns, R. (1989). The development and validation of a test battery for detecting and monitoring everyday memory problems. *Journal of Clinical and Experimental Neuropsychology, 11*, 855–870.

Wilson, B., Cockburn, J. and Halligan, P. (1987). *The Behavioural Inattention Test*. Fareham: Thames Valley Test Company.

Wilson, B., Forester, S., Bryant, T. & Cockburn, J. (1990). Performance of 11–14 year-olds on the Rivermead Behavioural Memory Test. *Clinical Psychology Forum, 30*, 8–10.

Wilson, B. A., Ivani-Chalian, R. & Aldrich, F. K. (1991). *The Rivermead Behavioural Memory Test for children aged 5–10 years*. Bury St. Edmunds: Thames Valley Test Company.

Wilson, B. A. & Moffat, N. (1984). *The clinical management of memory problems*. London: Croon Helm.

Wilson, B. A. & Patterson, K. (1990). Rehabilitation for cognitive impairment: Does cognitive psychology apply? *Applied Cognitive Psychology, 4*, 247–260.

Winocur, G., Oxbury, S., Roberts, R., Agnetti, V. & Davis, C. (1984). Amnesia in a patient with bilateral lesions to the thalamus. *Neuropsychologia, 22*, 123–143.

Winocur, G. & Weiskrantz, L. (1976). An investigation of paired associate learning in amnesic patients. *Neuropsychologia, 14*, 97–110.

Witt, E. D. (1985). Neuroanatomical consequences of thiamine deficiency: A comparative analysis. *Alcohol and Alcoholism, 20*, 202–221.

Wong, C. K. (1990). Too shameful to remember: A 17-year-old Chinese boy with psychogenic amnesia. *Australia and New Zealand Journal of Psychiatry, 24*, 570–574.

Wood, F. B., Brown, I. S. & Felton, R. H. (1989). Long-term follow-up of a childhood amnesic syndrome. *Brain and Cognition, 10*, 76–86.

Wood, P., Murray, A., Sinha, B., Godley, M. & Goldsmith, H. J. (1983). Wernicke's encephalopathy induced by hyperemesis gravidarum. Case reports. *British Journal of Obstetrics and Gynaecology, 90*, 583–586.

Woods, B. T., Schoene, W. & Kneisley, L. (1982). Are hippocampal lesions sufficient to cause lasting amnesia? *Journal of Neurology, Neurosurgery and Psychiatry, 45*, 243–247.

Young, A. W., Newcombe, F., Hellawell, D. & De Haan, E. (1989). Implicit access to semantic information. *Brain and Cognition, 11*, 186–209.

Zelinski, E. M., Gilewski, M. J. & Thompson, L. W. (1980). Do laboratory tests relate to self assessment of memory ability in the young and old? In L. W. Poon, J. L. Fozard, L. S. Cermak, D. Arenberg & L. W. Thompson (Eds), *New directions in memory and aging*. Hillsdale, N.J.: Lawrence Erlbaum Associates Inc.

Ziegler, D., Kaufman A. & Marshall, H. E. (1977). Abrupt memory loss associated with thalamic tumour. *Archives of Neurology, 34*, 545–548.

Zola-Morgan, S., Squire, L. R. & Amaral, D. G. (1986). Human amnesia and the medial temporal region: Enduring memory impairment following a bilateral lesion limited to field CA1 of the hippocampus. *Journal of Neuroscience, 6*, 2950–2967.

Zurif, E., Gardner, H. & Brownell, H. (1989). The case against the case against agrammatism. *Brain and Cognition, 10*, 237–255.

Glossary of Abbreviations

ACoA	Anterior communicating artery
AMIPB	Adult Memory and Information-processing Battery
AVLT	Auditory Verbal Learning Test
BP	Brown-Peterson Task
BRMB	Boston Remote Memory Battery
CAT	Computerised axial tomography
CET	Cognitive Estimation Task
CHI	Closed-head injury
CO	Carbon monoxide
CRM	Continuous Recognition Memory Test
CVA	Cerebrovascular accident
DMTN	Dorso-medial thalamic nucleus
ECT	Electroconvulsive therapy
EFT	Embedded Figures Test
FAS	Word fluency test
FSIQ	Full-scale IQ derived from WAIS (q.v.)
FSIQ–WMSMQ (q.v.)	Discrepancy score obtained by substracting WMSMQ from FSIQ (q.v.)
HSE	Herpes simplex encephalitis
LTS	Long-term store
MQ	Memory quotient derived from WMS (q.v.)
MRI	Magnetic resonance imaging
NART	National Adult Reading Test
PI	Proactive interference

PCA	Posterior cerebral artery
PD	Parkinson's disease
PLE	Paraneoplastic limbic encephalitis
PTA	Post-traumatic amnesia
RA	Retrograde amnesia
RBMT	Rivermead Behavioural Memory Test
RMT	Recognition Memory Test
SR	Selective Reminding Test
STS	Short-term store
TEA	Transient epileptic amnesia
TGA	Transient global amnesia
VC	Method of vanishing cues
WAIS	Wechsler Adult Intelligence Scale
WAIS-R	Revised version of WAIS
WCST	Wisconsin Card Sorting Test
WE	Wernicke's encephalopathy
WKS	Wernicke-Korsakoff Syndrome
WMS	Wechsler Memory Scale
WMS-R	Revised WMS

Glossary of Amnesic Patients Cited by Initial

BD (Hanley et al., 1989) Post-HSE
BJ (Dusoir et al., 1990) Paranasal penetrating head injury
BS (Parkin et al., in prep.) Carbon monoxide poisoning
BW (Williams et al., 1989) Third ventricle tumour
BY (Winocur et al., 1984) Bilateral thalamic lesions
CB (Parkin et al., in prep.) ACoA aneurysm
CG (Della Sala & Spinnler, 1986) CO poisoning
CM (Parkin et al., 1991) Non-alcoholic WKS
DRB (Damasio et al., 1985) Post-HSE
ER (Talland et al., 1967) ACoA aneurysm
GO (Talland et al., 1967) ACoA aneurysm
HM (Corkin, 1984) Bilateral temporal lobectomy
HO (Stewart et al., 1992) Post-HSE
HW (Moscovitch, 1989) ACoA aneurysm
IG (Stuss et al., 1988) Thalamic infarction
JB (Parkin et al., 1988) ACoA aneurysm
JE (Brown et al., 1989) Thalamic infarction
JK (Conrad, 1953) Post-HSE
JR (Parkin et al., in prep.) Thalamic infarction
LE (Parkin et al., 1992). WE in a young woman
LP (De Renzi et al., 1987) Post-HSE
MK (Starr & Phillips, 1970) Post-HSE
MP (Parkin & Barry, 1991) ACoA aneurysm (partial callosal disconnection)
MRL (Beatty et al., 1987) Anoxia

NA (Squire et al., 1989) Paranasal penetrating head injury
PZ (Butters, 1984) WKS
RB (Zola-Morgan et al., 1986) Bilateral hippocampal lesions
BC (Stuss et al., 1988) Thalamic infarction
RK (Parkin & Hunkin, in press) Hypothalamic glioma
RW (Delbecq-Derouesne et al., 1990) ACoA aneurysm
SS (Cermak & O'Connor, 1983) Post-HSE
TC (Wood et al., 1989) Post-HSE in childhood
TJ (Parkin & Hunkin, 1991) Late temporal lobe necrosis

Author Index

Subject Index

www.ingramcontent.com/pod-product-compliance
Ingram Content Group UK Ltd.
Pitfield, Milton Keynes, MK11 3LW, UK
UKHW011010180926
475701UK00004B/667
* 9 7 8 1 1 3 8 9 7 7 0 0 6 *